AS-Level

ICT

The Revision Guide

Editors:
Thomas Harte, Simon Little, Rob MacDonald, Chrissy Williams.

Contributors:
David Astall, Marie Gibbs, Colin Harber-Stuart, Nick Jackson, Gavin Lawrence, June McKenzie, Kate Redmond, Edward Robinson, Karen Scott, Rachel Selway, Sonia Stuart, Barry Thomas, Jennifer Underwood, Richard Vickery.

Proofreaders:
Cornelia Adamson, David Astall, Sonia Stuart, Laurence Stamford.

With special thanks to Neil Hastings, whose love of databases and teletext made this book possible.
Also thanks to Peter Spencer, who polished off numerous curly wurlys whilst giving his love and support.

Published by Coordination Group Publications Ltd.

This book is suitable for **AQA** and **OCR**. It's extremely **simple** to use...

For **AQA unit 1** — you need these pages...
p10-21 and p66-129 (the assessment advice stuff is on p128-129).

For **AQA unit 2** — you need p2-9 and p22-65.

For **OCR unit 1** — read through sections 1 to 8, following the instructions at the top of pages about where to skip pages.

For **OCR unit 2** — look at the assessment advice on p130-131. These pages will point you to the relevant parts of the book.

Finally, p132-133 give some general exam tips.

ISBN: 978 1 84762 141 2
Groovy website: www.cgpbooks.co.uk
Jolly bits of clipart from CorelDRAW®
Printed by Elanders Hindson Ltd, Newcastle upon Tyne.

Contents

Data, Information and Knowledge

These pages are for AQA Unit 2 and OCR Unit 1.

Welcome to AS ICT — the riveting study of Information and Communication Technology. To start with, you need to be clear on some very basic definitions. Close your eyes and make a wish, and all your ICT dreams will come true.

Defining Data and Information

ICT systems produce information (as output), using technology to store, process and transfer data (the input). The difference between these terms is quite subtle, but really important to understand:

1) **Data**
Data is **raw facts and figures** before they have been processed. The computer doesn't understand what the data means and it has **no meaning on its own**.

> **e.g.** Examples of data could be the strings of characters '19091985' or 'VD51FGD' which may be input into the computer, processed in some way and then output.

2) **Information**
Information is **data** that has been **given a meaning** by being put into context or processed into a useful format. If you know what a string of characters means, then it **becomes information**. It can be expressed as:
Information = Data + [structure] + [content] + meaning.

> **e.g.** '19091985' may be a product code for an item or it may be the date of birth of a person (19th September 1985) — it becomes information once you know what it refers to.

3) **Knowledge** ***This bit is OCR only.***
Information becomes **knowledge** when you use a **rule** or a **set of rules** to manipulate the information.

> **e.g.** If you know that 19091985 is a person's date of birth (19th September 1985) you can work out that the person is aged 18 or over and so is eligible to vote. You've used a rule which states 'if age>= 18 the person can vote' to get knowledge from information.

ICT systems provide information to a **human user** or to another **ICT system** as input. They always have the following components.

1) Data and Information — like we've defined above.
2) People — to enter the data and interpret and use the information.
3) Procedures — to make sure that the data input produces accurate information.
4) Hardware and Software — to store (hardware) and process (software), data and information.

He enjoyed the new system as the output was normally a 24" pizza.

The Data Cycle — Input, Process, Output, Feedback

A **data cycle** is the **overall process** of data being converted into output that is useful to the end user. After data is input, it can be processed or temporarily stored, after which it is output as information. Feedback takes aspects of the output to be input and processed again.

Make sure you **understand the diagram**, and go through the example below carefully so you're clear on all the stages.

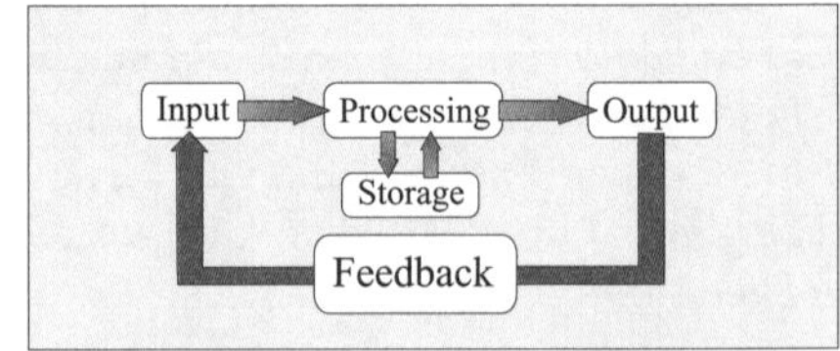

Example: *Recording a sale at a supermarket using EPOS — (Electronic Point of Sale)*

A. **Data is entered at input stage.** *E.g. bar code is read and validated.* **Information** is converted into **data** before it is input. *Product details (name of item, size, manufacturer etc.) are given numbers.*

B. **The data is processed by the computer.** *E.g. product details are found, stock level is updated.* Data from a database is **read** and **stored temporarily** in RAM. *The product details and price of the item are found. The stock record is reduced.*

C. **The processed data is output.** *E.g. an itemised receipt is produced. The total cost is displayed on the till screen and a receipt can be printed.* Some information **feeds back**. *Details of items that need reordering are stored.*

The supermarket might not be the most exciting example in the world but every system, no matter how complex, processes input into useful output.

Data, Information and Knowledge

Your **Data** Needs to be **Top Quality**

The **quality** of the data that is input is very important. If it's inaccurate or out of date or unreasonable, then it doesn't matter how wonderful the computer program is; it will still produce incorrect results. You can sum this up with the word: **GIGO**, which means '**garbage in, garbage out**'. Data must be **accurate**, **reliable, up-to-date**, **complete**, **reasonable** and **correct**.

There are **Different Data Types**

When data is stored in a computer, it can be stored in **different ways** depending on what it is used for. Here are some examples:

1) The data may be a **number**, in which case it may be a whole number (integer) or have a decimal part (real number).
2) Alternatively, it might be a group of **characters** (letters and numbers) in which case it is called a string.
3) Thirdly, it might just represent one of two **conditions** (e.g. "true" or "false") — this is called a Boolean type.

Data Types and Examples

Integer e.g. 2003, 18

Real number e.g. 147.35, 0.0034

String e.g. ABC435, Benjamin, CQ117YT

Boolean e.g. True or False, On or Off, 1 or 0

Different Methods can be used to **Convey Information**

Information can be represented and conveyed in different ways:

1) **Text** — this method is **easily understood** and can be very **detailed**. However the reader must be able to understand the **language** or **subject** that the text is written in or about. Lots of text is also **difficult to read**.
2) **Graphics** — images and symbols are **not language-specific**, so graphics can convey meaning easily. However if symbols are used, they must mean something in the **country or culture** of the user in order to be understood.
3) **Animation and video** — these can be used to **explain text** and can convey lots of information, although if you miss the start of a piece of animation or a video clip then you might not understand what follows.
4) **Sound** — this could be **speech** or simple sounds with a **specific meaning**, e.g. alarm / warning sounds.
5) **LED** — can be used in **noisy** environments, but they need to be clearly **visible** and the **meaning** understood.

Practice Questions

Q1 Draw a data cycle diagram and label it fully.

Q2 Describe the components involved in an ICT system.

Q3 What does GIGO mean?

Exam Questions

Q1 It is important to be able to distinguish between data and information. 21092002 is an example of data.

a) Give two reasons why "21092002" is a piece of data, not information. (2 marks)

b) Give one example of what information "21092002" could be converted into. (1 mark)

c) Explain the process of changing information into knowledge and give an example using your answer to (b). **This part is OCR only** (2 marks)

Q2 Using the example of data collected from a questionnaire, explain these three parts of an information processing system:

a) Input of data. (1 mark)

b) Processing of data. (1 mark)

c) Output of information. (1 mark)

Aceing your exams will be a data remember (groan...)

You need to make sure you've nailed the subtle differences between the meanings of the terms 'data', 'information' and 'knowledge'. The examples on this page are just the beginning. Try and think of more real-life examples that might crop up in an exam — otherwise it'll be: data = F, information = ICT AS result: F, knowledge = oh dear, I seem to have failed.

Data, Information and Knowledge

These pages are for AQA Unit 2 and OCR Unit 1.

Blimey — another two whole pages on data and information? Although there is some encoding thrown in for good measure — must be your lucky day! Just kidding. It's all good stuff though, so dive in and make with the learning.

Data can be Coded

1) When information is entered as data in a computer it is often stored in a coded form.
2) For example, when entering a person's gender into a database it is usually stored in a one character field as either 'M' or 'F'.
3) Other examples of coding that could be used in a library database are in this table:

Information	Data (in code)
Gender	'M' or 'F'
Membership Type	'F' (family) or 'I' (individual)
Book Status	'L' (on loan) or 'A' (available)
Barcode	'1 78082 645 3' (contains product details)

Advantages of Coding

1. **Less memory** is needed to store the data (e.g. M rather than Male).
2. It's **quicker** and more convenient to enter a code rather than typing the full name.
3. Data entry can be **validated** more easily, to make sure that the data input is reasonable.
4. If the data is in **standardised** format then it can be compared and organised.

Disadvantages of Coding

1. It may be difficult to **remember the codes** (though a drop-down list can be used as a reminder).
2. **Accuracy** may be lost when coding the information (e.g. giving grades for work instead of percentages).
3. Some codes are difficult to **understand** (e.g. a bar code).
4. Difficult to **track errors** — the code may be valid but it might not be correct.

There Can be Difficulties with Coding Value Judgements

1) A "**value judgement**" is a judgement made by an individual person.
2) Trying to **code information** based on value judgements can be problematic because you're relying on one person's opinion. You might end up with very **different data** if someone else made the judgement instead:
   - For example, suppose an Internet researcher called Clive has to give websites a **star grading** (from 1 to 5 stars), based on how **user-friendly** he thinks they are.
   - But, another researcher, Cliveta, might review the same websites and give **completely different ratings** based on her own judging criteria.

Data Sources can be Direct or Indirect

Before you can code data, you have to get your hands on some. There are two ways of doing this:

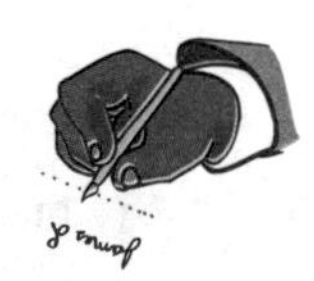

1) **Direct Capture**

Direct data capture is when specific data is collected for a specific purpose, e.g. on a census form. The data is then entered into a computer and processed, e.g. to find out how many people there are in the country and what the age distribution is.

2) **Indirect Capture**

Data that has been collected, e.g. membership details for a gym, may be passed on (with the member's permission) to another company, e.g. a sports shop, and used for a very different purpose, e.g. sending out advertising leaflets. In this case, it's called **indirect data capture**.

Data, Information and Knowledge

There are **advantages** and **disadvantages** to both of these data capture methods. ***This bit is OCR only.***

	ADVANTAGES	DISADVANTAGES
Direct	The source and collection method is **known** and **verified**. The **exact** data needed can be collected. Information being collected can be **changed** in response to **answers**.	Range of data collected may be **limited**. Data may **not be available** — location/time.
Indirect	**Large range** of data available that **could not** have been collected **directly**. Data from **different locations** and **time periods** can be available. Some of the data may have **already** been **analysed**.	Do not know if any **bias** was placed on the collection. **Accuracy** of the recording of data is **uncertain**. May not have all the information about **how, when and where** it was collected. The **original information** might not be **available**.

Information Sources can be Static or Dynamic

- **Static data** is usually found on a **CD-ROM**. Static information sources, once created, **do not change**, so the information may become **out-of-date**. The information can be relied on to be **accurate**, as it has usually gone through a checking process, but the amount of information held is **limited**.
- **Dynamic information** is usually found on a **website**. Dynamic information sources are **updated** regularly or can be **changed**. This means it is usually up-to-date and large amounts of information can be held. Dynamic web pages can be **linked** to a database and the user can retrieve information from this by entering details into a form on the webpage. The information may not always be accurate, as **no checking process** may have taken place.

Internet vs CD-ROMs as Information Sources...

CD-ROMs

1) All **software** needed can be included on the CD-ROM.
2) But if **errors** are found then the changes need to be sent to **everyone** who has bought the CD-ROM.
3) You may need to search **lots** of CD-ROMs to find the information you want.
4) CD-ROMs can be **lost**, **stolen** or **broken**.

The Internet

1) Lots of information can be found from **different sources** with different opinions.
2) Any errors found can be **changed** quickly and easily.
3) It's often hard to know if information on the Internet is **accurate** or **reliable**.

Practice Questions

Q1 Give three advantages and three disadvantages of coding data.

Q2 What is the difference between direct and indirect data capture?

Q3 Explain the terms static information source and dynamic information source.

Exam Questions

Q1 Data collected using a questionnaire needs to be stored and processed. Before this happens some of the data is coded.

a) Give three reasons why data may be coded. (3 marks)

b) For each reason, illustrate it with an example from a typical questionnaire. (3 marks)

Q2 A university codes data that has been collected before it is used.
Describe two problems the university might have as a result of coding the data. (4 marks)

Q3 The books supplied by a publishing company can be viewed on the company website.
Explain the advantages of using a website rather than a CD-ROM to show the books. (6 marks)

If you've got a code, buy an extra large box of tissues...

Unlike your revision, coding is good because it doesn't need too much memory and it's pretty darn quick. But beware of the pitfalls of coding — it can get difficult to remember and it's not guaranteed to be accurate. Which makes it kinda like revision actually. There's only one way round this mortal danger to your exam results — learn this page. Learn it good.

Value of Information

These pages are for AQA Unit 2 and OCR Unit 1.

Information is data put into a context. "Yes yes yes" I hear you cry, "we only covered this a couple of pages ago". Well, there's no harm in repeating things now and again, especially if your head is made of sand and blancmange like mine is.

Information Can Be Valuable

1) All information is **valuable to someone** (even utter rubbish can be of interest to somebody random).
2) Some information is **valuable to everyone**.
3) The better the quality of the information, the more valuable it becomes.

There is life beyond ICT. That strikes me as very valuable information.

Information Needs To Be Of Good Quality

Information is of **good quality** if:

1) there is enough of it to help people **make decisions**.
2) it is **accurate** and **up-to-date**.
3) it is presented in an objective way that **can't be misinterpreted**.
4) it is **relevant** to the person who wants to use it.
5) it is **easy to understand** and isn't buried in loads of useless information.

The classic example is the Internet — there's massive amounts of information on the Internet, but so many hours can get wasted sifting through web pages till you find some quality information.

Good Quality Data Is Reliable, Accurate, Up-To-Date, Complete And Precise

1) Information is produced by **organising data** in such a way that **meaningful** and **useful facts** can be gathered. The **quality** of the information depends on the **quality of the data**.
2) **Reliable** data is **collected from the right sources**. E.g. it's no good getting data on credit card usage from kids, nor is it always useful to ask for opinions rather than facts, as these are really hard to measure and record.
3) **Accurate** data is **recorded** exactly as it is and is **protected from being changed** accidentally or maliciously.
4) **Up-to-date** data is **recorded at intervals**. E.g. surveys on shopping preferences must take place regularly as shopping trends change with the time of year. If winter data is used to influence decisions to be taken about summer stock, the shops might be full of winter clothes in the summer. Just imagine the horror.
5) Data is **complete** when **all aspects are included** and **all possible sources are used**. E.g. a survey of five people is not as complete as a survey of 500, and any survey where many questions are left unanswered will give inaccurate results.
6) **Precise data** has **no possible alternative interpretation**. E.g. the recording of someone's weight is precise if it is measured, but the recording of how much they think they weigh is likely to be inaccurate.

You Can Have Too Much Information

1) Information moves around the world fairly easily these days, but some of it is **uninvited**.
2) We have **junk mail** posted through our letterboxes every day. We get **unsolicited e-mails** (**spam**) in our mail boxes, which **slows you down** as you separate it from **useful information**.
3) The **Mail Preference Service** was set up to help people **remove their names** from mailing lists.
4) ISPs and e-mail providers offer **similar services** for reducing the volume of spam you receive.

Useful Information Can Fetch A Cracking Price

1) A CD-ROM with files on it listing the contents of your cousin Jenny's bathroom probably isn't worth anything (depends on what's in the bathroom), but a CD-ROM containing very **recent**, **accurate** and **full market research data** could be worth thousands to any company that could use the information.
2) A CD-ROM containing **old data**, with lots of **gaps** and **mistakes**, stored in a **hard-to-access format** might not be worth much more than the bathroom CD-ROM.
3) Information can be **immensely valuable** to the right person, if it's **useful** to them.

Value of Information

Ensuring Information Is Valuable Costs Time And Money

Organisations keep information that is useful to them, but the information will often have a "use by date" after which it is **too old to be useful**. Time and money have to be invested to keep the information **valuable**.

1) There needs to be enough staff to **update** the data.
2) There need to be **security systems** in place to ensure that the data doesn't get changed accidentally or maliciously.
3) There needs to be **enough storage space** for the data.
4) There needs to be effective software to **manipulate** and **organise** the data into **useful information**.

Producing Information Can Cost Money

Hardware is needed to collect, process and output information. This includes the cost of buying, upgrading and maintaining the hardware. As more information is collected and stored the back-up hardware may also need to be increased.

Technical support were not impressed by the new call centre.

Software needs to be purchased or upgraded. Technical support may be needed. Staff using the software may also need to be trained.

Consumables are items that get used in the processes e.g. paper and toner or ink cartridges.

Personnel are people working in the organisation. New staff may need to be hired to collate, enter, process and output the information. Replacement staff may be needed to cover staff on training courses.

Practice Questions

Q1 Describe four characteristics of good quality information.

Q2 Give one example of information that could be valuable to a company.

Q3 Describe five characteristics of good quality data.

Q4 Give two examples of costs involved in producing information.

Exam Questions

Q1 A ski holiday company marketing new ski packages to Andorra in 2008 wants to decide which resorts to promote. The data they are using was collected in 2001.

a) Give two reasons why the 2001 data might not be useful in predicting the popularity of resorts in 2008. (2 marks)

b) Describe two of the costs that would be involved in gaining more up-to-date information on what skiers want from a ski resort. (2 marks)

Q2 A mail order company takes new customer details over the telephone. They need the full address of the new customers in order to set up an account. Rather than ask the customer to give their full address, they have bought a database of postcodes from which the address can be read. The customer only needs to give the postcode and door number to complete their address details.

Give three advantages to the mail order company of using the database, rather than collecting the address information directly from the customers. (3 marks)

The answer to life, the universe and everything — that's valuable information...

...and I just happen to know the answer. And before you say "42! 42! 42!", it's not 42. But I'm not sure whether it's appropriate for me to exclusively reveal to a group of ICT students information of such incredible staggering importance... Oh go on then, here it is — "love". Isn't that nice? Does it give you a warm feeling inside? It's not really that, it's 46.

What can ICT do?

These pages are for AQA Unit 2 and OCR Unit 1.

While it's important to learn specific details to impress examiners with, you need to have an overview too. These two pages will go over the general capabilities and limitations of ICT. You know, things like "makes noise but not jam"...

ICT Systems Can **Create**, **Process**, **Store** and **Transfer Data**

1) ICT, basically, is the use of technology to **create**, **manipulate**, **store**, **exchange** and **transfer** data in a variety of forms (including textual, graphical, audio, video).
2) ICT systems include all types of **computerised systems**, **telephone systems** and **mobile communications systems**.
3) The term ICT refers to the **hardware**, the **software** and the **data** that make up the system.
4) ICT systems **process vast amounts of data** and **produce information** that people can use to make decisions.

ICT Systems Can Do Lots Of **Useful Things**

You can store vast amounts of data using ICT

Large ICT systems are capable of **storing millions of items of data**. E.g. online stores keep their product details online and the UK census is now also stored for access online. The census database holds data about millions of UK residents.

You can transfer data quickly and easily

High speed broadband Internet connections allow **huge amounts** of data to be transferred at very **high speeds** — this allows users to do things like **download** high quality music and video, **communicate** via video links and webcams and watch **live streaming** videos, e.g. news coverage. Improvements in **wireless technologies** allow high speed data transfer through portable devices like mobile phones, e.g. for Internet access.

ICT systems can give instant feedback on the data they store

Being able to **give instant feedback** makes ICT systems **very efficient**. E.g. **stock control systems** keep track of item levels — if they drop below a specified limit a reminder is produced to re-order the item. Another good example is **electronic funds transfer systems** — they allow electronic transfer of money between accounts instantaneously, but can also report transactions if a customer account doesn't have enough money in it.

You can search, sort and combine information

Searches and sorting of large amounts of data can be done very quickly. For example, internet searches allow you to search millions of websites in just a fraction of a second. The results of searches can also be **combined** with other items to **produce useful things** like reports, invoices or mail-merged letters.

ICT can carry out repetitive processes

ICT systems can carry out processes like **calculating figures**, **producing lists** or **controlling devices** over and over again without making mistakes or needing a break. E.g. the same **processing** is required when working out telephone bills — because many bills have to be produced the processing must be **fast and accurate**.

ICT can provide vastly improved security

Systems can **password protect** or **encrypt** the data and information stored on them. Without the correct code the file(s) cannot be accessed. Systems also run **anti-virus software** to preserve the files against corruption. Storing copies of information on multiple systems as **backup** protects against data loss.

What can ICT do?

But Using ICT Isn't Always Appropriate

Sometimes the hardware isn't up to the job

1) You can only **store** as much data as the **system has disk space for**.
2) The **speed** at which the system can retrieve and process data depends on the **speed of the processor**.
3) **Hardware failure** can cause loss of data and **disruption** to the whole system.
4) People use the Internet to do things like downloading videos, filesharing and video-chatting — as usage increases, **more bandwidth** is needed. The bandwidth cannot always keep pace with the **demand**.
5) As people get used to higher processing speeds they begin to **demand even more**. Sometimes developments **can't keep up** with the increasing demands. This in turn affects software which can become **obsolete quickly**.

Information provided by ICT systems is only useful if the software processes it effectively

If the software is **badly written** it can mean:

1) It doesn't **retrieve** the data in an **efficient** way.
2) It **can't organise** the data in a way that can be **understood** or is **useful**.
3) It **can't control** what data is entered.
4) It **can't back up** the data safely.
5) It **has bugs** which can cause the system to crash and lose data.

There can be compatibility problems when transferring data

Different types of hardware and operating systems **store and deal with data differently**, so one machine may not be able to deal with data sent from another machine. For example:

1) **Apple Macs** are different from **PCs** and process data differently.
2) **Spreadsheet** packages often can't open a database file and vice-versa.
3) Many companies now give their employees **laptop computers** with **wireless** capability so that they can work anywhere using e-mail and the Internet. But as many different types of wireless technology have emerged (Wi-fi, 3G, GPRS) a worker will only be able to use their laptop where the right type of wireless access point is available.

Practice Questions

Q1 List three general capabilities of ICT systems.

Q2 Describe two ways in which hardware can limit the effectiveness of ICT systems.

Q3 Describe two ways in which software can limit the effectiveness of ICT systems.

Exam Questions

Q1 ICT systems can input and validate data. Give three other examples of things an ICT system can do. (3 marks)

Q2 ICT stands for Information and Communication Technology.
Explain the term "Communication Technology" in this context. (2 marks)

ICT — but I'm limited by my inability to get near the kettle...

That's because all the other writers, editors, examiners and teachers are hogging it. Oh yes, it's a busy busy morning at CGP central today. The office is humming with activity, and some calming music is being piped in for us. The only down side is that I'm imagining it all and have therefore clearly gone insane after only one section. Oh well, on to section two then...

Input Devices

These pages are for AQA Unit 1 and OCR Unit 1.

Hardware is all the physical parts of a computer system — monitors, disks, keyboards, printers, etc. It can be split into three categories — input devices, storage media and devices, and output devices. And that's what this section covers.

Different Systems Need Different Types Of Input

All systems need **instructions** of some sort and these generally come **from the user**.

- Some systems need **text**. This can be typed in by a user or read from a document.
- Some systems need high-quality **pictures**, and some produce line drawings and need accurate input of lines.
- Other systems use **video** images, and must be able to receive these images.

Input devices are chosen for their **quality** and **ease of use** in dealing with the type of input required.

All Systems Use One Or More Input Devices

Here are some examples:

Device	Type of Input	Characteristics and Limitations
Keyboard	• text • numbers • some cursor movement	• Most conventional computer systems have a QWERTY keyboard with a numeric keypad and function keys — people are **familiar** with them and they are **versatile** for experienced users. • Most **instructions** can be done **from the keyboard**, although some can be quicker with a **mouse** (e.g. most keyboards have arrow keys to move the cursor through text, but it's often quicker to use the mouse).
Mouse	• cursor movement • click/double click • drag • scroll	• Most conventional computer systems have a mouse or other pointing device — people are **familiar** with them and they are designed to **fit easily** in your hand. • They are easy for **beginners** to use with a graphical user interface. • **Extensive** use can cause repetitive strain injury. • Instructions can be **slower** with the mouse **than with the keyboard** (e.g. to copy and paste requires at least four mouse clicks whereas it only requires two keystrokes, Ctrl+C and Ctrl+V). • Some **optical mice** have trouble on certain surfaces, making the cursor move erratically or wander on its own. **Ball mice** used to pick up dirt which affected their performance, but they're hardly used these days. • **Wireless mice** can cause problems as they always require a supply of **batteries**. Low battery power can affect the **performance** of the mouse.
Scanner	• images • text	• A scanner uses reflected light to **read data** from a paper document. This data might be a picture or text, in colour or in black and white. • **Special software** is required to interpret what the scanner reads, especially if it is text. • The **quality** of the input depends on the **resolution** of the scanner. A high quality picture needs a high-resolution scanner.
Touch screen	• press • drag	• Touch screens are often used on terminals in **public places** and also on portable devices like mobile phones and mp3 players. • The user **touches** one part of the screen with their finger or a pointing device, and this acts the same way as clicking a mouse. • Using a touch screen means that a **surface** for a mouse is **not required** and means, in a public place, that the **input device can't be removed**. • It is **difficult** to **pinpoint small areas** on a touch screen and so buttons, menus, scroll bars, etc. must be large enough to be accessible.

Input Devices

There Are Also **Other Types** Of **Pointing Device**

Graphical user interfaces make use of pointing devices, such as a mouse or touch screen, as a way for the user to **give instructions**. Other types of pointing device are:

- **Trackball** — this is like an **upside down mouse**. The ball is on the top and you use your finger or the palm of your hand to move the cursor around on the screen. There will be **switches** around the trackball, which act in the same way as mouse buttons. Trackballs were used on laptops but are now mainly used as **aids** for people with disabilities like **arthritis or RSI** in the hands or fingers.
- **Trackpad** — these are also used on **laptop** computers. The pad is sensitive to the **movement** of a **finger** over the surface and the movement of the finger moves the cursor on the screen. Again, **buttons** are provided like mouse buttons and there is no need for a mouse or surface.

Both these devices can be difficult to get used to if you are used to using a mouse.

Some Systems Use **Special Types Of Keyboard**

1) A PC keyboard usually has a set of QWERTY keys, a numeric keypad and a set of function keys. This makes it **very flexible**, but **quite big**.
2) Some systems **don't need all these functions** and so they only have **part** of the keyboard.
   - A **cash machine** will only have a numeric keypad as only numbers will be entered.
   - A **mobile phone** (or touch tone phone) uses a numeric keypad but assigns letters to each key to allow text input as well.
   - **Touch tone phones** are used to select from menus on computerised call systems.

Concept Keyboards Don't Have **Traditional Keys**

1) A concept keyboard uses **sensitive areas of surface** rather than actual keys.
2) Different areas of the surface will **input different commands**.
3) Concept keyboards are useful in areas where dirt or liquid makes it **impractical** to use a conventional keyboard.
   - Many **fast food restaurants** use concept keyboards for entering customer food orders into their system.
   - Concept keyboards are used in computer controlled diagnostic systems for **testing car engines**.
4) Special areas of the keyboard will perform a **particular function** depending on the software it's used with.
5) This type of keyboard is very **specialised** and will be used with one particular system. It's not flexible enough to be used like a conventional keyboard.

Practice Questions

Q1 Make a list of the main types of input that can be used by different computer systems.

Q2 List three types of pointing device.

Q3 Give three different examples where keyboards are used as an input device (other than QWERTY keyboards).

Exam Questions

Q1 The World Wide Web is a collection of information often accessed by navigation through a graphical user interface. People can access the Internet from many different systems, including their home PCs, laptops, mobile telephones and public Internet terminals.

For two of the systems mentioned above, give an example of an input device that could be used to navigate a web page, and evaluate its use. (6 marks)

Q2 Describe one benefit and one limitation of concept keyboards. (2 marks)

Have you seen my new concept trousers? — they're a bit of a hard wear...

Hardware is a bit of an odd one — in theory, you already know it all. I mean, everyone knows how to use a keyboard and a mouse, don't they? Well... it's not quite that simple. You have to make sure you can remember all the ins and outs of all the different kinds of hardware input devices. It's easy to pick up marks on these questions, as long as you've learnt it all.

Input Devices

These pages are for AQA Unit 1 and OCR Unit 1.

Some input devices, like keyboards and mice and scanners, are general purpose — they provide a range of different types of input. Other input devices are designed specifically for one type of input. Like badgers. No, wait... What?

Scanners Are Used To Read Different Types Of Input

1) Scanners are used to **read** information from documents and **store** it in a computer system.
2) The data is read by the scanner and **interpreted by software**.
3) If the document is made up of **text**, it might be scanned then converted using **Optical Character Recognition (OCR)** software. This does the best it can to translate the image it gets into text but it **doesn't always get it right**. Even so, with large volumes of text it is still often **quicker** to scan and edit the text than to type it in.
4) **Bar codes** are scanned by specialist scanners. The scanner is driven by **specialist software** that interprets the bar code. A bar code reader will **only** be able to read bar codes.

Special Devices Are Used To Input Pictures And Drawings

A **graphics tablet** is used to input line drawings (e.g. engineering plans) into a computer. The user has a **stylus** (like a pen), which draws on a **graphics pad**. Drawings can be done from scratch or can be traced by moving the stylus over an existing drawing. A graphics tablet can only input lines but the tablet may have special areas for **giving instructions** for changing colour, line thickness or other features.

A **light pen** is a pointing device used to point to a position on the screen. It's especially useful for the input of line drawings — it works by drawing the line **on the screen** rather than on a tablet. Light pens can also highlight objects on-screen during a presentation.

- For photographic images a **digital camera** will capture an image and input it into a computer.
- For video images a **digital video camera** can feed a series of images into the computer. The **resolution** of the camera in both cases will determine the quality and size of the image it captures.
- A **webcam** is designed to be connected directly to a computer system so that it can feed its video images straight to a website, rather than store them first and then upload them. Webcams are also used in videoconferencing, and on instant messaging services so people can talk 'face-to-face'.

Some Devices Are Designed For A Very Specific Purpose

Data can be stored in a way which means it can be input **straight into the computer** as long as the **right device** is used.

1) Magnetic strips on credit card or train tickets hold data identifying card details or ticket details. A **magnetic card reader** is able to read the strip and decipher the details.
2) A **chip and PIN** card has a small integrated circuit which holds similar details to a magnetic strip, but also holds the PIN number of the card in encrypted form, so it can be authenticated as it is being used. A **special reader** is used to read the PIN from the card.
3) Magnetic ink is used on some documents and a special **Magnetic Ink Character Recognition (MICR) device** is used to read the magnetic characters. This system is extensively used in banking systems where magnetic characters are printed on cheques to give the cheque number, sort code and account number. The characters are read by a machine so that bank operators only have to enter the date and the amount of the cheque and the person it is to be paid to. This also makes cheque forgery more difficult.
4) An **Optical Mark Reader (OMR)** is designed to read marks made at particular points on a form. The reader knows what parts of the form give particular information and uses reflected light to see if there is a mark in any of those places. Common uses of OMR are on National Lottery tickets and school registers.

Input Devices

Some Devices Are Designed For Use **Without Human Intervention**

1) Environmental control systems, engine management systems and process control systems use a **variety of sensors** as input devices.
2) These sensors might sense heat, light, movement, humidity, magnetism or pressure.
3) Computer systems can **take the inputs** and **act appropriately**. For example, if a temperature sensor gives a temperature reading below what is required the system might turn on a heater.

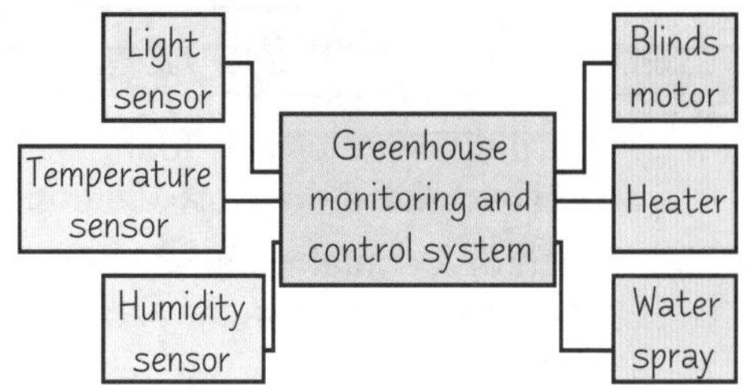

Physically Disabled People Sometimes **Need Special Devices**

Physical disabilities can prevent people from being able to use **conventional input devices** like keyboards and mice. A range of devices has been designed to cater for **different disabilities**:

1) A **foot-mouse** is a mouse controlled by the user's feet rather than their hands. This device has the same capabilities as a conventional mouse but is designed for those who are unable to operate a mouse using their hands, or to reduce the risk of injuries such as carpal tunnel syndrome caused by extensive mouse usage.
2) For blind users, **braille keyboards** can be used for typing.
3) **Concept keyboards** are also very useful for disabled users who can't use the conventional keyboard and for very inexperienced or very young users. Large areas of the keyboard have particular functions, often indicated by a picture to help the user.
4) People who are unable to make any movement will need very special devices to communicate with the computer. Some examples of these special devices include:
   - **microphone and headset** to operate and use software run by voice-recognition.
   - **puff-suck switches** used in place of a mouse button and operated by exhalation and inhalation.
   - **eye-typers** allow their user to select keyboard keys by staring at particular places for a given time.

Practice Questions

Q1 Make a list of input devices that can be used to input graphical images.

Q2 Explain how MICR devices work.

Q3 What sort of input devices might be used in an environmental control system?

Q4 Give three examples of input devices designed to help physically disabled users.

Exam Question

Q1 A photographic company wants a computerised system to store new and existing photographs so that they can be printed on T-shirts along with a slogan requested by the customer. They buy a T-shirt printing machine and a thermal printer capable of producing photo-quality output.

Name three input devices they will need and say what each will be used for. (6 marks)

Input devices? Frankly my dear, I don't give a damn...

Make sure you know all these — we're moving on to backing storage next. So go over them until you've got them all down. It's all pretty straightforward though, and none of it's too taxing... Which means that I have a few minutes to ask you what goes black-white-flag black-white-flag black-white-flag? Simple — a nun rolling down a hill with union jack pants on...

Backing Storage

These pages are for AQA Unit 1 and OCR Unit 1.

*A **backing store** (also known as a **secondary store**) is any data-storage area outside the computer's main memory.*

***Hard Disks** are the Main Internal Backing Store*

1) **Hard disks** are usually found inside computers. They're **rigid** circular plates that have been **magnetised**, and each **hard drive** usually contains several disks stacked on top of each other.
2) Each disk contains lots of **concentric tracks**, and these tracks are divided into **sectors**. The data is stored in the sectors. Most disks can store data on **both sides**.

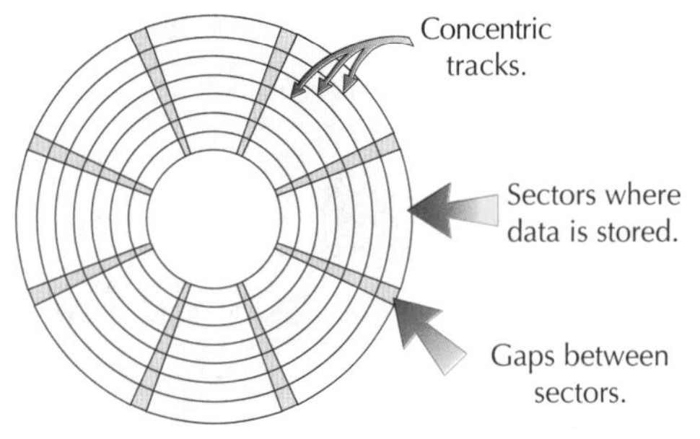

3) The disk **rotates** at between 5,400 and 10,000 revolutions per minute (rpm), and **read/write heads** (one on either side) float just above the surface of the disk. They're so close that a speck of dust would ruin the hard drive — so the disk drive is kept in a **sealed unit**.
4) The main benefit of hard drives is that they have a **large capacity** — hundreds or thousands of **gigabytes (GB)** (1 gigabyte = 1024 megabytes) are now common.
5) One potential problem is that the hard drive is usually housed **inside** the computer, so it's not easy to use it on a different machine (though you can buy removable hard drives). Also, if there's a problem with the hard drive, all of the data stored on it may be lost.
6) **External** hard drives are now readily available and quite affordable, so they're a good option for storing large amounts of data, and are portable.

***Optical Discs** are the Main External Backing Store*

Optical discs include **compact discs** (CDs) and **Digital Versatile Discs** (DVDs). They store digital data as **pits** (i.e. little indentations) on the surface of a **reflective disc**. The data is **read** by moving a **laser beam** across the surface of the disc and reading the change in position of the reflected beam.

There are three different types of CD:

1) CD-ROMs can only be used to **read** data — and they hold around **650 megabytes (MB)**.
2) CD-Rs are sold as **blank CDs**, but can have data **written** onto them only **once**. After that they work in the same way as CD-ROMs. Both CD-ROMs and CD-Rs are known as **WORM** disks — "Write Once and Read Many times".
3) CD-RWs are also available. RW stands for **Read and Write**. They are like a CD-R but can have old data **deleted** and new data **written** onto the disc.

We've been to Optical moon. We've followed Mr Spool.

DVDs are like CDs but **hold much more data** — up to **8.54 GB** a side. As a result they can store whole films digitally. You can get DVD-ROMs, DVD±Rs and DVD±RWs. These work in the same way that CD-ROM, CD-R and CR-RWs do. DVD-RAMs are like DVD±RWs but are made to be more suitable for frequent updating and changing of data than either DVD±RWs or CD-RWs.

Blu-ray discs are like DVDs but again **hold much more data** — nearly **6 times** as much as a standard DVD. They're used for storing movies in **high definition.**

For several years, Blu-ray was in a 'format war' with a rival format HD-DVD. The formats were very similar, but incompatible with each other. Blu-ray finally won the battle in Feb '08 when HD-DVD's main producer, Toshiba, ceased production allowing Blu-ray to become the industry standard.

Backing Storage

Flash Memory is often used in Memory Sticks...

1) Flash memory is often sold in **pen type devices** (often called pen drives or memory sticks) so that you can easily connect it to your computer using a **USB** socket. They usually store between **1 and 32 GB** of data.
2) Memory sticks are small and tough. They let you easily **transfer** data between different computers.
3) Although flash memory is a lot **slower** than the computer's main RAM, it's often **faster** than a hard disk. So some operating systems, such as Windows Vista, let you use memory sticks as a **temporary storage area** between RAM and the hard disk. That can lead to a faster computer, depending on the software you use.
4) The main disadvantages are that they are **easily lost** or stolen and more **expensive** than DVD–RWs, say.

and Memory Cards

1) Flash memory is also used to make small **memory cards**. They come in lots of different shapes and sizes, but most are close to rectangular and about the size of a **coin**.
2) Memory cards are used by **digital cameras** and some **mobile phones** and **MP3 players**. Many computers come with slots for memory cards, which means that you can use them for reading and writing files just like a **memory stick**.

Magnetic Tape can Back-up Large Amounts of Data

1) **Magnetic tape** is often used when large amounts of data need to be backed up. The data is written to and read from the tape in the same way as in a **video recorder**. Tapes can store as much as **800 GB**.
2) With magnetic tape, very large amounts of data can be stored relatively **cheaply**. This makes them ideal for backing-up a whole **hard drive**, or even a whole network.
3) However, **access time** is **slow**, because the **read/write head** can't go directly to a particular piece of data — it has to wind through the whole tape. This is called **serial** or **sequential access**.

Floppy Disks and Zip Disks have Had Their Day

1) A **floppy disk** is a circular piece of **magnetised plastic** protected by a **hard plastic** sleeve.
2) The amount of data a floppy disk can hold is **tiny** by today's standards — about **1.4 MB**.
3) Accessing data is **slow** and they only last about **6 months** if used regularly.
4) **ZIP disks** are like floppies, but much more solid and reliable. They can store up to **750 MB**. But they're much more expensive than optical media.
5) Floppy and ZIP disks have now all but **vanished**, replaced by more modern technologies.

So long, Mr Zip.

Practice Questions

Q1 What's the main internal backing storage used in computers? Describe its features.

Q2 Describe the different types of optical storage media available.

Q3 Give two examples of storage media that use flash memory and list their advantages.

Q4 List three types of magnetic storage media, describing their main advantages and disadvantages.

Exam Question

Q1 An insurance company uses a variety of software and stores many data files in its computer systems. Choose three different types of backing storage media and explain how the company might make use of these media. (6 marks)

If the Grand National was sponsored by IKEA — I'd be backing "storage"...

It might seem like that long list of backing storage media is a bit pointless to learn, but it's information that will be useful to you in the long run. It's always good to keep these things swimming around in the old noggin, cos you never know when they'll come up. And once you have learnt them, you can spend some quality time inventing puns to put into CGP books.

Output Devices

These pages are for AQA Unit 1 and OCR Unit 1.

An output device is any hardware used to communicate processed data to the user, e.g. monitor, speakers, printer.

Monitors** Are A Pretty Obvious **Output Device

The main considerations for choosing a monitor are **size**, **picture quality** (e.g. resolution, colour depth) and **cost**.

1) Monitor **size** is measured in inches diagonally from corner-to-corner of the screen. Typical sizes for normal home or office use would be around 17″ to 22″. They also come in different **aspect ratios** — the different **width and height** of an image depending on the capabilities of the monitor.
2) **Resolution** tells you how many **pixels** (dots) the monitor can display. Most new monitors can show at least 1280×1024 pixels. **Dot pitch** tells you the distance between pixels — lower values give sharper images.
3) Most new computer systems will have flat-panel screens using **TFT** (thin-film transistor) **LCD** (liquid crystal display) technology. These are thin, lightweight and portable compared to the old **CRT** (cathode ray tube) monitors which have virtually died out now.
4) **Plasma** screens are also popular — these can give better picture quality especially for larger screen sizes (e.g. between 35″ and 50″). This makes them suitable for more specialist uses, e.g. presentations, hotels, gyms.
5) LCD and plasma have pretty much replaced CRTs in the **TV market** too (apparently everyone now must have a flat screen TV as big as the living room wall. Personally I'm still happy with Edna, my 14″ B&W CRT).
6) These newer technologies do have some **disadvantages** though. LCD screens don't always give as good picture quality as CRTs and can be hard to view at angles. Some LCDs can struggle with moving images, giving a smearing effect. Plasma screens are **hot** to touch and are prone to image **burn-in** if screen savers aren't used.

Inkjet Printers** Are The **Cheapest

1) **Inkjets** are the most popular printers for home use. They spray jets of ink as the paper is fed past the print head.
2) There are **three** different ways of **controlling the flow** of ink. Some printers have nozzles with **crystals** which change shape when an electrical current is passed through them. In others, the ink is **heated** so it expands and pushes through the nozzles onto the paper. **Continuous flow printers** squirt ink continuously from the nozzles, and the unused ink is electrically charged and diverted back by charged plates.

Laser Printers** Are **Ace** But A Bit More **Expensive

Laser printers are the **most versatile** output device. They set up pages in full before printing and have four main parts:

1) **Electrostatic rotating drum** — has an electrical charge.
2) **Laser** — etches onto the drum a negative image of the page to be printed. Where the laser hits the drum the electrical charge is removed.
3) **Toner cartridge** — contains ink. When the drum passes over the toner cartridge the ink is attracted to the charged areas of the drum. The ink is then transferred onto the printer paper.
4) **Fuser unit** — heats the paper to fuse the ink onto it.

*The **User** Needs To **Think About What They Want** From Their Printer*

Initial Cost
Inkjets are very cheap to buy. At the moment a colour laser printer is still fairly expensive, but the cost of laser printers is coming down all the time.

Resolution
When looking for documents of a high quality, laser printers offer good resolution with a high dots-per-inch (dpi). Some inkjets are pretty good too though.

Speed
Laser printers have a high page-per-minute print rate, although the best inkjet printers can also print very fast.

Running Costs
Laser printers are often more cost effective than inkjet printers if you print a lot of pages.

Output Devices

There Are Some Other **Specialist Printing Devices** Too

1) **Graph plotters** are commonly used with **Computer Aided Design (CAD)**. They work using an automated arm that disperses ink, as it moves over the paper. This is often designed to handle large paper sizes and outputs high quality vector graphics (e.g. needed in architectural plans).
2) **Dot matrix printers** used to be used with PCs, but these days they're just used for things like receipt printing. They print a series of dots that appear to form characters at normal reading distance. They can be very useful where carbon copies are to be printed simultaneously.
3) **Thermal printers** are often used in till receipts and fax machines. They work by transferring an impression onto paper using heat.
4) **Braille printers**, also known as **embossers**, are used to create sequences of raised dots on paper. This device is intended for the blind and visually impaired.

Actuators Control Physical Movement

Actuators are output devices that are able to move and perform simple mechanical tasks. There are **three main types**:

1) **MOTORS** are powered by electrical signals from the computer.

   a) **Stepper-motors** are ones where the signal moves the motor in a series of tiny but accurate steps. Flat-bed scanners are usually powered by stepper-motors.

   b) **Servo-motors** are ones where the signal enables the motor to move continuously at high speed. These are used to power computer-operated drills.
2) **HYDRAULIC ACTUATORS** are powered by **fluid pressure** controlled by the computer. This makes them **slow** but very **powerful**, so they're useful for heavy lifting or equipment.
3) **PNEUMATIC ACTUATORS** are like hydraulic ones but are powered by **air pressure** instead. They're **less powerful** than hydraulic systems but **more responsive**, and are often used to power robots on fast-moving automated production lines.

Finally, here's a Couple More **Random** Output Devices...

1) **LCD projectors** are often used by companies for **presentations**. They basically project a computer's output onto a large screen, so can be used to show text, images, videos, etc.
2) **Speakers** are another fairly obvious output device for any system requiring sound. In some cases, speakers might be used as the **primary** output device, e.g. speech output for a visually-impaired person.

Practice Questions

Q1 Describe the main differences between TFT, LCD, plasma and CRT monitors.

Q2 Compare the relative advantages and disadvantages of inkjet and laser printers.

Q3 List four other specialist printing devices.

Q4 Name and describe the three types of actuator.

Exam Questions

Q1 A construction company employs architects to draw up plans for building layouts using specialist software. There is a proposal to upgrade an existing A4 inkjet printer to a more sophisticated output device that can produce precise printed copies of plans in a larger size.

Name a device that would be appropriate for this and say why. (2 marks)

Q2 A school IT room needs a paper output on a network. A laser printer has been installed by the school.

Give two reasons why the school might have decided on a laser printer. (2 marks)

Simon can't hear his lecturer properly — he needs better speakers...

I always forget monitors are output devices. I like having everything on paper you see, so I can dribble tea on it and get jam in between the sheets. I did try that with my computer once, but some of the keys stuck together so that every time I pressed the "b" key, the keyboard would type "swertyuiop". I had to give up after the spellchecker had a breakdown.

Systems and Applications Software

These pages are for AQA Unit 1 and OCR Unit 1.

What did the software driver say to the software? "Get off my bus, your ticket's clearly already been used and if you're not going to buy a new one then stop wasting my time." Or... "it's important to understand what drivers do".

Software Can Refer To All Kinds of Programs or Data

1) The term **software** refers to all the actual programs or data that a computer system uses — it's basically all the stuff stored electronically that you can't see. **Hardware**, by contrast, is all the physical bits that you can see.
2) There's two types of software — **systems** and **applications** software. Make sure you understand the differences between the two.

> **Systems software** is a set of programs that organise, utilise and control hardware in a computer system.
> **Applications software** is designed to make use of the computer system for specific purposes (see below).

3) Systems software includes **operating systems**, **drivers** and **utilities**. Operating systems are covered on p20-21.

Software Drivers Let the Computer Control the Hardware

Computer systems are made up of many devices, e.g. CD drive, printer, network card.
A **software driver** (or device driver) is a program **designed to control input, output and storage devices**.

1) Drivers allow **communication** between the operating system and hardware devices.
2) They also mean the devices can be **configured** by the operating system to work as intended.
3) It used to be the case that whenever a new piece of hardware, e.g. a CD drive, was added to a computer system, a driver would need to be installed before it would work. This would usually be supplied on a disk with the hardware.
4) These days, '**Plug and Play**' devices are a lot more common, where the drivers are **loaded automatically** when a new device is added. This is much less hassle all round.

System Utilities Are Programs That Perform Specific Functions

Here are some of the tasks that system utilities carry out:

Compression
System utility programs **convert data into a format** that takes up **far less memory space**. Compression software is particularly useful when data is being sent from one computer to another. Communication of data is faster when the file size is reduced.

File conversion
Each file saved on computer has a **file extension**, e.g. .doc, .xls. The extensions are **related to the specific application** used to create the file. A utilities program enables applications to **open** a file with a **different extension**. For example, MS Word can open a .wps file created by the word processor in MS Works even though its own files have an extension of .doc.

Keeping configuration files
These contain information on **system parameters**. When a program is run, it may need to look at configuration files to see which conditions it should adapt to.

Applications Software Can Be Generic or Task-Specific

1) **Generic software packages** are for everyday use and are very common. They're things like word processors, spreadsheet applications, desktop publishing software, and database applications.
2) They can be used for **lots of tasks**, not just one specific job. For example, spreadsheet packages can do things like sort numbers, produce simple databases, create charts etc.
3) **Task-specific** software packages can only be used for **one particular purpose**, e.g. payroll software can be used to process wages, but you can't use it to write a letter or draw a graph.
4) Task-specific software is usually used for a **specialist application**, so the user needs training in both the software and the subject area, e.g. CAD / CAM or music editing.

> When you're talking about applications software, make sure you **don't use the specific name** of a program (like Excel, or something) — always use **a description** (like **spreadsheet application**, or **word processor**).

Systems and Applications Software

Standardisation Can Affect The User's **Hardware and Software**

In an ideal world, all hardware and software would be built and work to the same set of standards. Unfortunately in IT, there are many different standards and most are not compatible with each other.

- **Hardware** needs to be **compatible** with a system's **software**. If a company decides to upgrade its software to a newer version, it may find that the old hardware will not work with the new software. Replacing the old hardware could then be very **expensive**.
- Different **operating systems manufacturers** e.g. Microsoft®, or UNIX®, have set standards so that applications will work on their operating systems. But there is **little compatibility** between manufacturers. This means that a presentation package written for one operating system **may not work** on another.
- As computers **age**, various components such as the processor or graphics card, may need **upgrading** so that they'll work with newer software and other newer systems. When computers reach a certain age, it may not be feasible to upgrade and instead the **whole computer system** will need replacing.
- **Technical Support** — if few people use the hardware or software, e.g. an older version of a software package, sources of technical support will be very limited and possibly expensive.

Lack of Standardisation Can **Also Affect Companies**

If companies merge and they use different hardware and software, this can cause problems.

1) The systems may not **communicate properly** — this can lead to incorrect data being passed between them.
2) **New equipment** might have to be purchased.
3) Staff may need to be **re-trained**.
4) There may be a **lack of technical support** available for those unfamiliar with the merged system.

The results of the merge between KFC and Orange were quite brilliant.

Practice Questions

Q1 What is system software?

Q2 What do software drivers do?

Q3 Write one sentence to explain each of the following terms: compression, file conversion and configuration.

Exam Questions

Q1 An insurance company has been formed through the merger of three smaller insurance companies.
Explain two effects the lack of hardware standardisation could have on the new company. (6 marks)

Q2 An operating system is software that controls and monitors hardware and applications.
There are often many system utilities supplied with an operating system.

Describe two examples of system utilities likely to be included. (4 marks)

Dear old Mary needs a new driver — Driv'er? But I 'ardly know 'er...

Because most drivers load automatically, a lot of computer users don't tend to ever know what they are or what they do. But you get the extra special pleasure of finding out, because you're doing AS ICT. It's hardly the most thrilling topic in the world, but just think how impressed your friends and family will be next time you tell them all about what you've learnt...

Systems Software — Operating Systems

These pages are for AQA Unit 1 and OCR Unit 1.

It's easy to take Microsoft Windows® for granted, but don't forget that there are other successful operating systems too. Some of them are named after fruit. But I don't like apples. Why couldn't they call themselves Banana, or Coconut?

The **Operating System Controls** All The **Applications**

1) An operating system is essential computer software that **controls and monitors all the applications**.
2) It provides an **interface** between the **user**, **software** and **hardware** and is sometimes called the "heart of the system".

There Are **Two Main Operating Systems** For The **PC**

Microsoft Windows

Microsoft Windows®, the most popular operating system, provides a **Graphical User Interface** (GUI) for the user. This was originally based on the **Disk Operating System** (DOS) developed by Microsoft®. MS-DOS is still used behind the GUI in older versions of Windows®, providing some of the control and monitoring.

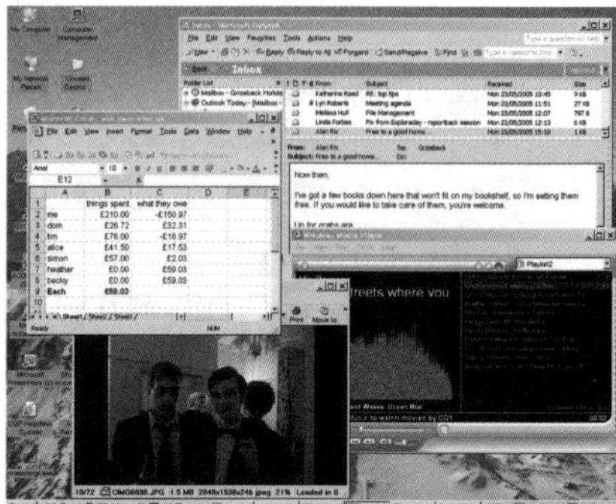

Linux

Linux is a rival operating system to Windows®. Although it's nowhere near as popular, the fact that the basic system is **free to download** and **open to development** by end users has led to its growth.

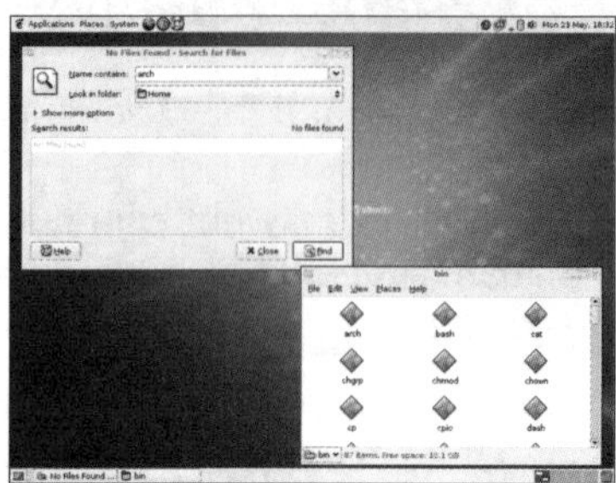

An **Operating System** Does **Various Different Things**

1) **Allocates internal memory**
When several applications are running at once there are often great demands on memory. An operating system handles the **allocation of RAM** to try and maximise scarce resources.

2) **Schedules programs and resources**
Again related to several applications running simultaneously, **processing has to be prioritised** to prevent programs freezing and to allow the computer to run efficiently.

3) **Monitors the system's input and output devices (IO)**
An operating system may have to **prioritise various input and output devices** so that they work efficiently, e.g. being able to display characters on screen as they are typed on a keyboard while at the same time another document is being printed.

4) **Logs errors**
Although an operating system tries to cope with all this multi-tasking, there are situations when memory is insufficient and applications or devices fail. An operating system has to provide **error messages** to the user.

5) **Checks for unauthorised access**
Different access privileges such as read only, read / write can be granted to users. An operating system controls the **granting of these privileges** and **regulates users** accordingly.

Systems Software — Operating Systems

Don't Forget About Apple Macs

1) Considered by some to be **more stable and efficient** than Microsoft Windows®, the Apple Mac operating system provides serious competition to PCs.
2) These work on a completely **different processor and systems architecture** to PCs.
3) Apple Mac computers are used extensively in the **graphic design industry**.

Operating Systems Can Multi-Task

1) Because lots of programs need to be run at once (especially in a windows environment), operating systems need to be able to **multi-task**.
2) Multi-tasking makes it appear as if multiple programs are **running simultaneously**, but it's generally just an **illusion** caused by the fast processing speed of the CPU. The CPU **divides its time** between the various tasks.
3) **Multi-core** processors are becoming more popular. These do allow the CPU to **actually** run different programs simultaneously. These can **speed up** applications, but only if the **software** has to be designed to use multi-core processing.

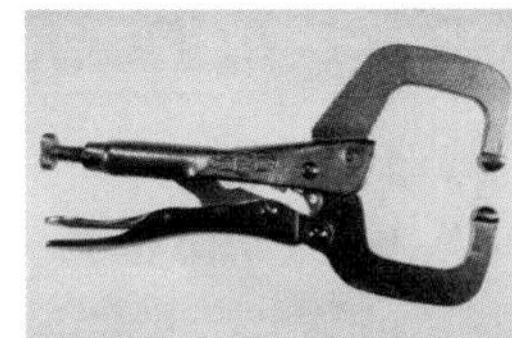

The tools used by the new operating system were getting curiouser and curiouser...

There Are Different Types of Operating System

1) **Single user system** is the name given to operating systems where one user has access at a time. These are the familiar operating systems usually associated with PCs.
2) **Multi-user systems** allow more than one user to access and use the computer at the same time. This can be seen in Local Area Networks (LANs), with computer servers that are accessed by multiple users.
3) **Distributed systems** use more than one computer system to run an application. These are common to networks, particularly LANs where one application has to be run at different sites.
4) **Batch processing** is where data is first collected together into batches before being input into the system at a later time, usually when there isn't a great demand for processing from other areas.
   For example, banks usually collect cheques that have been paid in throughout the day in various branches. They batch these and process them overnight.

Practice Questions

Q1 Describe the differing characteristics of Microsoft Windows® and Linux.
Q2 Name the five main things an operating system does.
Q3 Define multi-tasking and explain why it is useful for an operating system to be able to do this.
Q4 Name four different types of operating system.

Exam Question

Q1 A neighbour, who is a novice user, is purchasing a new PC.
An operating system is pre-installed on the computer.

a) State three tasks that are performed by an operating system. (3 marks)

b) What type of operating system would you expect to be supplied with the PC and why? (2 marks)

Dr. Foster uses leeches and a pump — it's not a great operating system...

Betcha by golly gosh wow gee blimey bananas... That was an action packed double page, wasn't it? Okay, okay. No. It really wasn't. But you know what (yes, I know, you've heard it all before) it really is useful information. Loads of people who use computers every day don't know this stuff — crazy... It's up to you to learn it all, so you're not one of them.

Human-Computer Interaction

These pages are for AQA Unit 2 and OCR Unit 1.

A Human-Computer Interface (HCI) lets users tell the computer what to do, and allows the computer to ask the user for input or display results. It's like show and tell, only with text prompts and error messages instead of fun.

The User And The Computer Interact Through The Interface

1) Users use an input device to **tell the computer what they want it to do** (usually a mouse or a keyboard).
2) The computer will **respond** to the user's requests and **ask for input** when it needs it (usually on a screen).
3) The interface is what **connects** the two.

A System Designer Will Aim To Create A Good Interface

A good HCI will:

- be **easy to use** for inexperienced users.
- give information about what **processing** is happening.
- be **consistent** so that the user becomes familiar with it quickly.
- have facilities for more experienced users to **customise** the interface.
- always do **what the user expects**.
- respond to user instruction in a **reasonable time** and **report on the progress** of a process.
- be **clear**. The user shouldn't have to think about what is required — it should be **obvious**.
- not require too much **effort** on the part of the user, e.g. minimum number of keystrokes, minimum mouse movement.
- reduce the possibility of mistakes by **checking** the user's input.
- have **help** available for the user when they need it.
- not require the user to **remember many commands**.
- take the user's **health and safety** into consideration, e.g. use colour schemes that are easy on the eyes, use screen layouts that don't require too much eye movement, minimise the number of times the user is required to click on things, use pre-emptive text to reduce the amount of typing required.

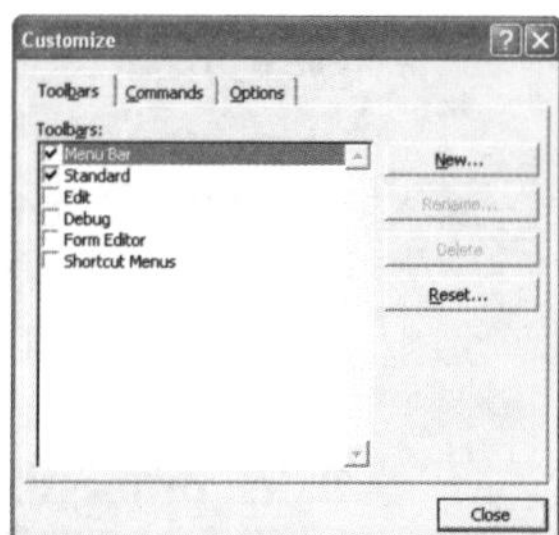

Interfaces can be of four kinds — **menu-driven**, **graphical**, **command line** or **natural language**.

Menu-Driven Interfaces Guide The User

1) Menu-driven software works with **windows-based operating systems**, such as Windows® or Mac OS®, and with **command-based operating systems** such as DOS® or UNIX®.
2) A menu-driven interface **guides the user** through a set of menus, letting them choose what they want to do.
3) Many **call centres** use this interface for directing telephone calls. When you phone the call centre, the system gives you choices and asks you to press a number for the one you want, then you're given a new set of choices.

Many Systems Have A Graphical User Interface (GUI)

A GUI will often have:

1) **Windows** — all input and output happens in a window which can be closed, moved, resized or minimised to help keep the screen clear.
2) **Icons** — buttons, check boxes, options buttons, etc. can be clicked on to change settings or to give instructions.
3) **Menus** — users can select instructions from menus.
4) **Pointer** — a pointing device (e.g. mouse, touch screen, trackerball, light pen) moves a cursor around the screen so that the user can control the windows, icons and menus.

Over-interaction with computers can have unwanted side-effects.

Human-Computer Interaction

Graphical User Interfaces Are Great For Beginners

1) Graphical user interfaces tend to be **intuitive**. This means that once you know about buttons, scroll bars and other controls, you can generally guess what you need to do next.
2) There is often **context sensitive help**, and the interface will be designed to make it as easy as possible for the user to enter data.
3) Because of all the features added to make the GUI easy to use, the actual software can sometimes be **quite slow** as processing time is taken up by the interface.
4) Also, in order not to confuse the user with too much information, **many commands are hidden** and must be found using help manuals.

Command-Line Interfaces Can be Powerful And Fast

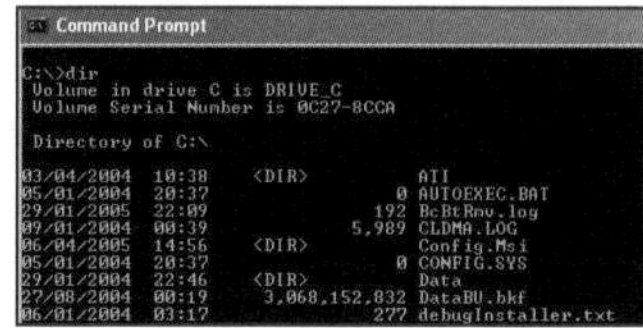

Command-line interfaces consist of a simple prompt screen into which the user types commands for the computer to carry out. A good example is MS-DOS®.

This kind of system can be very **quick** and **flexible** if you know what you're doing. It's good for computer programmers and other IT specialists who really understand how the system works.

But they're no good for your average computer user with no programming knowledge.

It's Much Easier When All Our Software Looks Similar

1) Many Windows applications use a **common interface** so that they all become easier to use.
2) For example, they all have similar File and Edit menus and some shortcut keys (Ctrl+X, Ctrl+S) do the same in all applications.
3) This means that when you get a new application, a large part of it will already be familiar, making it quicker to learn.

Natural Language Interfaces respond to Everyday Human Phrases

1) **Natural language interfaces** are designed to **understand human phrases**. The input may be through **typed text** or, in more advanced systems, **human speech**.
2) Using natural language can create an interface that is **easy to use** and reduce the need for **specialist training**.
3) However, it has **some problems**.
   - The processing is quite intensive and this can make the responses relatively **slow**.
   - People use **different phrases** to mean the same thing, so it's hard for the software to understand everything.
   - Natural language can be **ambiguous**, and computers can't distinguish between **different contexts** yet.

Practice Questions

Q1 Define the term "Human-Computer Interaction".

Q2 State five features of a good Human Computer Interface.

Q3 Name the three different types of HCI.

Exam Questions

Q1 Describe three features that should be considered when designing a HCI for complete beginners. (3 marks)

Q2 Give two advantages and two disadvantages of GUIs (graphical user interfaces). (4 marks)

After my PC crashed for the thirty-third time, the HCI I used was a mallet...

Tra-la-laaa... Oh wouldn't it be nice, just once, to be able to let loose on a dodgy PC with a mallet? Like a rock star? Or to throw a monitor out of a window after it's been playing up? Oh the fun we'd have. Of course, that sort of thing results in criminal prosecution and, from what I hear, that's not a very good thing. Hm. Perhaps I'll just sit in and revise instead....

Types of Processing

These pages are for AQA Unit 2.

*Here's a little section all about processing information. There shouldn't be anything too stressful here — it's just going through the different types of processing. Oh, and just remember — pizza, fizzy drinks **bad**, fruit and veg **good**!*

The Method Of Processing Is Chosen To Suit The Purpose Of The System

There are **three** distinct methods of **updating a system's data**:

1) **Transaction processing systems**
2) **Batch processing systems**
3) **Interactive processing systems**

Booking Systems Use Transaction Processing

1) In transaction processing, the computer responds to your request **there and then**.
2) Ticket reservation systems, cash machines and online-shopping sites all use **transaction processing**.
3) The **transaction** is the action that takes place, e.g. booking the ticket, withdrawing cash or placing the order.
4) With a booking system, all the booking information needs to be **entered** and **confirmed** before the actual booking is made, i.e. before the transaction is **processed**.
5) Transactions are processed **one at a time**, which means that **double-bookings** are impossible.

Example — Booking a Seat on a Plane (or 'The Ballad of Bob and Cecil')
Bob and Cecil both want to book a seat on the **same plane**. They go on to the airline's website at the same time and are both told that there are seats **available**. But, before they can actually **book** a seat, they need to enter all of their **details** and **confirm** the booking. Bob enters his details quicker than Cecil and **successfully books** a seat. When Cecil has entered all his details and pressed "confirm", he is told there are **no seats available**. The good news — the seat is not double booked. The bad news — **Cecil is angry**.

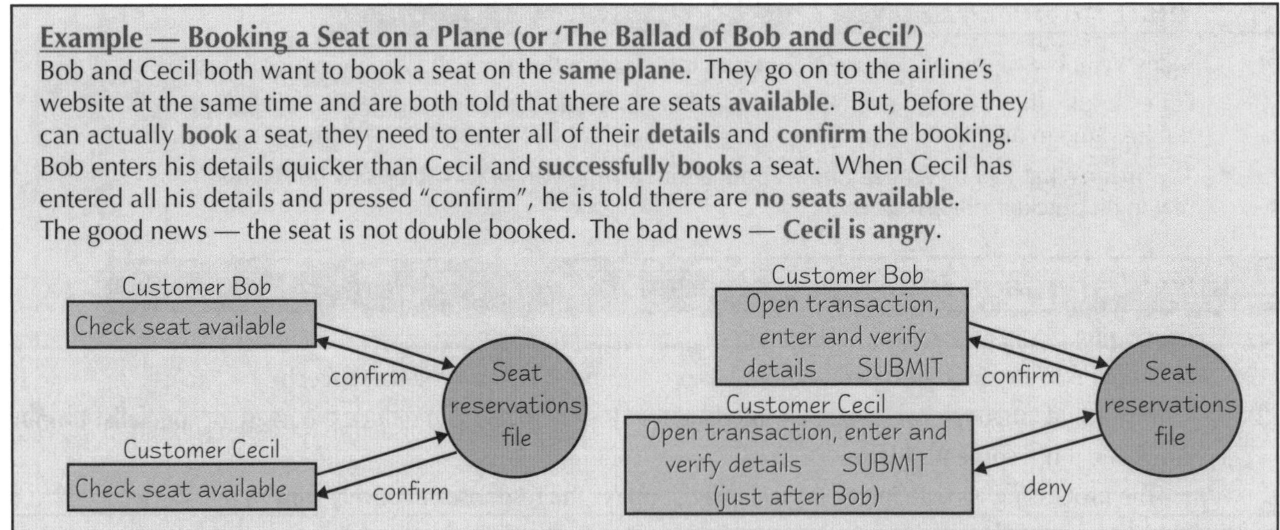

Batch Processing Systems Process Data at Regular Intervals

1) **Batch processing systems** work by collecting **large** amounts of **similar** transactions together over a **period of time** and updating them **all at once**.
2) Batch processing is used by companies that need large amounts of data to be processed regularly, e.g. utilities and telephone companies.

E.g. when a **gas company** reads meters they will collect all meter readings together with details such as the address or number of the gas meter. Once a set of readings have been collected, the data is input into the gas billing system all in one go and a set of gas bills are generated. When the bills are being generated, there is no input from the user at all.

A computer batch-processing some data (ish)

Types of Processing

Interactive Processing Lets You and the Computer... *Interact*

1) **Interactive processing systems** respond to actions from the user — you **interact** with them.
2) An interactive system is often **a front end** to a transaction processing system.

E.g. when you **shop online** you are using an interactive system. You can check if an item is in stock, check the price and can place an item in the basket and view what's already in there. Once you place the order, you're making a transaction, which then updates stock levels and billing information files.

The table below gives a nice summary of the three methods of processing you need to know, along with some lovely examples to remember for the exam.

Method	Examples	Reasons for using this system
Batch processing	production of gas bills, electricity bills, bank statements, credit card statements, invoicing, payroll	All transactions are processed together when the system is not busy, often overnight or at the weekend. This means access to the master data is always available during main working times. However, data becomes out of date until the next update.
Interactive processing	online booking systems, online banking systems, games software, design software	The user can check the state of data at any time and it will be up to date. Allows the user to control a system (e.g. a computer game) as the system responds to each user action. In an online booking / ordering system, it allows the user to look up and check information, e.g. prices, billing address, etc. before submitting their booking / final order.
Transaction processing	booking systems, invoicing and ordering systems, stock control systems	Transactions are made one at a time, which prevents two processes changing the same data, e.g. double booking a seat on a flight. However, there's no feedback from the system until a whole transaction has been submitted (unless it has an interactive front end).

Practice Questions

Q1 Explain what transaction processing is, using an example.

Q2 Explain what a batch processing system is, using an example.

Q3 Explain how transaction and interactive processing are different.

Exam Questions

Q1 For the following, recommend a suitable method of processing and say why that method is most suitable.
- a) a flight booking system. (2 marks)
- b) an end of month invoicing system. (2 marks)
- c) kitchen design software. (2 marks)

Q2 A large national bank updates customers' bank accounts overnight with deposits made during the previous day.
- a) Name an appropriate type of processing that the bank could use for this operation. (1 mark)
- b) Give three features of this type of processing. (3 marks)

Now here's some things EVEN BETTER than this page...

tea

potatoes

Scary goats

cars

the recorder

floating pylons

seals

fake heads

Ben

Data Backup and Recovery

These pages are for AQA Unit 2 and OCR Unit 1.

Backing up data is very important. Oh yes it is. Think of all those lovely Kylie MP3s you've got on your home computer. Are they backed up? No? But what if your computer suddenly dies? Noooooo.... Now, do you understand?

Data Needs To Be Backed Up

1) There are lots of ways that data can be lost — hard drives can **fail, viruses** can destroy or corrupt data, computer systems can be damaged in **fires** or **floods**, or files might just be accidentally **deleted**.
2) If a company suddenly lost all of its data, the results would be **disastrous**. Even if it only lost **some** data, it could still be **fairly** disastrous.
3) So the moral of the story is — it's really important that there's a **system** in place for regularly **backing up** data so that it can be **restored** if there's a problem.
4) Backing up basically involves making a **copy** of the computer system's data onto a suitable **storage medium**, e.g. magnetic tape, external hard-drive, DVD.
5) The backup should be **removed** from the **site** or stored in a **fireproof safe** — it's no good having the backup sat by the computer if the building burns down.

Data can be backed up on:

- Optical discs (CD-R / CD-RW / DVD±R / DVD±RW)
- External hard drives
- Pen Drives
- Magnetic tapes
- Zip drives

There are Different Methods for Backing Up

Global Backups

- A **global** backup is when you copy **all** of your data files to a second backing storage medium.
- If you lose your data, it's fairly **quick** and **easy** to **restore**.
- The downside is that the backing up process can be very **slow**, especially if you've got a lot of data.
- This can be a problem especially if you need to back up data **regularly**. For example, a company might find itself in a situation where the daily backup isn't finishing before the next one needs to start.

God's global backup

Incremental Backups

- **Incremental backups** only copy files that have changed since the last back up.
- Only backing up the altered files makes it **much quicker** than doing a global back up.
- **Restoring** from incremental backups can take a long time as the data needs to be **rebuilt** from all the separate backups.

Mirrored Hard Drives

- With this system, a second hard disk keeps an **exact mirror copy** of the main hard disk — the mirror is updated at the **same time** as the main disk.
- If the main disk fails, the mirror hard disk is **immediately available** and fully **up-to-date**.
- The mirrored disk may be part of the same computer system, or in more sophisticated systems, it can be at **another location**.
- Mirroring systems can be **very expensive**.

A Good Backup System might Combine Several Methods

1) Backups need to be **regular enough** so that if the whole system was lost and had to be restored from a back up, the data would still be **useful** to the users.
2) Depending on **how much data** is changed and processed, it may be necessary to back up the data once a week, once a day, or even more often, e.g. in the case of a booking system.
3) An **effective system** for backing up is often to **combine** global and incremental back ups. So for example, a company might do a global back up **once a week** and incremental back ups **every day in between**. If all data has to be recovered then there will be a maximum of **seven** backups to recover from.
4) There will also be a system for how long backups are **kept**. So a company might keep daily incremental backups for a **week** before **overwriting** them, but keep weekly or monthly **global** backups for a **longer period**.

Data Backup and Recovery

Companies Need To Plan For a **Worst Case Scenario**

1) In the event of a problem, it's really important for a company to get its systems up and running again as **quickly as possible**.
2) It's the responsibility of the IT department to **check regularly** that the backup process is working properly and to have a **recovery plan** in place.
3) The recovery plan might involve transferring the backed up data onto **replacement hardware** and installing the new hardware.
4) This all needs to be done as **quickly as possible** to ensure minimum disruption to the company — remember **time is money**, etc, etc.
5) The recovery plan should be **tested regularly** to make sure it's going to work. It's not a great idea to wait until something goes wrong to see if the recovery plan actually works...

Data can be **Archived** for Long-Term Storage

1) Archiving is the **storing** of data that is not being actively used, but **may be needed** at some point in the **future**.
2) The data is **copied** to a suitable **storage medium**, e.g. DVD, but then the **original data** is **removed**.
3) The main purpose of archiving is that it **frees storage space** on the main computer system, but the archived data is still available should it ever be needed.

Old pop bands are often liquidised for archiving. They can always be reformed at a later date.

Practice Questions

Q1 What's the difference between global and incremental backups? Give an advantage of each.

Q2 Describe a backing-up system that uses both of these methods.

Q3 Explain the difference between backing up and archiving.

Exam Questions

Q1 The owner of a small newsagents uses a computer to manage the orders and deliveries. Every week the owner copies the files onto a re-writable CD and puts the disc into a drawer next to the computer.

a) State three problems of this method of backing up. (3 marks)

b) Describe a more appropriate backup procedure. (4 marks)

Q2 A company is reviewing its backup and recovery procedures.

a) State three items that should be included in a backup procedure. (3 marks)

b) State three actions that should be part of a recovery procedure. (3 marks)

Don't back your data up into a cactus — you'll make it cry...

Awwww who's a little bit of data... Awww look at the cute ickle bit of data. Awww diddumms... But seriously: make sure you've got all this info about backing up data down. It's an easy way to pick up marks, and it's also an important lesson. I mean, just imagine what would happen if the ambulance service or the police force lost access to their whole systems.

Networks

This page is for AQA Unit 2 and OCR Unit 1.

Welcome to Section 4 — Communication Systems. This first double page on networks has a lot of info crammed in, but soldier through and you'll be rewarded with some nice, relaxed TV chat at the end of the page.

Computers Can Be **Networked** or **Stand-Alone**

1) If you have a home computer, it's probably a single computer not linked to any others, i.e. a **stand-alone** machine.
2) However, most computers nowadays are **linked together in a network**, either to other computers in a building or on a site (**LAN**) or to other computers around the world (**WAN**).

Definition of a network: computers linked together allowing resources to be shared and data to be transferred.

Advantages of Networking

- Hardware (e.g. printers, hard disks) can be **shared**.
- Software and data can be easily **shared** and **transferred** between machines.
- A user can access their files **from any computer** on the network (this is called 'hot-desking' — an employee doesn't have a particular desk in the office, but can use any of them).
- **Management of files** (e.g. backing up of data) can be done automatically and access to certain facilities (such as the Internet) can be controlled.

Disadvantages of Networking

- **Extra equipment** (e.g. network cards, cables, servers, etc.) is needed, and more specialised knowledge to oversee it.
- If the network **breaks down**, you won't be able to access your data or run programs if they're centrally stored.
- Users have **less control** over how computers are set up.
- Networks can be **slow** when there are lots of users.
- There's an increased risk of being infected by **viruses** from other people's machines.

Make Sure You Remember the Difference Between **LANs** and **WANs**

1) **LAN** — A **Local Area Network** is a collection of computers and peripherals in one building or site which are connected together using cable or a wireless connection.
2) **WAN** — A **Wide Area Network** connects computers over a large distance to other towns or countries using telecommunication links. There has been a large increase in the number of WANs in recent years, due to the reduced costs of transferring data and the demand for more instant communication.
3) The biggest example of a WAN is, you guessed it, the **Internet**.

There Are **Different Ways** to **Connect** to Networks

Computers can be linked to a network in various ways depending on the type of network.

1) LANs are usually linked **using cables** such as unshielded twisted pair (e.g. UTP CAT5).
2) **Fibre-optic backbones** (a high-speed line or series of connections in a network) can be used giving very fast links.
3) **WANs** use **long distance** communication technologies, e.g. telephone networks, satellite links or radiowaves. **Mobile phone** networks use **microwave** transmission which works over a relatively short distance.
4) Satellite and radiowave are examples of **wireless communication**.

Standard **Protocols** let Devices **Communicate**

1) When IT devices like workstations or computers are linked together to form a **network**, they must be able to communicate with each other.
2) Even though the hardware or the software is not the same, the communication links between them have to be compatible, therefore modern computer networks set **protocols** (rules) so that data sent from one computer can be understood by another computer.
3) If these **standards** were not in place then it would have a devastating effect on industry as IT devices would not be able to communicate with each other and data would be corrupted.

Different types of protocol:

IP — Internet Protocol

TCP — Transmission Control Protocol

FTP — File Transfer Protocol

HTTP — Hypertext Transfer Protocol

Networks

This page is for AQA Unit 2 only.

Learn the **Right Terms** To Talk About **Linking Networks**

1) A **bridge** is a device used to connect two LANs that use the same communication protocol.
2) A **repeater** is used to boost (amplify) the signal on a LAN which covers a long distance.
3) A **gateway** is used to link together different types of networks, e.g. two LANs that use different communication protocols, or a LAN to a WAN as shown in the diagram.

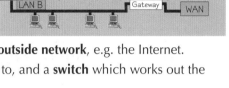

4) In homes, the gateway is the **Internet Service Provider (ISP)** that links the home computer to the Internet. In businesses, the gateway is the computer that links all the workstations on a **local network** to an **outside network**, e.g. the Internet.
5) A gateway uses a **router** which decides where the data needs to be sent to, and a **switch** which works out the pathway to send the data along.

Networks Need **Particular Hardware** and **Software** To Work

Hardware
- Each computer on the network needs a **network interface card** (**NIC**) and a **connection** (either with a cable or wireless) to the network.
- There's usually a **main central computer** (**server**) which often stores shared programs and individual files.
- To connect to a WAN, like the Internet, a **modem** or **gateway/router** will be needed.

Software
- The server itself needs a **network operating system** and software to manage and control the network.
- Network software will usually allow data **compression**, **encryption** and **error correction**.
- Each machine may need a **browser** to view Internet / intranet pages.
- **E-mail** software will be needed to communicate across the LAN and beyond.
- If an Internet connection is required then the server will need **connection software** and software to stop unauthorised access from outside the LAN (a **firewall**).

Bandwidth Tells Us **How Much Data** Can Be Transferred In a Given Time

1) **Broadband** transmission allows **many signals to be transmitted at once** and is very fast. It's particularly useful for multi-media transmission (sound, video and text simultaneously).
2) The term **bandwidth** refers to the **maximum amount of data** that can travel over a **data transmission channel** in a given time period — i.e. how much data can be sent from one computer to another **in any given time**.
3) Bandwidth is **NOT about the speed** of transmitting the data but about **how much data** can be transmitted. The **more bandwidth** there is available, the **more data can be moved**, e.g. video requires a large bandwidth because of the large amount of data which is being transmitted per second.

Practice Questions

Q1 Why has there been an increase in the number of WANs over recent years?

Q2 Explain the following terms when talking about networks: "repeater", "bridge", "gateway", "router" and "switch".

Exam Questions

Q1 There are ten employees in a local tourist office.
Each employee uses a PC connected to a local area network (LAN).

a) Give four benefits to the office of using a network, rather than standalone PCs. (4 marks)

The office is part of a national tourist board that is connected together over a Wide Area Network (WAN).

b) Discuss the differences between a LAN and a WAN. (6 marks)

c) Give two benefits to the tourist board of using a WAN. (2 marks)

I'm Network Technician Jack Bower and this was the longest page of my life...

If you've ever watched 24, you'll have heard the word protocol a lot, they love it... "you can't do that, it's not protocol", "Dammit, I don't care about protocol, I'm going to kiss you...", "Coffee please, milk, no protocol"... I bet those episodes will make a lot more sense now that you know what protocols are — standards to help computers communicate over networks.

Networks

These two pages are for AQA Unit 2.

Right then — here's the second instalment on networks. Better make sure you grab a hold of something tight, because this ride's going to go so fast you'll wish you'd never got on to page 30... wheeeEEEEEEEeeeeeeeeeeeeeeeeeeeeeeeeeee...

Networks Can Be Arranged In Different Ways

1) Networks can be arranged in various ways, depending on the number and type of computers on the network and how they are going to be used. Each way has its own advantages and disadvantages.
2) The way a network is arranged is called the **topology** of the network.

Bus Networks Are Based on a Single Connecting Cable

1) **Bus** networks (also known as **line** networks) have **one long cable**, known as the backbone, with the file server, workstations, computers and other devices attached along it.
2) Each connection point is called a **node**.
3) Every computer along the line receives each signal sent which means if there's a lot of **traffic** (computer activity) or a large number of computers, the communication can be **slow**.
4) It's **cheap** as it doesn't use much cabling, but if there's a **break** in the backbone then the whole network will **stop working**.

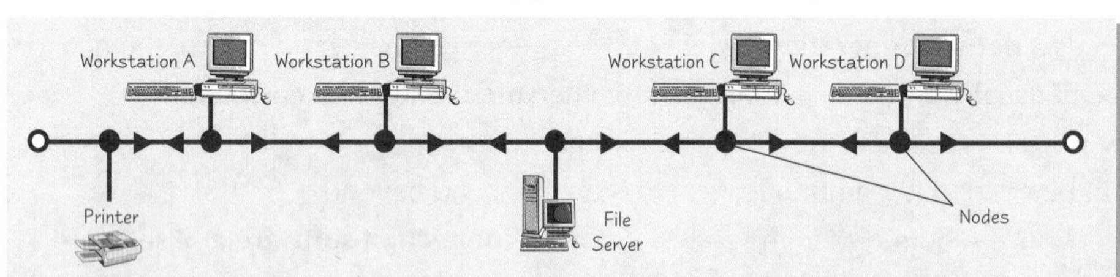

fast network

slow network

Star Networks Give Each Computer its Own Connection to the Server

1) In a **star** network each computer has its **own separate connection** to the file-server.
2) It's **faster** than a bus network — heavy use on one workstation doesn't affect performance on the others (as long as the server has the capacity to cope).
3) If one cable fails, it doesn't affect the other computers, meaning the network is **more fault tolerant**.
4) The layout makes it easy to **add or remove individual computers**.
5) Star networks are **more expensive** because more cabling is required.

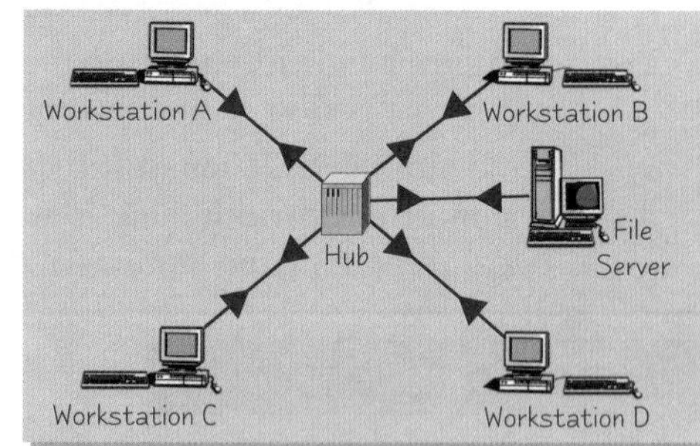

Data Flows Round Ring Networks in One Direction

1) In a **ring** network, the computers are linked together by cables into a circle. The data only flows **one way** around the network.
2) It's relatively **cheap** and **fast** although it can become slow if there is a lot of traffic.
3) It's suitable for a **small** number of computers — up to around 15, say. It doesn't need a file server because data is stored on the individual computers rather than centrally.
4) This makes it **difficult** to add or remove computers, and also means if **one** computer breaks down, the network stops working.

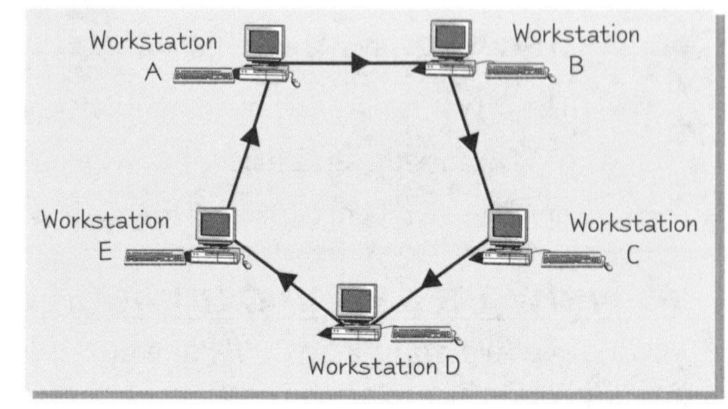

Networks

There Are Two Types of LAN

There are two types of local area network:

1) **Peer-to-peer** — this is when a small number of computers are linked and can communicate but there is no central file server. It is easy and straightforward to set up and the software to do so is often contained in the operating system.

2) **Client-server** — this is where there is a main server that controls the network. The computers linked to it are called clients, hence the name **client-server network**. It requires specialised software running on the server and is needed when there is a reasonably large number of users (say over 10).

The server controls the following:

- **Storage** of user's files.
- **Printing** over the network.
- **Access** to the network using user-names and passwords.
- Automatic **back up** of data on a regular basis.
- **Storage of some software** such as applications packages (though some may be stored in the client machines).

In a peer-to-peer network these facilities are the responsibility of individual users.

Wireless Communication means you Don't Need the Cables anymore...

1) A **wireless network** is very useful for connecting portable laptops to a network or connecting computers in temporary buildings where cabling would be difficult.

2) Wireless networks require a transmitter, which transmits via an antenna to wireless network cards on the networked computers.

3) Wireless networks are usually not as fast as conventional networks.

4) Also, the antennae have a limited range and may require line of sight.

Practice Questions

Q1 What are the differences between the star, ring and bus network topologies?

Q2 What is a peer-to-peer network?

Q3 What are the advantages and disadvantages of wireless networks?

Exam Questions

Q1 A small publishing company has four computers that are linked together using a peer-to-peer network. The company is expanding and buying a new suite of ten computers which will need to be networked and linked to the existing computers.
The manager has been advised that the company should change to a client-server network.

a) Explain the difference between a peer-to-peer network and a client-server network. (2 marks)

b) Why is a client-server network more suitable for the new situation? (3 marks)

Q2 A secondary school is installing a new local area network of computers and a decision has to be made whether to use a bus topology or a star topology.

a) Briefly describe in words the difference between these two topologies and draw a diagram of each configuration. (4 marks)

b) Give ONE advantage of a bus topology compared to a star topology. (1 mark)

c) Give ONE advantage of a star topology compared to a bus topology. (1 mark)

LAN LAN LAN your boat gently down the stream, merrily merrily merrily merrily, wireless is a dream...

Wireless technology is a bit scary if you ask me. How long is it going to be before everyone has wireless implants in their brains to connect them directly to the Internet ... Imagine that. All the rubbish on the Internet being fed into your brain. The 92% of your brain you don't use will probably be used to store MP3s and podcasts. Oh yes, it's going to happen.

The Internet

These pages are for AQA Unit 2 and OCR Unit 1.

"Internet" you say? Tell me about this strange new technology...

Getting **Connected** to the **Internet**

1) In the early days of home Internet, everyone used **dial-up** connections which were very **slow** and meant you couldn't use the phone while connected to the Internet.
2) These days, more and more Internet users have **broadband** connections which give **much** greater download speeds and mean you can still use the phone, yippee...

> **Typical dial-up speed: 56 kbps (kilobit per second)**
> **Typical broadband speed: 8 Mbps (megabits per second) i.e. ~143 times quicker**

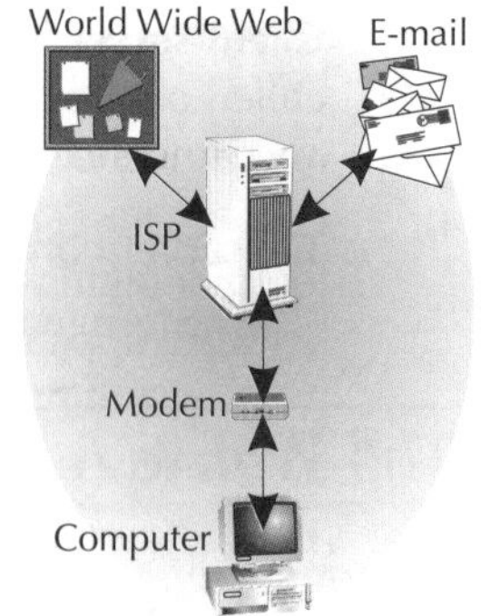

3) Dial-up connections are OK if you only need the Internet for **basic tasks** like checking e-mail, checking train times, etc. But the Internet is increasingly being used for a **wide range of activities** — downloading music, sharing videos, online gaming, web TV and broadcasting. For most of these uses, a broadband connection is **essential**.
4) You can get broadband through your **telephone line**, **cable TV** service, mobile **phone network** or even by **satellite**. The companies that provide access to the Internet are called **ISPs** (Internet Service Providers).
5) As well as connecting users to the World Wide Web (WWW), ISPs usually provide other services such as **firewalls** and **e-mail facilities**.

Hardware

1) A **modem** (modulator / demodulator) may be needed to **convert** the computer's **signal** into a form that can be understood by the **communication system** being used, e.g. telephone system.
2) If you want a wireless system (Wi-Fi) at home, you can get a wireless modem **router** (modem and radio transmitter in one) to plug into your phone socket. You can then connect as many computers as you like to the Internet from **anywhere** in the house, as long as they have a **wireless adaptor** to receive the signal.

Software

1) The main piece of **software** you need to view web pages is a **browser**, such as Internet Explorer®, Netscape® or Firefox®.
2) Your browser might need extra pieces of software called **plug-ins** to enable it to view certain pages properly, e.g. to play certain file types, watch videoclips or streaming media.
3) **Firewall** and **anti-virus** software are a must to keep your computer safe, though these are often provided by the ISP.

Web Page Addresses Are Made Up of Different **Bits**

Web page addresses are called **URLs** (Uniform Resource Locators). They're made up of various different parts:

http://www.cgpbooks.co.uk/index.html

http — **hypertext transfer protocol**. This is the way data is transferred over the Internet. Most browsers will add this bit of the URL automatically.

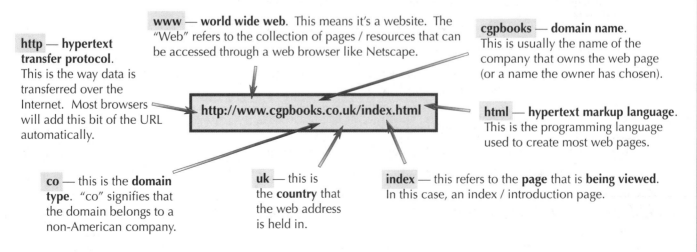

www — **world wide web**. This means it's a website. The "Web" refers to the collection of pages / resources that can be accessed through a web browser like Netscape.

cgpbooks — **domain name**. This is usually the name of the company that owns the web page (or a name the owner has chosen).

html — **hypertext markup language**. This is the programming language used to create most web pages.

co — this is the **domain type**. "co" signifies that the domain belongs to a non-American company.

uk — this is the **country** that the web address is held in.

index — this refers to the **page** that is **being viewed**. In this case, an index / introduction page.

The Internet

Search Engines Help Users *Find Information* on the *Web*

1) Web **search engines** use automated programs called **web crawlers** to collect information about web pages.
2) A web crawler basically "reads" the web, following the links from each web page it visits, trying to cover as much of the web as it can in a systematic way. As the Internet contains **over 6 billion** web pages, web crawlers have plenty of work to keep them busy, especially with websites being updated constantly.
3) Search engines use the information from web crawlers to compile an **index**. When you do a **keyword search**, the search engine uses its index to find the best sites to match your search. This is how search engines can appear to search millions of pages in a fraction of a second.
4) **Google**, the most popular search engine now, was one of the first search engines to use a different technique for **ranking** the importance of pages. Previously, most search engines ranked pages based on how often a keyword appeared on the pages. Google's system ranks pages based on how many **links** pages have to them.

The *Web* is only *Part of the Net*

1) A lot of people think that the World Wide Web and the Internet are the same thing. Not so.
2) The **Internet** is basically just a huge collection of linked computer networks.
The World Wide Web is a system of **interlinked documents** (web pages) accessed **through** the Internet.
3) Some of the other major uses of the Internet include:

- **e-mail, instant messaging** and **online chatting**
- **remote access** (e.g. extranets — see below)
- **ecommerce** (e.g. online banking, shopping)
- **econferencing** (online meetings over different locations)
- **streaming content** (e.g. online broadcasting, webcams)
- **file sharing** (e.g. FTP and peer-to-peer networks)

Intranets are Used by Many *Businesses* and *Organisations*

1) An **intranet** is like a mini-Internet that runs over a **single company's network**. It uses Internet protocols and has similar facilities, e.g. web pages, but it can only be accesssed by authorised users, e.g. company employees.
2) An **extranet** is similar, but it allows people, e.g. external businesses and customers, to **connect from outside** (via the Internet). Users are given **passwords** so that they can access data on the company's **internal servers**. Extranets need **extra security** to stop external users from hacking in.

Advantages of Intranets

1) The intranet can be **customised** to serve the company's needs most effectively.
2) Communication and data retrieval is usually **faster** as everyone is on the same network.
3) It cannot be freely accessed by external users, so the data stored there is more **secure**.

Disadvantages of Intranets

1) It **costs** a lot more to set up and maintain an intranet, than to just let users share files using e-mail or a local network.
2) Only certain users with **specialist knowledge** or training are able to amend or update the intranet.

Practice Questions

Q1 What hardware do you need to connect a computer to the Internet?

Q2 What's the difference between an intranet and an extranet?

Exam Questions

Q1 At first, the Internet could only be accessed by using a personal computer.
Name two other devices that can now be used to access Internet services. (2 marks)

Q2 Explain what is meant by each of the following terms:
a) browser
b) search engine (4 marks)

I've heard that the Angling Times needs an Extranet...

Ha haha haha. Cod, that's an awful joke. Well, just make sure you know your plaice — use this revision guide wisely and you're bound to do well. Follow the golden rules: don't get crabby, don't flounder, don't carp on about your troubles — that way everything will work out okay and you'll have a (wait for it) — a — a — a right, cracking, old whale of a time.

The Internet

These pages are for AQA Unit 2 and OCR Unit 1.

The Internet is dominating the world of commerce, education and entertainment. It's constantly expanding, bringing many problems as well as benefits. So get your world-domination-problems-and-benefits-caps on and we'll get started...

E-mail is the One of the Biggest Uses of the Internet

1) E-mail is big. It's been estimated that around **50 billion** e-mails are sent every day. That's quite a lot.
2) E-mail lets people send **text** and **attachments** to another person with an e-mail account **via the Internet**. These attachments can take the form of **sound**, **images** and lots of **other files**.
3) E-mail accounts are often provided by the user's **ISP**, which is then normally accessed through their own computer. Most of these accounts will also have an option that lets users **access their e-mail remotely**, so they can access their e-mail on any online computer in the world.
4) There is also a huge choice of purely **web-based e-mail** available (e.g. Hotmail, Yahoo etc). Most of these will have an option that lets users **forward mail** to an ISP account set up on their own computer.

Benefits of Using E-mail

- It's **fast**, as messages can be sent around the world in a few seconds.
- It's **cheaper** than posting or faxing documents.
- The same message can be sent to **lots of people** at the same time.
- The recipient **doesn't need to be on-line** when the e-mail is sent as it is stored centrally and can be retrieved later.
- Attachments can be sent **easily**.

Problems with Using E-mail

- The people sending and receiving the e-mails must have **their own e-mail accounts**.
- You need access to a computer that has the right software to use e-mail. These things are **expensive** if you don't already have them.
- Messages can get **delayed** by problems with the ISP or with the web-based e-mail provider.
- Messages can become **corrupted** during transit.
- Destructive **viruses** can be sent via e-mail.
- Users often get sent lots of **spam**, despite the filtering and other systems devised by e-mail providers to avoid this.

"Spamming" is when unrequested bulk e-mails containing commercial messages and adverts are sent out.

Bulletin Boards and Weblogs Spread the News

There are other popular ways to communicate over the Internet besides e-mail:

1) People can place information on **electronic bulletin boards** for others to read (and sometimes comment on).
2) Websites provide **listings** and **classified ads** for local communities — everything from available jobs to pet dogs for sale can be found and many of these listing sites are free.
3) **Weblogs** (or "blogs") are also becoming an increasingly popular way to keep an online diary or journal, letting users choose if they want to let everyone view their page, or just a select group.

Web 2.0: The Interactive Web

1) Back in its early days, using the web to most people simply involved browsing **static web pages** which were largely just a collection of **text** and **images**.
2) Over the years, the ways that people use the web have gradually **changed** and **expanded**. There's now a lot more **interactivity**, **communication** and **sharing** of information.
3) This has led to the coining of the term **Web 2.0** referring to this new "version" of the web that has evolved.
4) Examples of this include **chat forums**, **social networking sites** (e.g. Myspace and Facebook), **video sharing** sites (e.g. YouTube and Googlevideo) and **Wikis** (e.g. Wikipedia) which allow users to easily create websites as a team effort.
5) Anyone can **create or contribute** to a website and put their own **views and opinions** on it which means not everything you read is necessarily **true**. All content found on websites should be **carefully considered** and only trusted if the **source is reliable**.

The Internet

Money Changes Hands Over the Internet

1) **Online shopping** is becoming more and more popular. Here's some of the reasons customers love it...

- Huge choice — buy goods from anywhere in the world and choose from thousands of stores.
- Prices often better than in the shops because online stores have lower costs and there's more competition.
- Comparison websites can search for the best deals on price and delivery costs.
- Convenience — a shop's website runs 24/7, 365 days a year. They also benefit customers who can't leave the house, who live in remote areas or have no transport.

2) There's lots of benefits for **companies** too...

- Can advertise and market goods online, increasing customer base.
- Can communicate quickly with suppliers, staff and customers, including via e-mail.
- Online stores save money on cost of staff and of retail outlets.
- Online stores increase sales as they can be accessed by customers 24 hours a day.
- Delivery companies have also benefited as there is an increase in parcels being delivered

3) Other activities where customers might be spending or transferring money include online **banking**, **auctions**, paying **bills**, buying **tickets**, **gaming** sites and downloading **music** and **films**.

There are **Disadvantages** to **Spending on the Internet**

- The popularity of online shopping isn't great news for everyone. **High street shops** lose out as more people choose to shop online instead. This is especially bad for smaller businesses as the Internet tends to be dominated by massive sites like Amazon and eBay, making it harder for **smaller companies** to **compete**.
- Customers can also lose out — despite improvements in money transfer systems, a lot of people are still worried about **the security risks** of giving out their card or **bank details** over the Internet. The Internet can be a haven for **fraudulent activity**.
- Shopping for products online also causes problems when **tax and import regulations** differ between the country the goods are coming from and the one they're being delivered to.
- Alternatively, the goods that you've bought **may never arrive** — at least if you go into a shop you know you'll be **walking out** with whatever it is you've paid for.
- Online shopping needs to be **delivered**, and some companies need a **signature** — if you're not at home when your purchases are delivered it's pretty **inconvenient**. It might end up **costing you more** to get them delivered again or to go and pick them up.
- Even then, you might not get the **exact goods** you ordered. If you're doing your food shopping online, it's possible that any out-of-stock items will be **substituted by others** that aren't as good.
- To shop online, you need a computer and an Internet connection, which can be **expensive** to **install and maintain**.

Practice Questions

Q1 Give two advantages and two disadvantages of using e-mail over normal post.

Q2 Give five reasons why people might exchange money on the Internet.

Exam Questions

Q1 A friend remarks that they send all their letters by normal post.
Suggest two reasons why they might consider sending e-mails instead. (2 marks)

Q2 Explain, using examples, the advantages and disadvantages to customers of shopping on the Internet (9 marks)

I blog, you blog, he/she blogs, we bloog, you bleg (pl.), they blaggered...

Blog's such a stupid word, isn't it? Can't imagine Jane Austen keeping a blog. Or William Shakespeare. Course that could have something to do with how they didn't have computers back then. So yes. Blogging. E-mail. Make sure you know it.

Other Communication Systems

These pages are for AQA Unit 2 and OCR Unit 1.

Now you've gotten to grips with the Internet, it's time to take over the animal kingdom... as my auntie Mavis used to say. These next pages look at some of the other ways we crazy things called human beans like to communicate.

Good old **Fax Machines** are Still In Use

A fax machine **scans** a document, **encodes** the data and **transmits** it via telephone (or online computer) to another fax machine.

Uses

Fax machines tend to be used in open offices and are used to send **non-personal documents** in business (e.g. paper invoices, pencil sketches / design ideas that are on paper). Some people still use them **at home** too.

Advantages

A hard copy is immediately received by the recipient which **cannot be electronically altered** (very useful for legal documents).

Disadvantages

You cannot **receive** documents unless the fax machine is **switched on** and **connected** to the telephone line.

The **quality** tends to be poorer than in e-mail.

Copies can't be sent to **multiple recipients** in one go.

Problems with the **hardware** can cause delays, e.g. paper jams.

Voicemail and **Call Routing** are **Automated Phone Answering**

Voicemail (also called voice messaging) is a **computerised answering service** that automatically answers your call, plays a greeting in your own voice and records a message. After you retrieve your messages, you can delete, save, reply to or forward the messages to someone else on your voicemail system. This is very useful for individuals, or for small businesses who need to be able to record messages people leave for them out of office hours.

Call routing is used more often in bigger companies — it's a **digital answering service** that uses a **central storage system**. This means incoming callers can listen to the menu choices, press the **appropriate keys** for who they want to speak to, then be directed to the right person.

Some systems are more complex, e.g. the Odeon Cinema phone line lets you book tickets without talking to a human being, or some banks guide you through security checks and let you transfer money via an automated call routing system.

Call routing is an efficient, automated system which means **less time is wasted** on the telephone.
But, it is very **impersonal**, and callers can get stuck within **complex menus** when they have a query.

Transport Systems Give **Info** to **Drivers** and **Control Traffic**

There are various different types of transport system that help give information to drivers quickly and efficiently:

1) **Sensors** by the sides of roads and pads or strips on the road surface can be used to **monitor** traffic flow.
2) **Matrix signs** are used to warn drivers of **delays** or adverse **weather conditions**.
3) **Active Traffic Management** systems can be used to control the flow of traffic and stop traffic jams before they happen. In these systems, sensors monitor the traffic flow and the **speed limits** along the road are **changed** to keep the traffic moving — it's all controlled by computer. These systems have been used on several motorways in the UK.
4) **In-car navigation systems** ("Sat Nav") use GPS (Global Positioning System) and map data to pinpoint your location and can give you directions to your destination. They can sometimes access live traffic information from special transmitters to guide you around traffic jams. This is very useful but is usually pretty **expensive**.
5) Up-to-date information about traffic flow, accidents and weather can even be **texted** to your **mobile phone** (but you'd need a passenger to read the information as UK drivers aren't allowed to use mobiles in cars).

Bluetooth — it's not **Blue** and There's **No Teeth in it**

1) Bluetooth is a technology that lets your computer, mobile phone, PDA — in fact anything with a Bluetooth chip **communicate** to other devices by **radio** instead of cables.
2) It's useful because it not only saves on cables, but lets you easily **synchronise two devices** for transferring data.
3) So if you want to send a picture from a mobile phone to a printer, you just **switch on** the Bluetooth and place the two devices together (i.e. within about 10 m of each other) and then send. Because it uses radiowaves, you **don't** need to have **line of sight**.

Apparatus required for a Bluetooth upgrade.

Other Communication Systems

Digital TV** has **Taken Over

From 2007 to 2012, the old style **analogue** TV broadcasting in the UK will be phased out in favour of **digital TV**.

Digital TV can do **a lot more** than the old analogue TV. It gives a much more **interactive service** where you have more control over what you're watching. Digital TV has already been around for many years through **satellite** and **cable TV**, but after the switchover, everyone should be able to receive digital through a **normal aerial**.

Uses

Digital TV gives lots of **interactive features**, e.g. for a football match, you can choose the camera angles and commentators you want (or even better, get **expert commentary** when watching your favourite **BBC celebrity dancing show**). With some digital services, you can even carry out e-shopping, e-banking (and in the future, e-voting).

Advantages

Better picture quality than analogue.

It gives viewers a more **interactive** TV experience — just press the **magic red button**.

It provides viewers with **far more choice** (lots of extra channels and services).

It allows the viewer to use the TV as a **two-way communication** device.

Disadvantages

It needs a **digital receiver** or a digital TV to decode the signal — everyone has to fork out for one of these as part of the switchover.

After the switchover, most homes will be using **more energy** with their new digital equipment. This isn't great for the environment...

Webcasting and Podcasting** are basically **Internet Broadcasting

What is "Webcasting"?

Webcasting is the use of the Internet to **broadcast** audio or video transmissions using **streaming media technology**. So it's just like TV and radio broadcasting, but done over the Internet. In fact, most radio stations and many TV stations now do **webcasting** simultaneously alongside their normal broadcasting.

OK, so what's a "Podcast" then?

A **podcast** (the 'pod' comes from iPod®) is a file (e.g. MP3) produced to be played back on a portable device, like an iPod®. The basic idea is that you **subscribe** to a podcast **feed** — it could be a TV show, radio station, band, anything really... Then, each time a **new podcast** is available (e.g. a new episode or song), software on the user's computer (called a **podcatcher**) automatically detects and downloads it. The same software automatically **transfers** the podcasts onto the **portable device** when it's connected.

Many educational establishments are turning to **online courses** with lectures and exercises being provided through **webcasts** or **podcasts**. This **reduces costs** and means they can reach a much **bigger audience**.

Practice Questions

Q1 Give one advantage and two disadvantages of using a fax machine.

Q2 Explain how "Sat Nav" and Active Traffic Management systems work.

Q3 Explain the difference between webcasting and podcasting.

Exam Questions

Q1 Some car manufacturers have installed in-car information systems which can give up-to-date details of traffic problems across the country. Explain two benefits of having these in cars. (4 marks)

Q2 By 2012, all analogue television services will be switched off in favour of digital television. Give three benefits of digital television over analogue. (3 marks)

Monsieur, with these blue tooth gags, you are really spoiling us...

I think it's great that we're ditching analogue TV — digital's much better. I watched "Finding Nemo" with my baby brother and he actually tried to climb into the TV so he could go swimming. Actually, I take it back. I don't want digital TV, I want a swimming pool in my living room. By the way, learn everything on this page, 'kay? There's lots here but you need it all.

Other Communication Systems

These pages are for AQA Unit 2 and OCR Unit 1.

Well, this has been a pretty short section. Just two pages left and there's nothing to it. Which reminds me, I saw Eastenders last night. There's nothing to that either, is there? They're just one step away from a plot involving aliens...

Mobile Phones are Everywhere Now

1) Mobile phones work by sending **microwave** radio signals to and from a nearby **base station** (usually within about 10 miles if the reception is good). The base stations **relay** your signals through one or more telephone **networks** to connect you with the person at the other end.
2) Mobiles are **massively popular** now and as technology improves, they are **merging** with other communication systems to create **brand new systems**. For example, a typical handset as well being a "phone" might also be a **camera**, **video camera**, **radio**, **mp3 player**, **alarm clock**, **personal organiser**, ... dishwasher, vending machine, shoulder to cry on... OK, maybe scrub the last three.
3) Some measures have been taken to **control** the use of mobiles. Using a mobile while you're **driving** is now **banned** (unless you've got hands-free). Video/camera phones have been banned in **court rooms** and **exams** to stop illegal filming.
4) The problem is, because these devices are so small and widespread, it's really hard to **stop** misuse. For example, phones have been used by children to **film bullying** and post it on the Internet.

Mobiles do everything these days.

Advantages	Disadvantages
Compact and **lightweight** for carrying around. Can use them **almost anywhere** (so long as you've got network coverage). You can use them for **a lot more** than phoning. Even if you don't use it much, it's great to have one for **emergencies**, e.g. car breaking down.	It can still be more **costly** to send messages by mobile phone than with other devices. Many people are concerned about the possible long term **health risks** from the radiation they give off. Hard to **control misuse**, e.g. driving, illegal filming.

Teleconferencing and Videoconferencing are Very Useful

1) **Teleconferencing** is a way of connecting one set of users to another **over the telephone**, making it feel as though everyone is sitting round the same table.
2) **Videoconferencing** is very similar, but also allows the users to see each other.
3) They're mostly used in **business** to allow multinational companies to hold meetings with employees in different locations. **Home use** is also increasing, with webcams giving users visual communication as they chat online.

Advantages	Disadvantages
It saves on **travelling costs** as users don't need to meet at a common meeting place. Meetings can be held **at any time**.	**Expensive equipment** is needed. The technology is still **not perfect**, so synchronisation can be poor (especially with video conferencing). No substitute for direct **human interaction**.

Teleworking Lets Employees Work From Home

1) These days, many employees work from home and send their work to the office using ICT — this is **teleworking**.
2) Teleworking refers to the use of **any communication device** to transmit work to the head office, so it includes e-mail, ftp sites, fax, phone, webcams etc.

Advantages	Disadvantages
Employees working from home can work flexible hours and are often more **satisfied employees**. Companies require less office space, which **cuts costs**. Employees don't have to travel to work, which reduces pollution and money spent on transport.	Workers can feel **isolated**, and lonely because of lack of personal contact with co-workers. There is no clear separation of work and home life, which some people find **stressful**. There are often more **distractions** at home.

Other Communication Systems

EDI is basically a *Giant Electronic Mailbox*

1) **Electronic Data Interchange** (EDI) is a way of sending documents from one company to another, using a **telephone network**.
2) The sender's computer can talk to the receiver's computer, regardless of what machines or software are being used by both. EDI is an electronic mailbox, taking data straight off one computer and putting it on another.
3) This is used primarily in business to **transfer items** like orders, letters and invoices. It has also recently been used to transfer **exam results** from the examination boards to schools and colleges.

Advantages	Disadvantages
It's very **straightforward** and can transfer massive amounts of data at once. Nothing has to be printed off and posted, so it cuts down on **paper waste** and **postage costs**. It **cuts down on human error** — data goes straight from one machine to another and is processed online.	EDI software can be **too expensive** for small companies.

Remote Databases are used *Mostly* in *Business*

1) Remote databases allow users to connect to a company's database via a **WAN**, e.g. via the Internet.
2) Remote databases are frequently used in **business**, (especially leisure and tourist trades) allowing customers to know exactly what is on offer and to have their booking confirmed straight away.
3) You often connect to remote databases when using the **Internet**, e.g. when you're finding train times and booking tickets, searching a library catalogue, buying theatre, cinema, plane tickets etc...

Advantages	Disadvantages
Since you connect directly to the database, the information is always **up-to-date** and you can make bookings **immediately**. It's **cheap** for businesses as it "cuts out the middle man".	There's always a danger of data being **hacked** as it is transferred to the computer system. When the database is open to many users, e.g. a website booking system, it's easy for **mistakes** to be entered and hard to **spot** them.

Practice Questions

Q1 Mobile phones have recently been banned from some public buildings. Give a reason for this.

Q2 What is "teleworking"?

Q3 Explain what EDI means.

Exam Questions

Q1 A sales representative for Puppet Publishing is working on her laptop in a hotel away from the office. Describe two ways in which she can use ICT to send a report to her office. (4 marks)

Q2 A firm of UK engineers is designing a new bridge with an American company. It has been suggested that the best way the two companies can stay in contact during the project is to use videoconferencing.

a) Explain what is meant by the term 'videoconferencing'. (4 marks)

b) Give two advantages and two disadvantages to the companies of using videoconferencing to discuss project progress instead of arranging actual meetings. (4 marks)

Have you seen ma wicked new phone? — Oh no, I forgot to bling it...

Well, bang goes another section — just make sure you know it inside out. It's pretty easy to pick up marks on these communications questions, as long as you know what you're talking about and don't wander off the point into a large hedge where there's a bird I used to talk to my friend Tracey about but she lives in London with my — oh look a penny.

ICT in Industry and Manufacturing

These pages are for AQA Unit 2 and OCR Unit 1.

This section will give your life a much needed dose of salty ICT goodness. Or, to put it another way, it will go through everything you need to know about ICT in the real world, in a very clear and straightforward fashion. Smashing.

Industry Wouldn't Work Without ICT

ICT is used in many different ways in manufacturing and industry, from initial design to control and ordering.

1) It is used in **administration** — e.g. payroll systems, clocking on and clocking off, communications (e-mail, telephone, fax), word processing and accounting, general office management and co-ordination.
2) It is also used to **order** and **keep track** of raw materials needed in the production process.
3) ICT is also used to create **designs** and **models**, and to **test** and **manufacture** them.

CAD stands for COMPUTER AIDED **DESIGN**

CAM stands for COMPUTER AIDED **MANUFACTURE**

CAD is Very Useful in the Production Process

CAD is used by manufacturers and engineers to **design** things that will be built e.g. toasters, cars, bridges, buildings. CAD is usually **vector-based** software, which is very powerful and often needs a lot of memory to run.

e.g. a factory production manager may use CAD to model the effect of a particular design on manufacturing schedules.

Benefits of CAD

1) CAD software provides **three-dimensional representations** of designs on a screen (even though basic design may have been done in two dimensions), which can be rotated to be viewed from any angle.
2) It produces useful **information**, e.g. data on parts lists, requirements for different materials and components, wiring schedules etc.
3) **Higher output** because time-consuming tedious tasks are removed, e.g. many calculations are done by the software.
4) CAD software can **create simulations** which help **test** how the product will perform, e.g. in car plants, CAD can simulate car crashes in safety tests.

Drawbacks of CAD

The down side is that professional CAD systems require **complex**, **powerful** and **expensive** hardware, and the users need to have a lot of **training**.

CAM is when the Machines are Controlled by Computers

If the machines used in manufacturing or testing are controlled by a computer, it is a CAM system.

Benefits of CAM

1) Production of parts is **faster** and **more reliable** because machines do not get ill, go on strike or have a bad day.
2) The **quality** is more **consistent**.
3) Production can continue day and night, so **output** is **greater**.
4) Some **difficult or unpleasant jobs** can be done by robots.

Limitations of CAM

CAM machines are designed for particular functions, and though they can be programmed, e.g. to cut at a different angle, they cannot be switched between totally different tasks.

Robots / Robotic Arms can do Nasty Jobs for us

- **Dangerous** e.g. involving the use of explosives, welding, working with chemicals, monitoring radiation, cleaning up contamination.
- **Unpleasant** e.g. where working conditions are poor and uncomfortable (e.g. cold or wet).
- **Boring** e.g. jobs which need continuous repetition of tasks, e.g. working on an assembly line.
- Jobs that require **physical strength** e.g. lifting heavy car parts, putting piles of newspapers onto palettes or loading and unloading machines.
- Jobs that need **fine motor control** for example assembling watches or computer microchips.
- Jobs where **delicate objects** are handled.

ICT in Industry and Manufacturing

CAD and CAM have **Changed People's Jobs**

CAD and CAM systems (particularly CAM) have affected many workers all around the world.

1) Many jobs have become **automated** and are either fully or partly carried out by machines. For example, in the car industry, all spray painting of cars is now done by robots.

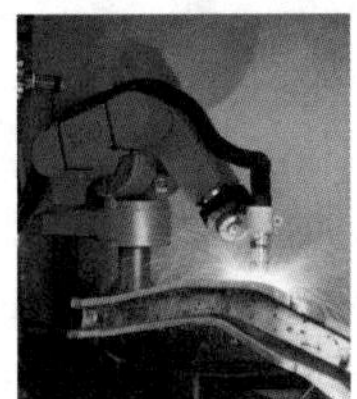

2) Some jobs have **changed**. The workers produce the **same goods** in a **different way**. For example, where a draughtsman used to produce drawings using pencil and paper, now they use CAD.

ICT in Industry — Positive Points for the Workers

- Sometimes using ICT can make a job **more interesting and efficient**. For example, a draughtsman can use CAD software to produce a drawing and then experiment **easily and quickly** by making changes to find the best solution.
- **New jobs** are created to design, produce and control the machines. (Many of these new jobs are not in manufacturing, but are more likely to be, for example, in IT support).
- Although retraining is often needed when humans doing manual jobs are replaced by robots, **gaining recognised qualifications** can improve workers' employment and salary expectations.

ICT in Industry — Negative Points for the Workers

- Some workers are **too old or uneducated** to adapt to new working practices. Others may **live too far away** from new employment opportunities.
- Some communities which grew up around a manufacturing industry have become '**ghost towns**', because people have moved away to find new employment.
- Many industries have become completely **dependent** on ICT. If the ICT fails, the industry cannot go on until the problems have been fixed.
- Some workers **do not like change** and are unhappy with being forced to change the way they work.

Practice Questions

Q1 What do CAD and CAM stand for?

Q2 Describe two different ways CAD is used in manufacturing and industry.

Q3 Give three benefits of using CAD in manufacturing and industry.

Q4 Give four examples of the sorts of jobs robots are used for.

Exam Questions

Q1 Describe, by means of examples, the ways in which the introduction of ICT into manufacturing and industry can eliminate some jobs, transform others and create some new jobs. (6 marks)

Q2 ICT has brought benefits to a number of different areas.
Give two uses of ICT in manufacturing companies and describe the benefits that can be gained. (4 marks)

I want robot arms that will do my homework...

CAD and CAM can get pretty complicated. The good news is that examiners don't want to know if you're a trained CAD system operator. What they want to know is that you understand the processes at work in industry and how they affect the workers. Examiners also want to know how to make their drab, loveless lives better, but that won't help your ICT exam.

ICT in Commerce

These pages are for AQA Unit 2 and OCR Unit 1.

Most money transactions, especially purchasing goods and being paid a salary, now get carried out electronically. So, here's a little tip: sticking a tenner in a CD drive won't help you buy stuff off eBay, though it makes a great noise.

Customers Can Get Cash Any Time

1) In the old days we used to have to carry cash around all the time. If the banks were shut when we ran out, it meant we had **no access** to money and no way to pay for things.
2) Now we have **credit** and **debit cards**, and most banks and supermarkets have **ATMs** (Automated Teller Machine — i.e. cash machines) so we can get money **at any time**.
3) ATMs have electronics to read the **chip** inside the card or the **magnetic strip** on the back. The user types in their **PIN** (Personal Identification Number), to **verify** that they are the account holder.

Customers No Longer Rely on Cash

Cash is readily available, but there are also more options to pay electronically, so we're becoming a **cashless society**.

Credit and Debit Cards

These allow users to buy goods directly without using cash.

Data identifying the card is read using the embedded **chip** (or the **magnetic strip**).

Money is removed **instantly** from the customer's bank and put in the shop's account, so no physical cash needs to change hands.

These transactions are called "Electronic Fund Transfer" (**EFT**) or "Electronic Fund Transfer at Point of Sale" (**EFTPOS**)

Cheques

These allow users to pay for goods directly without using cash.

UK cheques have a line of **magnetic ink** on them which contains the cheque number, account and sort code information.

This data is read using **MICR** (Magnetic Ink Character Recognition), see p.12. The cheque then takes up to 7 days to be verified.

Direct Debit and Standing Orders

These are used to pay bills on a regular basis.

They directly **link** individual bank accounts to the company that needs to be paid.

Standing Orders — you tell the bank what to pay.

Direct Debits — you authorise an outside company to ask your bank account for payment.

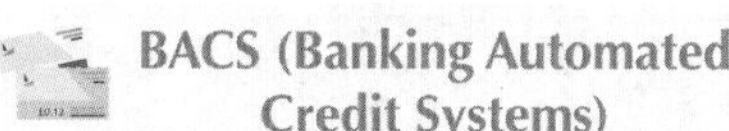

BACS (Banking Automated Credit Systems)

This is used by most companies to pay employees' **salaries**.

Employees receive a **payslip** but **no paycheque**, as money is transferred into their account electronically.

An electronic file of the company's payments is produced and transmitted to **BACS** who process the payments on behalf of the company.

This makes the whole process more **efficient**, with less likelihood of delay or loss/theft of money.

Utility Bill Cards

Rather than pay a bill all in one go, users are able to pay a **little bit** at a time.

The user transfers money from his account onto the card. Money is gradually taken off the card by the company providing the utility, as and when that utility is used.

As the amount of money left on the card gets smaller, the user then has to **"top up"** the card with money again.

Online and Telephone Banking

Users can pay bills and view accounts from their **own homes** using the Internet, digital television or telephones.

Smart Cards

They look like credit cards, but they only have a chip — there's **no magnetic strip** at all. The chip is used to store any sort of information, and is not necessarily just used to find the card owner's details in a larger database. Things like **satellite television subscription cards** are smart cards.

Being a Cashless Society has Advantages and Disadvantages

Advantages	Disadvantages
No need to carry cash	Some transactions incur administration fees
Can shop from home by phone, digital TV or the Internet	Many traders unwilling to install expensive equipment
Less chance of being mugged	Some people prefer cash
Less money in the shops and banks to be stolen	Cash sales are usually quicker
	Security problems with sending money electronically

ICT in Commerce

Loyalty Cards Help Supermarkets to **Target** their Customers

1) Most supermarkets now issue **loyalty cards** to their customers.
2) The supermarket uses loyalty cards to **keep an eye** on their customers. Every time a customer uses their card, the details of every item bought are recorded, e.g. where, when, in what quantity and how it was purchased.
3) In this way the supermarket can build up a picture about the **spending habits** of their customer base. It can then target individual customers by encouraging them to buy products that match their **shopping profile**.
4) Every purchase gives the customer **reward points** which can be **redeemed** later on for money off or free products. The supermarket can use this to **boost sales** of certain products by offering extra reward points on them.

Be wary of free gifts from your supermarket. They may just be keeping an eye on you...

A **"One Card" Society** Could Be **On The Way**

1) At the moment we use lots of **different cards** for different things, which is confusing because so many of them can be used in different ways. A plan has been formed to replace the different cards with a **single card**.
2) The main **problem** with only having one card is that if you lose it or it is stolen, then you **lose your identity** and it becomes much easier for a stranger to get access to all of (not just one area of) your finances.

Online Shopping is Amazon-ly Popular now...

Online shopping allows people to **order goods** through the web or digital television, and have them **delivered directly to their home**. I'd love to rabbit on and on about it now, but it's covered on p35.

Practice Questions

Q1 What is meant by a "cashless society"?

Q2 How are smart cards different from credit and debit cards?

Q3 Give two advantages and two disadvantages of being a cashless society.

Q4 Give an advantage and a disadvantage for a customer of having a supermarket loyalty card.

Q5 Give an advantage and a disadvantage of a "one card" society.

Exam Questions

Q1 A local building society branch has just installed a new Automated Teller Machine (ATM).
a) State one advantage for the building society of installing an ATM. (1 mark)
b) State two advantages for the branch's customers of the new ATM. (2 marks)

Q2 Gordon has bought a beginner's book on surfing from a company's online store. He has since received catalogues selling surfing equipment through the post, and is also receiving e-mails about surfing lessons and holidays abroad.
(a) Why has Gordon been receiving the e-mails and the catalogues? (2 marks)
(b) State why many people are quite wary about ordering goods using credit cards over the Internet. (1 mark)

"**Cash** in on revision tips for extraordinary results" — yeearg...

I'd be a lot less cashless if I had someone else's identity, I'll tell you that for nothing. Well, get learning all the ideas on these pages, as they're pretty important. If you can answer all the questions above then you're well on the way. Just be sure to remember cashless old me when you're rich and famous, having achieved stardom through extraordinary AS ICT results.

ICT in the Home

These pages are for AQA Unit 2 and OCR Unit 1.

Home ownership of ICT devices is growing all the time. You should know about different kinds of ICT and how the use of all this ICT is changing home life. Not like my mum. My mum still thinks she can delete the Internet with one click.

More People are Using **Computers** at **Home**

In 2007, **more than 60%** of people in the UK regularly used the **Internet**. This figure is growing all the time. The amount that computers get used in the home is also **increasing**.

Typical computer use in the home includes:

- **Creating personal data**, e.g. using address books, using spreadsheets to do accounts.
- **Storing information efficiently**, e.g. using computer filing to store documents, using e-mail folders to store important e-mails (such as registration details, or records of online purchases).
- **Finding information** easily on the Internet, e.g. cinema listings, research for schoolwork.
- As a **word processor** for typing documents, e.g. personal letters, coursework, creative work.
- **Designing web pages**, e.g. to display family photos, as part of a school course.
- **Communicating** with friends, family or others using e-mail, instant messaging (e.g. MSN / Yahoo Messenger) and social networking sites (e.g. Facebook / MySpace).
- **Downloading music**, e.g. sites such as iTunes allow users to legally download songs for a price.
- Used to **play CDs or DVDs** — can be a useful alternative when the telly's being watched by someone else.
- Doing **homework**, e.g. drawing graphs on a spreadsheet program, revising and researching schoolwork using the Internet, etc.
- **Playing games**, e.g. online or on CD-ROMs/DVDs.
- **Online shopping**, which lets users compare prices more easily than going round the shops and so can save a great deal of money, time and effort (see p. 35).
- **Online banking**, which many users find more convenient as they can do it 24 hours a day, instead of relying on the bank's opening times and potentially wasting time queuing at their local branch.

More People are **Working From Home**

1) The number of people working from home is increasing as **communication links improve**, e.g. faster broadband Internet connections, fax machines that display received material digitally, rather than on paper.
2) Many people are able to do all, or large parts, of their work from home using e-mail, telephones, faxes and computers. This is called **teleworking** (see p. 38)

Having a **Home Computer** has its **Problems**

1) Some children spend so much time in front of their computers that they don't learn valuable social skills and **lose the ability to interact** successfully with people face-to-face.
2) Unlike in an office, users are **unlikely to be trained** to use the hardware and software they've bought, and can have great difficulty setting up and using it.
3) Parents can feel **pressurised** to buy **expensive equipment** because they see computers as being able to help their children, and because they want to keep up with the Joneses.
4) A major concern is that **children** are able to **access unsuitable websites**, e.g. pornographic sites, and that parents **don't know** how to stop it happening.

"Baby no want bottle. Baby want 30 inch flatscreen monitor. Wah."

ICT in the Home

Computers are *Not the Only* Type of *ICT* Found in the *Home*

A **large number** of devices found in the home are driven by ICT.

1) **Mobile phones** have a built in microchip to control many functions, e.g. messages (texting), address book, alarm clock, digital camera. Some include web browsers.

2) **Games consoles** like the Xbox 360 and PlayStation® 3 are powered by microprocessors and use digital media (DVDs and Blu-Ray discs) to play games, films and music.

3) In **washing machines**, microchips and sensors work together to control the washing cycle. Some washing machines have a wide range of programs and more sophisticated ones allow users to download washing programs from the Internet (though that's just silly, frankly).

4) **Other devices** controlled by microchip include Blu-Ray, DVD and CD players, digital alarm clocks, central heating systems, burglar alarm systems and home security lighting, microwaves.

Good Things about ICT in the Home

1) It's easier to **select** and **control** the things you want devices in the home to do, e.g. you can set a digital alarm clock using a remote control and you can choose what kind of wake up call you want.
2) The use of **microchips** in devices has made some **cheaper to produce**, e.g. digital wristwatches, so they are available to more people.
3) Cheap technology has led to the development of many devices which can improve our **quality of life**.

Bad Things

1) When microchips break they cannot be repaired and need to be **replaced**. Sometimes it is cheaper to replace the **whole device**. This has led to a wasteful "throw away" society.
2) Some people find it difficult to **adapt** to new devices and prefer the old-fashioned ones they could understand easily.

Practice Questions

Q1 Describe three things that computers are used for in the home.

Q2 What are the main problems with using home computers?

Q3 Discuss the pros and cons of using microchips in home devices.

Exam Questions

Q1 A friend remarks, "We don't have a computer in our house. In fact our house is an ICT-free zone". Explain, using three examples, why it is unlikely that their house is entirely free of ICT. (5 marks)

Q2 Many households now have Internet connections.

a) Give two examples of the ways children might use the Internet at home. For each example, discuss one benefit and one drawback of using ICT in this way. (6 marks)

b) Give two examples of the ways adults might use the Internet at home. For each example, discuss one benefit and one drawback of using ICT in this way. (Use different examples, benefits and drawbacks to the ones used in part a).) (6 marks)

Q3 The use of Information and Communication Technology (ICT) has brought benefits to a number of areas. State two uses of ICT in the home (other than the Internet) and describe the benefits that can be gained. (4 marks)

I go to work at one, take an hour for lunch, then at two I'm done — I WISH...

Imagine, if you will, working from a tiny bedroom, typing for 20 hours a day just to make ends meet, with cats wandering around miaowing to be fed, and kids mooching about the place demanding their pocket money, and the trains that blast by so loudly, so LOUDLY, SO LOUDDARGGHHHHHHhhhh... Anyway, just make sure you can answer exam questions about it.

ICT in Education

These pages are for AQA Unit 2 and OCR Unit 1.

Pretty much everyone uses ICT, from teachers to primary school kids to police officers. Which personally I find weird because in my day, teachers couldn't even work the remote control for the video. Does that still happen? Probably...

ICT is Used in Three Main Ways in Education

1) As a **tool**, to perform specific tasks, e.g. word processing, doing calculations, etc.
2) As a **tutor**, helping students to learn new information, e.g. learning via interactive presentations.
3) As a way to **manage, store and communicate information**, e.g. using databases to store pupil records.

ICT as a TOOL

- **Calculations and measurements** — calculators and spreadsheets save time on calculations and retrieval / display of information, graphing programs can produce graphs from numerical data, sensors and automatic measuring devices can be used in experiments, e.g. digital thermometers to record temperature.
- **Research** — classroom computers are connected to the Internet, which can be used as a source of information. E-mail allows pupils to share data and ideas with students from other schools.
- **Coursework / homework** — word-processing improves presentation and makes documents easier to edit, spreadsheets can be used to organise data and produce graphs for coursework reports.
- **Interactive display boards** — these can be used instead of a traditional whiteboard to display computerised teacher's notes and presentations. The board is basically a large projected computer screen which can be controlled by moving and clicking a special pen on the screen.

ICT as a TUTOR

- **Teaching programs** can give the students information, or teach skills using games. Students try to answer questions and feedback from the computer helps students improve their knowledge.
- **Integrated learning systems** (ILS) give students their own specific learning programme, set to their own ability. Software like SuccessMaker (for Key stage 3) contains full details of the curriculum being followed and records a student's progress, as well as highlighting their learning needs so teachers and the Head of Year are aware of them. However, such software is very expensive and needs highly-trained staff to manage and maintain it.
- **Distance learning** — Students work at home, taught directly by specially designed software for the course (e.g. on the Internet). The student also uses ICT to communicate with tutors and other students on the course.

ICT as a way to MANAGE, STORE and COMMUNICATE INFORMATION

- **Databases and computer filing** improves the efficiency of general administration, e.g. student's records can all be kept on computer for quicker access (see p.107).
- **Storage and communication** — Teachers can put teaching materials on a VLE (Virtual Learning Environment). This is a secure area on the school's computer system that students can login to and access from home. They can then revisit lesson notes and resources and submit work electronically.

There Are More Benefits Than Problems

Benefits	Problems
Students can use ICT in order to **present** their work more **neatly**.	ICT equipment is **expensive** to buy and needs experienced / trained staff in order to maintain it correctly.
Users with **special needs** are better catered for with ICT, e.g. more visual for students with hearing impairments.	
ICT can support many **different formats of teaching**, and so varies the ways in which students can be drawn into different subjects.	Hardware can be **unreliable** and breakdowns lead to frustration.
Some computer use, e.g. teaching programs, provides **immediate feedback** for students which is very useful.	Using ICT can mean that children **don't learn to do things by hand**, e.g. arithmetic and drawing graphs.
Sensors, measuring and calculating devices can help students better understand **mathematical concepts** in subjects like Science.	Use of the Internet in classrooms raises **security issues**, e.g. children accessing unsuitable websites.
Some applications **save a lot of time and effort**, e.g. programs that teach French vocab are quicker and more efficient than using paper.	**Plagiarism** has also increased as students find pre-written coursework online.
Using computers often encourages **collaborative work**, so students learn to work together.	

ICT in the Police Force

The *Police Force* Uses ICT in *Two* Main Ways

1) Communication

Many different forms of ICT help the police force communicate with:

1) **itself** (on a local and national level) — e.g. file sharing between different regions, e-mail for national communication, walkie-talkies and radios for local officers to communicate quickly with each other.
2) **international bodies** — e.g. sharing information (databases, files, images) with Interpol to help catch criminals.
3) **the general public** — e.g. the police can home in on criminals by getting the public to provide information. Large numbers of people can be shown mugshots, CCTV footage and crime re-enactions on the television or Internet, increasing the chance of getting useful information.

2) Organisation

1) The police use lots of different databases e.g. for storing fingerprint and DNA data. **HOLMES 2** (Home Office Large Major Enquiry System 2) is the main database used to pull all the information together into one place. **Details** of all crimes are entered into it and users can **search** and **analyse** the data.
2) Before HOLMES 2 was introduced, police officers had to **sift** through large numbers of documents **manually**. Now, HOLMES 2 helps officers to **keep track of evidence** and **reduce paperwork,** improving overall **efficiency**.
3) It lets **different forces work together**, providing one big HOLMES 2 incident room instead of lots of small ones around Britain, and holds details of all electronically-tagged criminals, so they can be easily located.

Benefits of ICT for the Police

Quicker and more efficient solving of crime:

Faster response times through improved communication.
Quicker at retrieving / sharing information from other agencies.
Forensic investigations more thorough with better technology, e.g. more precise scanning equipment retrieves more evidence.

Improving crime prevention, e.g. CCTV, burglar alarms.

Problems with ICT for the Police

ICT equipment is expensive.

Equipment can be unreliable.

Hacking is a constant danger — high security is needed so that investigations can't be compromised.

Practice Questions

Q1 How does the Internet provide learning opportunities for school children?

Q2 Give three examples of how ICT is used in schools.

Q3 Give three problems of using ICT in schools.

Exam Questions

Q1 The Head of a school decides to adopt an IT package to track pupils' grades and achievements. The package will be used throughout the school.

a) Identify two different potential users of this package. (2 marks)
b) With the aid of examples, suggest different ways that each user could use the package. (6 marks)

Q2 The use of Information and Communication Technology (ICT) has brought benefits to many of the public sectors, such as education, medicine, industry and commerce.

For both of the following, state two uses of ICT, and describe the benefits that can be gained. Your examples must be different in each case.

a) Education (4 marks)
b) Police (4 marks)

No Mr Holmes, please don't shoot me — I'm Holmes two...

Shucks. See, back in the good old days I was talking about in the intro, the police didn't know how to work videos either, let alone manage massively impressive databases of the gruesome and gore-tastic. Well, guess you'd better learn all this stuff, if not to improve your exam result, then at least to know what to watch out for when the rozzers are on your tail.

ICT in Medicine

These pages are for AQA Unit 2 and OCR Unit 1.

This double page is all about the ways that ICT wasn't used in the hit 70s TV forensic-detective show "Quincy M.E." or in the hit 90s show "Dr Quinn Medicine Woman". Pretty much.

Doctors' Surgeries Rely Heavily on ICT

1) **Patients' records** are kept on a computer **database**, making them **quick to find**, **well-organised** and **legible**.
2) This also means that a **hospital** can get **almost instant access** to anyone's records.
3) The **appointment system** is **computerised** so there are fewer double bookings and misunderstandings.
4) If doctors have trouble diagnosing a condition, they can refer to an **expert system**:

   An expert system is an application that combines artificial intelligence with a database of specialist knowledge. A medical expert system can be used to diagnose conditions from a list of symptoms entered by the user. It is programmed with a set of rules that tell it how to analyse the information in its database and form conclusions. It gives the doctor instant access to a vast store of knowledge — much easier than using chunky reference books.

5) Doctors and pharmacists can also refer to **online databases** for the most up-to-date **medications** and advice about **prescription levels**. This is useful because all the information is kept in one place and **regularly updated**.

ICT Can Help Unwell or Disabled People at Home

Here is a selection of the many ways that ICT can help people in their homes:

1) Using **self-diagnosis tools** such as the NHS Direct web site, people can often **get advice electronically**. They will, however, often be directed to seek out the advice of a qualified doctor as well, e.g. self-diagnosis of a sprained wrist could lead to trouble if it turns out actually to be broken — delayed medical attention could result in permanent damage to the wrist or other complications.
2) **Vital signs monitors** can be used at home to measure things like blood pressure, temperature and blood oxygen level, making it possible to **monitor** patients with a chronic condition or those recently discharged from hospital.
3) **Body chips** (including a microprocessor, sensors or a wireless radio frequency device) can be implanted inside people to monitor and regulate blood pressure, heart rate and cholesterol. Internal pacemakers for the heart also include a chip. This means that people are able to **go on with their daily lives** more normally.
4) Disabled people can use **ECUs** (Environmental Control Units) to interact with and manipulate one or more **electronic appliance**, e.g. television, CD player, lights, fan, etc. This can be done in different ways, e.g. **voice-activated equipment**, **special switch access**, a **computer interface** and **adaptations** such as X-10 units.

   The **BCS** (British Computer Society — www.bcs.org) does a lot of work in **raising awareness** of disabled people's ICT needs, and runs a support network.

   X-10 units act like remote controls for things that are already wired to a switch, e.g. one could be used to turn household lights on and off so that the user did not have to get up to use the switch.

5) Blind or partially sighted people can be helped by **Global Positioning Systems** (GPS) so that they know where they are. E.g. a GPS can be programmed to alert the user that the next bus stop is the one to get off at.
6) There are many ways in which blind or partially sighted people are able to use a computer.
   - Specialist **big screens** are available (up to 50 inches).
   - **Stickers** showing characters in **large print** can be stuck onto the keyboard .
   - **Magnification software** can zoom in on any part of the screen.
   - **Screen "readers"** use speech output to talk to the user and tell them what is on screen, and relay back what is being typed.
   - **Voice recognition software** is available as another way to command the computer.
   - **OCR** (optical character recognition) scanners can scan and "read" most printed text.
7) Many TV programmes are **subtitled** for deaf or hearing impaired people, and virtually all DVDs supply subtitles.
8) Deaf or hard of hearing people can use **hearing aids** which are custom programmed by a computer to match the person's hearing abilities.
   - An **audiograph** tests the patient's hearing by transmitting sound waves directly to the inner ear.
   - This is used to produce an **audiogram** (a kind of graph) of the test results.
   - The computer uses this information to **program** the **hearing aid** to give the best hearing improvement.
   - The hearing aid can be **reprogrammed** at any time.

ICT in Medicine

ICT has **Many Different Uses** in **Hospitals**

Virtually all hospital **administration** is carried out using ICT.

1) All patients' records are stored digitally by local surgeries, and are shared quickly and easily with hospitals.
2) Patients' records are then **updated** following hospital treatment and returned to the surgery.
3) ICT is also used to **track bookings**, **create appointments**, **write letters**, **update databases**, **monitor stock levels** of medical supplies and equipment and to **order more** when needed.

Surgery is increasingly being carried out with the help of ICT equipment.

1) **Robotics** are used in some medical operations because they allow surgeons to **control their surgical instruments** and require only the smallest of incisions on the patient. The systems usually consist of:
   - Minute cameras that are inserted into the patient to send images back to the surgeon.
   - Surgical instruments mounted on a surgical arm.
   - A viewing console where the surgeon sits in order to manipulate instruments using joystick-like controls.

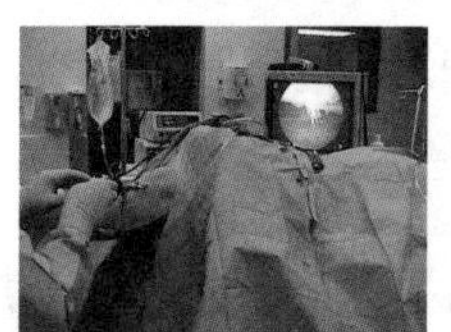

2) Surgery is also helped by **organ donation**. When an organ becomes available, medical staff consult a national **database of requests for organ transplants** so that they can then send it to the appropriate hospital.

ICT is also used on hospital **wards**.

- ICT helps nurses to **monitor** the blood pressure and heart rate of patients — input sensors collect data and send it to a microprocessor. If a **problem** is detected, an **alarm is sounded**.

ICT Plays a Big Part in **Medical Research**

1) Computer models can be used by researchers to **simulate** the effects of a new drug, virus or treatment on the human body.
2) Other researchers use a database of illness and conditions to **track trends** in the country and world wide.
3) ICT can also be used for **data collection**, e.g. using sensors to track temperature changes, **data analysis**, e.g. using a statistics package, and to **present findings**, e.g. using a graphics package to show results.

Practice Questions

Q1 Give five ways that ICT can help disabled people at home.

Q2 Give three benefits of using ICT in doctors' surgeries.

Q3 Give three examples of ways ICT is used in medical research.

Exam Questions

Q1 a) What is meant by the term "expert system"? (2 marks)

b) Explain how a doctor might use an expert system to assist diagnosis of ailments. (2 marks)

Q2 ICT-based systems exist that enable patients to diagnose their own ailments. Discuss the advantages and disadvantages of such systems. (6 marks)

"Doctor, Doctor, can you cure my acne?" — "I never make rash promises..."

Don't worry. The author of that gag has already been taken to the psychiatric ward for treatment. Well there's quite a lot on these two pages, isn't there? This stuff gets quite tricky and technical in places, but it's really important for you to know. You can see from the practice exam questions that some right nasty ones crop up on this subject, so get swotting now.

Working in ICT

These pages are for AQA Unit 2 and OCR Unit 1.

Whatever job IT professionals undertake, they must be able to show a number of other qualities as well as technical skill if they are to succeed in their careers.

There are **Certain Qualities** you **Need** in Order to **Work** in ICT

Good written skills

All professionals must have **good written skills**, as they enhance communication and lead to better understanding. In an IT context, different professionals will need good written skills for different reasons. For example:

- People working on a helpdesk would need to keep **clear and concise records** of all the problems that have been logged.
- Systems analysts need good written skills so they can give users **clear documentation** on the system and make appropriate recommendations in an understandable way.

In the exam you may be asked to describe qualities an IT professional needs. If you answer the question by writing about "communication skills" then you won't get as many marks as splitting this into good written skills and good listening skills.

Be able to communicate well orally

All professionals need to **communicate effectively**, and **oral** communication is a large part of that. For example:

- ICT helpdesk workers need to be **clear and direct** if giving instructions to users over the telephone.
- Computer programmers need to use more **technical terms** and "jargon" to discuss things at work with **precision**.

Good listening skills

The IT professional must also be able to **listen to users** and **co-workers** in order to find out what problems or instructions they have.

"...and we just CAN'T get it to record Hollyoaks."

Problem solving skills

The IT professional must be able to work in a **logical way** in order to solve problems. Although there are specific ways that specific problems may be solved, frequently they will need to attempt **different approaches** until they are certain what the actual problem is. Being **thorough**, **logical** and **systematic** is important for all IT professionals.

Approachability

Most professionals need to be **approachable** in order to make working with other people easier. For example:

- IT support professionals (in a large company) need to be approachable so users will **come forward** with problems.
- Programmers don't need to be approachable in the same way, but need to be **receptive to comments** from employers, and make superiors feel that he / she is willing to be approached with **feedback**.

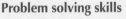

The team failed to communicate to Dave that they weren't using his horse idea anymore.

Ability to work in a team

Being able to work with other people is a big part of any profession. It's highly likely that an employee will be expected to work with others at some point, even if they don't get on. Successful teams are based around their members being able to:

- **Communicate Ideas** — To work in a team you need to be able to **listen** to other people's ideas, clearly **explain** your own ideas and engage in **constructive arguments** about whose ideas to use.
- **Follow Instructions** — There's not much point coming up with lots of ideas and then having everyone go off and do completely different things. Members have to know **what job** they have to do and how it fits in to the **overall objectives** of the team.
- **Work Independently** — It **wastes time** if members of the team constantly have to be checked on. Being able to do your job properly and **without supervision** helps the team **achieve** their goals more quickly.

Working in ICT

In Case That Lot Wasn't Enough, Here's a **Few More Important Qualities**

As if you didn't know that ICT professionals were brilliant enough already, here are a few more of their endless talents. What fascinating individuals they must be — like monks, but with computers and bad ties.

Is it 'cos I is macaque?

Technical competence

The IT professional must have a **strong technical competence**. This may seem a little obvious, but there you go. Another way of putting it is "don't hire a monkey to do an elephant's job."

Patience

Solving IT problems is about **finding solutions** — there is not always an obvious answer or quick fix. It can be a frustrating and time-consuming process, so the IT professional must have the ability to be patient and calm.

Self-motivation

This is important in any job. IT professionals tend to need to be very self-motivated. For example:

- IT support professionals, whilst typically responding to direct queries, also need to take it on their own **initiative** to find and introduce new systems that will better serve the users in the future.
- Programmers can find themselves working on very long projects, and they need to keep themselves motivated in order to continue working on the same thing for such a long time.

Flexibility

Many IT professionals need to be flexible about **when and where they work**. Those providing IT support may need to travel frequently between different sites, while systems analysts may need to work out of office hours when there are no active users accessing the system. All professionals may be called upon to **work extra hours** in order to get a job done.

You may be asked in an exam to explain what the different types of personal qualities are, or you may be asked to show the qualities required for a particular job. Remember to answer the question in relation to the job named.

Practice Question

Q1 List three qualities that would be needed by a person working in the IT industry.

Exam Questions

Q1 A company called "JP Direct" is recruiting a new member of staff for their support desk. The head of personnel asks the support desk manager to explain what personal qualities the right person for the job will need to have in order to be an effective worker.

State, with reasons, four personal qualities that the manager would want a new employee to have. (8 marks)

Q2 Virtually all companies now work with ICT systems. Many employ users who have little or no understanding of the ICT systems they are using, and who need help from IT professionals.

State two personal qualities that IT professionals should have that will enable them to help such people effectively, and explain why each quality would be needed. (4 marks)

U nede 2 av gd ritten skilllz if u wanna pas yr xmz — bling bling innit...

In the Church of the Unified Liberation of the Holy Mosaic, we live by three commandments: 1) thou shalt not forsake learning about working in ICT, regardless of other things thou could be doing instead; 2) by so doing thou shalt perform better than thou might otherwise have done in exams; 3) thou shalt not make up religions for the purposes of revision guides.

Working in ICT

These pages are for AQA Unit 2 and OCR Unit 1.

Ask most computer science students what they want to work as in ICT and they'll probably say something like programmer or webmaster. Or, ummm, security researcher.

Programmers *are Responsible for Computer Code*

Programmers are responsible for **implementing computer code**. So, they have to:

Write computer code

1) Programmers usually receive detailed **specifications** that explain what a computer program should include, how each part should **work** and how all the functions should **fit together**.
2) They then have to **create or write parts of the program**. Once all the individual parts are made, it's the programmer's responsibility to **fit them all together** and make the final program.

Debug computer code

1) Debugging means taking a list of the various ways in which a piece of software **doesn't meet its specifications** in unexpected or unexplained ways, figuring out the **causes** of these problems and **fixing them**.
2) Usually this means looking for the causes of **obvious** problems, such as the program unexpectedly **crashing** or **outputting garbage**, and **not so obvious ones** — such as why a database only processes 463 transactions an hour when it should be doing 2031.
3) Often that means reading **other people's code**, as programmers usually work in **teams**.

Document and maintain computer code

1) Even after a program has been released, programmers need to continue working on it so that **future versions** can be produced. It's also necessary because bugs can be discovered **after the software has been released** and need to be fixed.
2) Programmers need to **document their code** so that it can be maintained by other programmers. This is usually done by putting **comments** into the code and writing other documents that explain how the code they've written works. This is called **annotation**.

Webmasters *Rule the Web Universe*

1) Webmasters are responsible for the **maintenance of websites**.
2) If they work for a **smaller company** then they can be responsible for **every single detail** of a website — **designing the layout**, implementing it with **HTML and CSS code**, **testing it** with all the popular browsers, organising somewhere for the site to be **hosted**, and **correctly applying updates** to the version of the website that the public can see.
3) In **larger companies**, they tend to take more of a **supervisory role**. The webmaster is responsible for developing extensive documentation about the overall **look and feel** of the website, and how **specific parts** of it should work. The actual implementation is done by **web developers** and the hosting is organised by **web technicians**. So the webmaster is more like the **manager of the web department**.

Security Researchers *Try to Improve Computer Security*

1) Security has become an important part of ICT now that more and more machines are **connected together**, and people are using those machines for **more and more things**. People used to write computer viruses to **show off** and gain notoriety, but now they try to write software that infects machines to steal stuff like **credit card details**. So computer security is much more important now than it was a few years ago.
2) It's the security researcher's job to **find weaknesses** in existing systems, and to suggest ways to **make computers more secure** in the future.
3) Sometimes that means doing hands-on work like **pretending to be a hacker** and trying to break into your own computers. Other times it means quite dull **numerical analysis**.

Working in ICT

It's Good To Have **Specific Examples** *Up Your Sleeve*

Now that you're clear on the skills needed to be a successful IT professional (and I'm SURE you're just dying to become one), have a think about some specific jobs, so you can put all these qualities together in an exam answer.

Helpdesk Team Member — Doug Age 26

Oral Skills

Doug needs to be able to talk to users on the phone. He needs to be able to listen to what their problem is, and then offer advice in a clear and concise way.

Written Skills

Doug will need to log the problem and its solution clearly for future reference.

Patience and Approachability

Doug needs to convey a sense of calm, especially if the user is panicking. The user needs to feel confident in Doug's ability.

Flexibility

Doug needs to think about the user's needs and ability level, and work with them in mind.

Problem Solving and Technical Skills

Doug needs to be able to find the fault in the system as described by the user and solve it.

Systems Analyst — Rachel Age 31

Oral Skills

Rachel must be able to communicate with the user in a way that is jargon free.

Patience

Rachel needs to explain her findings clearly and patiently to users — they need to understand her conclusions and suggestions.

Approachability

Rachel will be working with users a great deal and therefore she must be easy to talk to, and appear friendly and trustworthy.

Problem Solving and Technical Skills

She needs to be highly skilled and trained so she can thoroughly observe the current system in operation.

Remember that the explanation is the vital thing in answering these questions — get all the qualities in your answer, but make sure you explain them properly and relate them directly to the job you're talking about.

Systems Analysts and Helpdesk Team Members are pretty obvious ones to go for.
Of course there's loads of other jobs you could have a think about too. Examples of these are:
Computer Technicians, Network Technicians, Systems Administrators, Systems Engineers, Security Engineers, Database Administrators, Programmers / Developers, Webmasters, etc.

Practice Question

Q1 Write an advert for an IT Helpdesk Team Member's job, in less than 35 words, listing and briefly describing the qualities you're looking for in an employee.

Exam Questions

Q1 The role of a programmer extends beyond simply writing computer code. Describe a programmer's job in relation to:

a) Debugging computer code (3 marks)

b) Documenting and maintaining computer code (3 marks)

Q2 Large companies have to employ teams of IT professionals because the workload tends to be too high for just one person. IT professionals are given specific jobs within a team. Describe the roles of the following people within the web department of a large company.

a) Web developer (2 marks)

b) Web technician (2 marks)

c) Webmaster (2 marks)

Hello, Helpdesk?...What do you call a man with a spade on his head?...

I never really understood that joke. How can you have a spade on your head? If he was going to be called Doug, wouldn't he have to have a hole in the ground on his head? Which, by the way, is impossible. Oh well — maybe next time I'll have a new employee at the helpdesk... someone with a really funny name. Like Archibald. Or Alan Titchmarsh.

The Effects of ICT

These pages are for AQA Unit 2 and OCR Unit 1.

In this section you've seen how ICT is everywhere... literally, everywhere. This raises some pretty meaty issues.

*ICT has Changed **National Patterns of Employment***

1) At first people were concerned that ICT would **replace workers** and lead to an **employment crisis**. But ICT has changed the **type** of jobs that people do rather than **reducing the size of the workforce**.
2) Companies now need people to be things like **network managers**, **technicians** and **website designers**, and they need other people to install and maintain ICT systems, and to train other staff.
3) ICT has also made life **easier** for a lot of people who have kept the same jobs — for example, databases allow you to **find** individual records a lot more easily than searching through a filing cabinet.

ICT Services** Have Changed **How Businesses Work

1) The increased use of ICT for communication and other services means that businesses no longer need to be as **centralised**. There's **less need** for businesses to be situated in **big cities** or to have all their **sites close together** — teleconferencing can be used to hold meetings between people at different sites, for example.
2) Teleworking (working from home) allows many businesses to reduce **overheads** and **space** to save money.
3) However, file sharing, e-mail and teleworking make it **more difficult** to keep information **confidential**.
4) The increased use of ICT has environmental implications too — on the plus side, teleworking means fewer employees **travelling** to work every day, and working electronically means that companies use **less paper**. But of course, all this ICT equipment uses lots of **energy**...

Teleworking and teleconferencing are covered on p38.

*But **ICT** also creates **Social, Moral** and **Ethical** Issues*

1) **Social** issues are those concerning how computers are **affecting the way society is organised**, and **how people act** and behave towards **each other**.
2) **Moral** and **ethical** issues are to do with right and wrong.

*There are **Three** Main **Moral** and **Ethical Issues***

Most people agree that these issues are the most important. But there are others. Remember the golden rule — it's up to **you** to form **your own opinion** about these issues.

Unrestricted Internet access — there are **very few restrictions** on what people can view on the Internet. Even laws that do exist about illegal content are very **hard to enforce** online.
While this could expose children to **offensive material**, greater controls are opposed by people who think that they would **restrict freedom of speech**.

Ease of copying computer files — it's now so easy to copy computer files that many people are **ignoring copyright and licensing** rules. The problem has become worse as computers are increasingly used for things like music and movies. Some people argue that this has created a new generation that are **comfortable with breaking the law**.

Increased government surveillance — at the minute the government requires ISPs to retain a list of all the **websites** visited by each internet user for **4 days** and details of who they've communicated with by **e-mail** for **6 months**. In the future governments could tell them to start keeping this information for **much longer**, or start keeping copies of the **contents** of the web pages and e-mails, without the user noticing any difference in their connection.
Some think that longer and more detailed records would help **fight crime**, but other people are worried that the government would just use any additional powers to **spy on the behaviour of the public**.

The Effects of ICT

There are **Five Main Social Issues**

Remember, what counts is not **which** issues you put into your answer, but **how you discuss** them.

'Information Rich' and 'Information Poor'

1) Computers **aren't cheap**, so not everyone can **afford** them.
2) Some people worry that this might create a **two-tier society** — those who are computer-literate ('information rich') and those unable to exploit the technology ('information poor').

The Internet's Changing How We Interact

1) The growth of **e-mail** and **home shopping** worries some people. They think that we will increasingly stay at home, becoming **less physically fit**, and communicating only via the Internet.
2) They also fear that Internet communication will cause people to lose **personal skills** and communicate only with people having similar views, resulting in **society** becoming **fragmented** and **depersonalised**.

Over-reliance on Technology

1) We **trust** technology all the time — to operate traffic lights, fly planes, control our money. But the more we rely on technology, the bigger the problems when things **go wrong**. Hackers can **exploit weaknesses** in ICT systems and use these for identity theft, e.g. to steal bank details.
2) Some people think ICT is **deskilling** society — we're gaining ICT skills but losing others that **aren't being replaced**.

Impact on Literacy

1) Some people think the increased use of **computers** is resulting in people spending **less time reading**.
2) Regularly using '**text speak**' and **autocorrect** functions in software could be damaging **literacy levels**.
3) As a result **education standards** will be lower and the workforce less capable — making society poorer.

Faster Pace of Life

1) It's argued that computers are increasing the **pace of life** (and **stress** levels).
2) Computer technology is **rapidly changing** — so people constantly have to **adapt** to new ways of working.
3) Computers can handle larger quantities of data, and process them much **faster** than manual methods — so humans have to **work harder** to **keep up** with the work generated.

Practice Questions

Q1 How has ICT changed patterns of employment in Britain?

Q2 Explain the issues associated with unrestricted Internet access, copying files illegally, and government surveillance.

Exam Questions

Q1 Discuss the implications of ICT upon the following areas:

a) National literacy levels (3 marks)

b) Reliance on technology (3 marks)

c) Personal skills and interaction (3 marks)

I doont fnk tat TIC as ad ne Fex on v litrusee wut i huv all red ee got...

That might be because, as my doctor once told me, my brain is "genetically similar to a potato". But enough about me. That's the end of Section Five, so pat yourself on the back, make sure you can answer the questions on each page, and then take a break... Did you enjoy it? Now, ICT friends, onwards and upwards to Section Six. It's a corker.

Malpractice and Crime

These pages are for AQA Unit 2 and OCR Unit 1.

The weak points of an IT system are often its users and the points at which it meets the outside world. Hardware can also be a weak point if it is not regularly maintained or if it is not capable of dealing with the system's demands.

Data Needs To Be Kept Secure

Data needs to be **kept secure** to prevent it being lost or changed accidentally or deliberately:

- **Accidental loss** of data can occur due to human error, natural disasters, power failures, and problems with the hardware and software being used.
- **Deliberate loss** of data can occur due to hacking, cyber crime, viruses and vandalism.

Physical Methods Prevent Access to a Computer in Person

1) Companies can restrict physical access to computers by **keeping rooms locked** when not in use.
2) **Security cameras** can be used to monitor corridors and rooms.
3) Many organisations are beginning to use **biometric devices** to provide physical security. These are things like **fingerprint scanners** or **iris scanners** which ensure that only authorised people can gain access to the computers.
4) **Fire and burglar alarms** can be installed.
5) An **Uninterruptible Power Supply** (a back up battery) can be installed to prevent loss of data if there's a power failure.

Logical Methods are Computer-Based Methods

Logical methods are applied to a computer by an administrator.

1) Folders can be set as "**Read-Only**" so no one can accidentally delete an important file. After writing files to disk, the disks can be **write-protected** with the same result.
2) Data can be **encrypted** to protect it when it is being transmitted. Encryption means taking plain text and applying an **algorithm** to it so it appears meaningless. Encryption stops anyone who has the data from being able to understand it without the **appropriate key**.
3) A **firewall** helps to prevent people hacking in to the computer system from outside.
4) As well as having **user IDs** (user names) and **passwords**, different users can be given different levels of access to parts of a system, e.g. they might only be allowed to view and change certain data depending on their job.
5) User ID and password procedures can also be used to log what each user is doing at any particular time — this is an **audit trail**. Audit trails are useful in helping pinpoint what happened after data has been compromised.
6) **Software logs** can be used to look at patterns of access to the computers. If a user begins to access computers at strange times then it could be that their user name and password are being used by someone else.
7) **Security software** e.g. virus checkers, anti-spam and anti-spyware, must be kept up-to-date with the latest versions installed.

Malpractice and Crime

Passwords Need to be Kept Secure

Companies that require their employees to have a password usually make sure that the following standard rules are used. These rules help to reduce the likelihood that a password will be guessed or hacked by someone else.

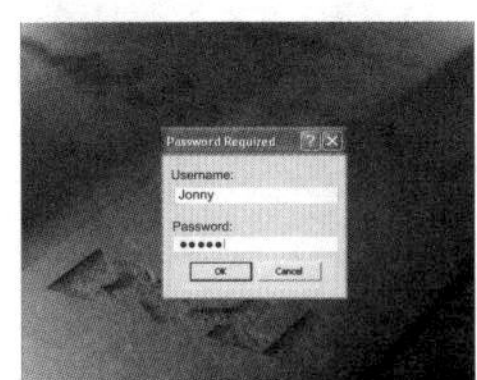

They'll never guess this, laughed Jonny, typing in a password with the same number of letters as his name.

1) Use a mixture of numbers and letters.
2) Don't use a recognised word or a word from a dictionary.
3) Change your passwords regularly — every month would be the ideal.
4) Make sure a record is kept (somewhere safe) of passwords used, and don't use the same ones again.

Backing Up Data Is Vital to IT Systems

The best way of keeping data secure is to keep several **copies** of it, and store each copy in a **different place**. Keeping copies means that if valuable or private data is lost, corrupted or stolen, the organisation still has the information stored somewhere. **For more on backup and recovery see page 26.**

- If data is **stolen** — a backup copy means that details like customer account passwords or other security information can be changed before the information can be used **fraudulently**.
- If data is **lost** — a backup copy can **replace** the data like for like (as long as it has recently been backed up — data that is subject to regular changes could be out of date, but the organisation would at least have a recent copy that takes less time to update, rather than nothing at all).
- If data is **corrupted or damaged** — a backup copy stored at a different location can be used as a replacement as it will not have been subjected to whatever **problem** damaged the original store.

Security, Privacy and Integrity — Make Sure You Know the Difference

1) Data **privacy** is the need for some data only to be accessed by, and disclosed to, authorised persons.
2) Data **integrity** is the correctness of data both during and after processing.
3) Data **security** is the use of various methods to ensure data privacy and data integrity as well as preventing the loss or destruction of data.

Practice Questions

Q1 Why is it important that data is kept secure?

Q2 Describe the types of things that could cause accidental and deliberate loss of data.

Q3 How can you reduce the likelihood of your password being hacked?

Q4 Explain the difference between data security, privacy and integrity.

Exam Questions

Q1 State three ways a company can prevent physical access to its communications network. (3 marks)

Q2 Give five measures that can be taken to protect data by the administrator of a network. (5 marks)

If you want to get to him, you'll have to come through me... and me... and...

Keeping data secure is absolutely vital — it benefits everyone. Just think, if you were a goldfish, you could finally solve the problems you'd been having with that pesky seven second memory, because you'd never lose any information. Also, if you were a goldfish, you could finally solve the problems you'd been having with that pesky seven second memory.

Malpractice and Crime

These pages are for AQA Unit 2 and OCR Unit 1.

Well this page isn't for the faint-hearted. Of course, there's no weighty discussions of abortion or vegetarianism, but in ICT-land, this stuff is pretty important. The bad news is you have to learn it all.

Computer Crime Is Any Illegal Use Of An ICT System

1) **Unauthorised access** to computerised information systems is an **offence**. If information systems are illegally accessed their data could be **altered**, **lost** or **used for illegal purposes**.
2) Computer crime is an increasingly big problem. These are some **common examples**:

- **hacking** into a system to **look** at its data.
- **hacking** into a system to **destroy** its data.
- **theft of data** from an information system.
- **theft of money** carried out by transferring money electronically.
- **theft of goods** by re-routing them.
- **illegal use of software** by copying or using it on more machines than there are licences for.
- **internet fraud** e.g. unsecure sites where criminals can get access to your credit card details.
- **introducing viruses** into a system to deliberately cause damage.

Malpractice Means Professional Misconduct

Malpractice means acting in an **unprofessional way**, that leads to **unauthorised use or loss of data**. For example:

- Staff might **forget to log off** or turn a workstation off, leaving it open for someone else to use.
- Staff might leave password details **lying around** somewhere they can easily be found.
- Staff might access unsafe software or websites and **introduce viruses** which can destroy the data in a system.
- The organisation might not have a **good backup system** and if there is a problem such as a power cut or a system crash, they will lose their data completely.
- The information system itself **might have faults** that allow anyone to get in, in which case the malpractice would have been by the system developer.
  For example, there was a case where a major bank's system allowed people to access other people's accounts.
- An organisation might **inadvertently process data** in a way that **causes distress or damage**.
  For example, a sales system user might accidentally record a payment to a wrong account so one person seems to have paid too much and another too little. One customer will be asked for a payment they have already made and will be inconvenienced by having to prove it.

Computer Crimes Are Committed By Hackers and Crackers

A **hacker** is someone who uses their technical knowledge to **access a computer system without permission**.

- Some hackers might access a computer system **just to show that it can be done** (some companies employ hackers just to test the security of their systems).
- Some hackers access a system to **use the software**.
- Some hackers access a system to **read or copy the data**.

A **cracker** is someone who uses their technical knowledge to **crack codes**, like passwords and other encrypted data.

- Some crackers **find out a password** then pass it on to a hacker, or use it to access a system themselves.
- Some crackers **translate encrypted code** that was being sent from one system to another.

Sure, they didn't look that dangerous. But Kev and his mates were the most lethal crackers in the business.

Malpractice and Crime

Malware is Designed To **Inconvenience** Or **Seriously Damage** Systems

1) **Viruses** are computer programs that attach themselves to (infect) known programs and can **replicate themselves** without the user knowing. They are activated when the main program is run. They are often designed to harm the computer system, e.g. by **deleting** or **modifying** data so that it becomes unreadable.
2) **Worms** are similar to viruses — they also replicate themselves but they don't need a host program to attach to. They are usually designed to automatically spread over **networks**.
3) **Trojan horses** are programs that **seem** to be doing something useful but are actually doing something malicious in the background. Hackers use Trojan horses to **get access** to a system while a user is doing a **particular task.**
4) **Time bombs** and **logic bombs** are malicious programs that become activated at a **particular time** (e.g. on friday 13th), or when the user does a **particular thing** (e.g. boot sector viruses activate when the system is booted up.)

Fraudsters, Obscenity, Pirates, Illegal goods — the **Internet**'s got it all...

There is so much **information exchanged** over the Internet that it is an **obvious target** for criminal or illegal activity.

1) **Bogus websites** can be set up that gather other users' **financial** and **personal** details that can then be used fraudulently. Online transactions have made credit card fraud easier too because data can be **intercepted** and card details can be **decrypted.**
2) Because there are no physical meetings between users on the Internet, it's possible to **buy** and **sell illegal items** like firearms.
3) It's possible to publish **fake personal details**, like name, age or address, without anyone else knowing in order to blackmail or stalk others, or to commit fraud with someone else's details.
4) It's also easy to **hide your identity** when using the Internet — personal details like e-mail addresses and instant messaging usernames are often not related to any **physical location** or person.
5) **Copyright infringements** occur regularly on the Internet as it's possible for users to **illegally download** and make **copies** of things like **pictures, music, videos or software** that should be protected.
6) A big benefit but also a big problem is the fact that **no one controls** the Internet. Many governments try to **block or filter access** to websites but they cannot control what is **uploaded** to them which might be **inaccurate, libellous or offensive material.** The Internet **can't be turned off** if someone doesn't like something on one of the websites, and it's simply impossible to police everything it contains.

Practice Questions

Q1 Give 5 examples of computer crime.

Q2 Define the terms "malpractice", "hacker" and "cracker".

Q3 What is a Trojan horse?

Q4 Why are online transactions targets for criminal activity?

Exam Questions

Q1 Describe three ways in which a company's staff can undermine the security of its information systems. (6 marks)

Q2 What is the difference between a hacker and a cracker, and how are they a threat to computer systems? (4 marks)

Q3 Identify and describe three types of malware that could infect a computer system. (6 marks)

Crime doesn't pay — unless you get away with it...

But seriously, it's not a good idea to indulge in any illegal activity. Prison's a pretty nasty place. I hear that Hitler's dog is there, and one of the Lassies is there (which one? The evil one...). Hang on. I'm actually just referencing an episode of the Simpsons where their dog is having an operation. How did I get on to that? What I meant to say was — this stuff is serious.

ICT Legislation

These pages are for AQA Unit 2 and OCR Unit 1.

Right then me hearties, time to knuckle down and learn a few specific legal things. No more of yer swashbuckling, timber-shivering parrot talk — I'm talking about real life, honest to goodness piracy. I mean computer crime laws.

The **Computer Misuse Act** Makes **Computer Crime Illegal**

If you hack into a computer system you can **read private data** or you could **copy or damage it**. Reading data isn't a serious crime like theft, but it is an invasion of privacy, and **laws are needed** to make sure that people don't do it.

1) General computer use grew during the 1970s and 80s, leading to **an increase in computer fraud**, e.g. stealing money out of people's bank accounts by changing data, and a new problem — **how to deal with deliberate access or damage to data**.
2) The term "hacking" became used for **breaking into someone's system without permission**. This is sometimes just people proving that they could beat the system for fun, but often it's to **steal** data or to damage a system.
3) **Prosecuting hackers proved to be very difficult** as existing legislation relating to theft, criminal damage and intercepting telecommunications **didn't cover hacking**. One such failed example was Crown v Gold where two journalists were acquitted of unauthorised access to the BT network in the 1980s.
4) This led to the **1990 Computer Misuse Act**, which identifies three levels of offence:

Level 1 Offence:
Unauthorised access to computer material —
e.g. 'hacking' and piracy.
This means viewing data you are not permitted to see, or illegally copying programs.
The **maximum penalty** is **6 months** in jail or a maximum fine of **£5000**, or both.

Level 2 Offence:
Unauthorised access with intent to cause a further offence —
e.g. fraud and blackmail.
This means gaining unauthorised access with the intention of committing a more serious crime (one that would get you a jail sentence of at least 5 years).
The **maximum penalty** for this is **5 years** in jail and maybe a **fine** too.

Level 3 Offence:
Unauthorised changing or deleting of files —
e.g. planting a virus.
This means modifying or deleting the content of any computer with intent to cause damage to programs and / or data (including deliberately introducing a virus). This can get you a **fine** and up to **5 years** in jail.

In order to prosecute someone, it has to be proved that they:
- **intended to gain access** to data or programs
- **didn't have authorisation** to do so
- **knew and understood** that they didn't have authorisation

In 2004 a British university student was given 200 hours community service for the "unauthorised modification of computer data and impairing the performance" of a computer system at the US Department of Energy. The student had used their disk space to upload movies, software and games, which slowed down their system.

But There Are **Lots Of Loopholes**

Some legal experts believe that the Act is too full of **loopholes** to be a real and useful deterrent.

1) Organisations often want to **hide** the fact that there is a **problem with their security** from the public — revealing this could damage public confidence in them and harm their reputation. As a result, companies often **avoid** involving law enforcement agencies and instead deal with matters **themselves**.
2) It's actually quite **hard to prove intent** — it's easy for hackers to argue that their actions were accidental.
3) The Computer Misuse Act is now at least 15 years old and it was written **before** the Internet became so **widely used**, making it a bit **out-of-date**. The person to be prosecuted is often a citizen of a different country to the one the computer system is in, making the process very difficult and confusing.

The British student who hacked into the US Department of Energy was prosecuted under British law even though it was American. But the same won't necessarily apply to a foreign national who hacks into a British system.

ICT Legislation

The Copyright, Designs and Patents Act (1988) Covers Illegal Copying

This law makes it **illegal** to steal or make unauthorised copies of software. The Act also covers CD-ROMs, music and books. It was introduced in **1989**. Individuals and organisations who break this law risk an unlimited fine.

Here's the main ways the law gets broken:

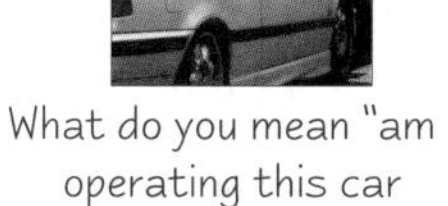

What do you mean "am I operating this car without a licence?"

1) **Using software without a proper licence.**
   e.g. if you have a licence to use a word processor on one stand-alone computer, but then you install it on all the machines in a network, you're breaking the law.
2) **Software piracy.**

   e.g. professional criminals producing multiple copies of games software and selling them.
3) **Illegally downloading material from the Internet.**
   e.g. downloading MP3 files from illegal sites to avoid paying for them, or copying text or images from the Internet and using them without receiving the copyright owner's permission or saying where you got them.

It gets more complicated when material is downloaded from **servers located in different countries**. Different countries have different copyright laws, and as no government has control of the Internet, the copyright laws in the country where the materials are being downloaded become more difficult to enforce.

When You Buy Software, You Buy A Licence For It Too

Single-user licence
You'll need one of these if you're buying software to use on one computer at a time. So you could install it on your home PC and laptop in theory, as long as you didn't use the software on both machines at the same time.

Multi-user licence
Companies need these when they want to use a piece of software on several different machines. The licences usually specify a maximum number of users who can use the software at any one time — it limits the numbers of active users, rather than the number of copies of software that are installed.

Network licence
This allows a company to share software with users over an internal network.

Site licence
This lets a company have an unlimited number of users of the software, within a particular location.

Different licences cost different amounts. You're likely to pay a fair whack more for a 30-user licence than a single-user one.

Practice Questions

Q1 Give an example of an offence for levels 1, 2 and 3 of the Computer Misuse Act.

Q2 What is currently the maximum sentence you could get for deliberately gaining unauthorised access to files, if it's proved that you didn't intend to commit any further crimes?

Q3 State three problems with the current Computer Misuse Act.

Exam Questions

Q1 Briefly explain three ways in which the law can be broken under the Copyright, Designs and Patents Act. (3 marks)

Q2 A small company has a multi-user software licensing agreement for a spreadsheet package specifying that there must be no more than 5 copies in use at any one time.

a) Describe what is meant by a "software licensing agreement". (1 mark)

b) Would the company be breaking the agreement by installing the software on 5 PCs and 3 laptops? Explain your answer. (2 marks)

Johnny Depp's been illegally downloading MP3s — It's a piracy issue...

Phew, good to get these pages out of the way. It's important to learn all about the legislation that's in place to deal with computer crime, even though it does have its loopholes. Criminals have been prosecuted successfully though, and it's only a matter of time before the law tightens up on these issues. But Johnny Depp can be exempt. Because he's a stunner.

ICT Legislation

These pages are for AQA Unit 2 and OCR Unit 1.

Ooh, more jargon on these pages. I know it's a right pain in the donkey, but learning all the proper words will make you sound much better in the exam. Anything's better than writing things like "him who did that thing with the wotsit..."

The **Electronic Communications Act** covers Communication and Data Storage

The 2000 Electronic Communications Act (ECA) was passed as the UK government wanted "to make the UK the best place in the world for e-commerce" and to "Create a legal framework so that people can be sure about the origin and integrity of communications".

The Act had two main parts:

- **Cryptography Service Providers** — companies or individuals providing services like data encryption or digital signature creation had to be part of an approved register.
- **Facilitation of Electronic Commerce, Data Storage** — this basically said that digital signatures would now be acceptable in legal documents, and covered how they'd be used.

The new ZT3529 (Stanley) provides data encryption, e-document signing, wood-cutting and can prepare a variety of hot and cold beverages.

1) Contracts signed over the Internet are as legally binding as those signed by hand. This increases the security of e-commerce as the contracts entered into are legally binding.
2) The complete acceptance and use of digital signatures will take time. The use of a digital signature is still not fully accepted when making a will or buying a house.
3) There is also a security risk. A government minister's digital signature was hijacked within 24 hours of its creation. A document, digitally signed by the Trade and Industry Minister had an additional statement inserted into it that opposed the government's cryptographic policy.

The **Freedom of Information Act** covers Access to Official Information

The Freedom of Information Act (FIA) came into force at the beginning of 2005 and deals with access to official information. This means you can find out information on any topic from any public authority including government, health service (hospitals and doctor's surgeries), schools and police.

1) Anyone can ask for information — there are no age limits.
2) You have to write to the public authority you think has the information you want, along with your name, address and a description of the information you want.
3) It's usually free but you may be asked to pay a small charge for photocopying and postage.
4) The public authority has to reply to you within 20 working days.
5) FIA is one of a set of Acts. Requesting information under the **wrong Act** will delay the information being received. For example, information **about you** needs to be requested under the **Data Protection Act.**

The Good Stuff

Information which was not accessible to the general public is **now available**. This means that public authorities **can't** take decisions and not tell anyone. The information is now available to those **who want it**.

The Not-So-Good Stuff

The public authority doesn't have to provide the information if:

- an **exemption** applies, e.g. if it's info that might affect national security.
- the request is **too vague** or if it's been asked for before.
- the **cost** of collecting the information exceeds a **reasonable limit**.

The authority also doesn't have to confirm or deny the existence of the information requested, a bit annoying really...

ICT Legislation

*The **Regulation of Investigatory Powers Act** covers Intercepting Communications*

The 2000 Regulation of Investigatory Powers Act (RIPA) was nicknamed the 'snoopers charter'.
It allows **lawful interception** of postal, telecommunications and digital **communications** in certain circumstances.

Communications may be **secretly monitored and recorded** in circumstances such as:

- the interests of national security
- investigating unauthorised use of telecommunications systems
- preventing or detecting crime

Communications may be **secretly monitored but not recorded** in cases such as:

- a company checking whether communications being made are business or personal
- monitoring calls made to anonymous telephone help lines

1) The RIPA Act allows companies to **monitor and record** communications for certain purposes, e.g. training, improving systems — this is allowed as long as the people involved in the communication have given their consent.
2) It requires **Internet service providers** to install systems for monitoring **e-mail** and **Internet activity** in order to assist law-enforcement agencies.
3) The Act has some **benefits** for companies — it allows them to check that their facilities, e.g. Internet and e-mail, are only being used for work purposes and that confidential company information is not being given away.

Sam thought he was enjoying Enrique in the privacy of his own home...

Little did Sam know...

4) Many people think that the level of monitoring RIPA allows is a breach of **trust, privacy** and **civil liberties**.
5) Some people are also concerned that there aren't enough controls on the **organisations** who are doing the monitoring.

The OCR specification needs you to be aware of any updates or changes to the Acts.

Practice Questions

Q1 What are the two main parts of the Electronic Communications Act?

Q2 Briefly describe two problems with the Electronic Communications Act.

Q3 Explain the purpose of the Freedom of Information Act. Describe the good and not-so-good stuff about it.

Q4 Under RIPA, give three situations where communications could be secretly monitored.

Q5 What must a company have before it can lawfully record phone calls?

Q6 Would you dance if Enrique asked you to dance? Would you run and never look back?
Would you cry if you saw Enrique cry? Would you save his soul tonight?

Exam Questions

Q1 Explain two benefits of the Electronic Communications Act to a company which sells books through a website. (4 marks)

Q2 Describe the main provisions of the Regulation of Investigatory Powers Act. (4 marks)

You can run, you can hide, but you can't escape the snoopers...

Phew, that would have been an incredibly dull two double pages if Enrique hadn't jumped to the rescue, like the hero he is. Don't worry about Sam though. He's not in love with Enrique, it's just a phase that he's going through... I recommend you learn all about the three Acts on this page before moving on, but if you feel like leaving, I'm not going to make you stay.

ICT Legislation

These pages are for AQA Unit 2 and OCR Unit 1.

Here we go. These are the last two pages about data protection legislation, and the last two horribly jargony pages in this section. Jargony. Hm. That's not a real word. But you know what is? Slouchy. How weird is that...?

The **Data Protection Act** Limits Information That Can be Held about You

Data organisations and government agencies collect and hold information about people. The 1998 Data Protection Act (DPA) was introduced to limit the amount of information that can be held.

There are a few specific terms you need to know:

1) A **data controller** decides how the data will be collected, created, stored, organised and used.
2) A **data processor** is the person or organisation who retrieves the data under the authority of the data controller (this could be the organisation that collected the data, or it might be a third party).
3) A **data subject** is the individual person who is identified by the data.
4) **Personal data** is data that relates to a living, identifiable person. Most personal data is stored on computers these days, but it could also mean paper-based records.
6) **Processing** is the obtaining, recording or holding of the information or data.
7) **Recipients** are given the data to do something with. They are usually employees of the data controller or are data processors.
8) A **third party** is the person who receives the data from the processing.

The **Information Commissioner** Is Independent From The Government

1) The **Information Commissioner** is an independent official, appointed by the Crown, to oversee the Data Protection Act 1998 and the Freedom of Information Act 2000. They must report to parliament once a year.
2) Their office maintains the **Public Register of Data Controllers**.
3) Any organisation that wants to process personal information **must be placed on the Public Register**. It's a criminal offence to keep and process personal data if you are not on the Public Register.

- The Information Commissioner is responsible for making sure that the **Data Protection Act is enforced** and that **all data controllers comply with it**.
- They give **advice** on issues relating to the Act.
- They give **examples of good practice** and **consider complaints** from data subjects.
- They ensure that the **Freedom of Information Act is enforced**.

Individuals Have **Rights** under the DPA

There are six main rights that an individual has:

1) **Right to subject access** — you're allowed to see what information a company holds on you.
2) **Right to prevent processing likely to cause damage or distress** — if the processing causes a high level of damage and distress you can ask the company to stop (although they're not always legally bound to comply).
3) **Right to prevent processing for direct marketing** — companies need your permission before using your personal data to send you marketing materials (this could be post, e-mails or telesales). If you receive unwanted mail you can ask to be removed from their mailing lists.
4) **Rights in relation to automated decision making** — some decisions are taken by a computer. You can ask that a person takes the decision, not a computer.
5) **Right to compensation for damage and distress suffered by the act being contravened** — if you can prove that the data controller did not follow the requirements of the DPA then you are entitled to compensation.
6) **Right to rectify, block or erase incorrect data** — if the data that is held about you is wrong, then you can get it changed.

ICT Legislation

A Data Subject's **Consent** Is **Not Always Needed** For **Data Processing**

Consent may not need to be given by the data subject, if:

- the data is necessary for **setting up a contract**, e.g. credit references.
- the data is necessary **by law**, e.g. attendance records in schools, production of accounts, details of donors to charitable organisations.
- the data **helps protect** the vital interests of the data subject, e.g. missing persons register.
- it is necessary for **administering justice**, e.g. National Police Database.
- it is required by **government** or it is in the **public interest**, e.g. tax records.

Some Data Must Be **Registered** But Is **Exempt From Subject Access**

Some registered data is **exempt from subject access**. This includes data that might:

- affect a **criminal investigation**
- affect the outcome of a **court case**
- affect a **tax assessment**
- **identify another person** (unless that other person has given their consent)

The **Data Protection Act 1998** Has **8 Principles** For You To **Learn**

The principles are stated below in a slightly simpler form than in the Act itself — you need to learn them all:

Principle 1) Data must be processed **fairly** and **lawfully**.
Principle 2) Data must be obtained only for **specified purposes** and must not be processed in any other way.
Principle 3) Data must be **adequate**, **relevant** and **not excessive** in relation to the purpose.
Principle 4) Data must be **accurate** and, where necessary, **up-to-date**.
Principle 5) Data must **not be kept** for longer than is necessary for the registered purpose.
Principle 6) Data must be **processed** in accordance with the **rights** of the data subject.
Principle 7) Measures must be taken to **prevent** unlawful processing or accidental damage / loss of data.
Principle 8) Data **must not be transferred** to a country or territory **outside the European Economic Area (EEA)** unless that country or territory has an adequate level of data protection legislation.

Practice Questions

Q1 Define the terms "data subject", "data controller" and "data processor".
Q2 Give four responsibilities of the Information Commissioner.
Q3 What is listed in the Public Register?

Exam Questions

Q1 A charity keeps data on all people who have ever donated anything to them. Their Public Register entry shows that they will keep data about the money and services that donors have given, along with identifying data such as name and address. The register also states that the data will be used for accounting, management analysis (of monetary information only) and direct marketing, and that the data will not be transferred to any other countries.

Explain which parts of the register entry may need the data subject's consent and which parts may not. (4 marks)

Q2 Data can be easily transferred from one system to another, regardless of where in the world those systems are.

Name two principles of the Data Protection Act 1998 which relate to the transfer of data between systems and explain how they do so. (2 marks)

Wow, this stuff is really, really interesting...

One more thing to add — sometimes consent is given implicitly, e.g. if you fill in a form, you know the data is going to be stored. Well anyway, it's pretty hard-going this stuff, and not the most interesting if I'm totally honest. Still all the hard work will be worth it in the end, trust me. Anyway, time for a chocolate break. Mini creme egg or chocolate elf? Decisions...

Health and Safety

These pages are for AQA Unit 1 and OCR Unit 1.

There are a few different health problems associated with computer use, and there is legislation to help protect people from these. The most important thing to remember though, is that this is the last double-page of this section.

There Are **Guidelines** To Help Us **Fix Health Problems**

1) Lots of the health problems caused by computer use can be prevented or reduced with **simple actions**.
2) Some actions are just recommendations, but some are covered by the **regulations set for employers**.
3) There are also guidelines for hardware and software **developers** to consider the health and safety **of their users**.

There Are **Different Ways To Help** With Each Problem

Here are some examples:

Problem	Causes	Prevention/reduction
eye strain (can cause blurred vision and headaches)	• **concentrating on the screen** for too long • constantly **refocusing eyes** between screen and paper • **glare** from light reflecting on the screen • sitting too **close** to the screen	• Take **regular breaks** from working at the screen — about 15 minutes every hour • **refocus eyes** every 10 minutes and make sure work areas are well lit • use blinds to **reduce glare** from the sun • sit at least one metre from the screen
repetitive strain injury (RSI) (can lead to carpal tunnel syndrome, ulnar neuritis and neck problems)	• Repeated **similar movements**, such as clicking mouse buttons or typing	• use **wrist rests** when typing • take **frequent breaks** • have the keyboard at the **right height** • press keys and buttons **lightly**
back and neck problems	• can be caused by **repetitive movement** • also **bad posture**, especially when sitting for long periods at a computer	• maintain **good posture** • take **frequent breaks** and **move around**
deep vein thrombosis (forming of blood clots in the veins)	• **sitting still** for very long periods of time	• take **frequent breaks** and **move around**
epilepsy	• screens which **flicker** at certain frequencies • **strobe effects** on screen displays	• **screen filters** can reduce flicker • use a high **screen refresh rate**.

Good Posture And A **Well-Designed Workstation** Are **Important**

1) You need to sit upright, keep your **elbows and knees at 90°** and your **feet flat on a footrest**.
2) Your **chair** should provide **back support**.
3) Your chair should also have **wheels**, to allow easy movement away from the computer.
4) Your eyes should be at least **1 metre from the screen**.
5) Your **keyboard** should be at the **correct height** (allowing you to keep your arms at 90°).

Hardware Should Be Chosen With **Health And Safety In Mind**

Hardware can be chosen to **minimise health problems**. For example:

- there are **ergonomic** mice and keyboards
- screens should be an **appropriate resolution and size** for the software they are used with
- printers and copiers should produce the **required quality** of document, e.g. if A3 is needed, an A3 copier should be available, rather than A4 being joined together manually.
- all equipment should work **within acceptable time limits**.

Ergonomic means that it's designed to minimise discomfort and injury.

Health and Safety

Employers Must Meet The **Regulations** For **Health And Safety**

The **Health and Safety at Work Act 1974** and **Health and Safety (Display Screen Equipment) Regulations 1992** cover **employers' responsibilities**, especially where employees work with computer systems. Employers must:

- pay for **regular eye tests** and pay for glasses if they are found to be needed.
- ensure **electrical equipment** is safe and **provide workstations** with space for movement and comfortable working.
- provide **chairs with height adjustment** and **back support**.
- ensure working conditions have **adequate light**, **reduced glare**, **good ventilation** and a **comfortable temperature**.
- plan work so that **regular breaks** can be taken.
- provide **health and safety training**, e.g. lifting techniques and fire and **emergency training** for employees.
- ensure the working environment is **safe** from **fire hazards** and **obstructions** e.g. trailing cables, boxes of paper.
- provide **trained first aiders**.
- allow **pregnant women** to work **away from VDU equipment** if they choose to (because the radiation levels have been linked with increased chance of miscarriage).

Some **Health Problems** Can Come **From Software**

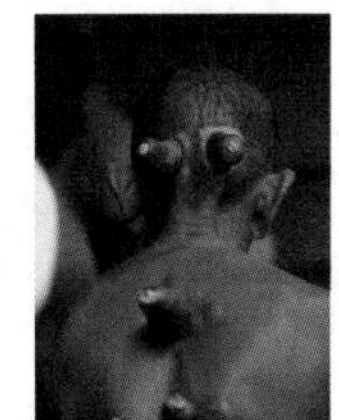

Horn growth is a common problem for spreadsheet users.

1) When new software is designed, there are **guidelines for the developers** covering health and safety factors linked to **poor software design**.
2) Changing to new software can cause **stress**, and this can lead to **fatigue** and **health problems** — the changeover should be as **smooth** as possible.
3) If **training** is required, it should be **available** to all who need it and should be **comprehensive** enough to allow users to be **confident** in using the software.
4) If the **user interface is too complicated**, this can cause stress — the user interface should be designed to be as **easy to use** as possible.
5) However, **experienced users** will become **frustrated** with a user interface that is too simple. An easy to use interface may feel slow for the experienced user and this may cause frustration and stress. **Shortcuts** can be useful in reducing this stress.

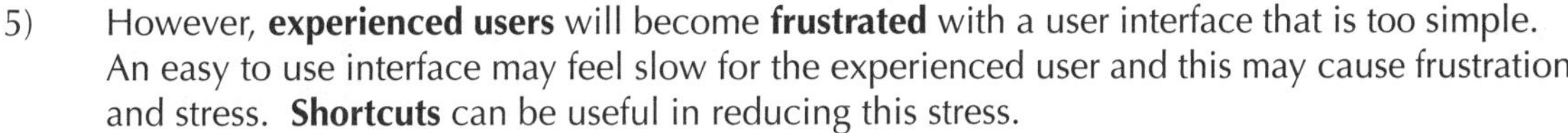

6) The new system must be **as good as**, or better than, **the old system**. A user can become frustrated if tasks that worked well in the old system are replaced with ones that are slower or more difficult.

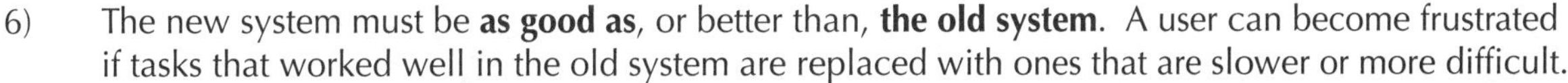

7) **Losing important work** is another cause of stress. Systems should be designed to allow work to be recovered in case of accidental loss through hardware or software failure.
8) Movement of the mouse, number of mouse clicks and number of keypresses should be **kept to a minimum** and a user should not be required to focus on one particular area of the screen for too long.
9) There are also guidelines explaining that **some colour combinations** place **less strain on the eyes** than others.

Practice Questions

Q1 List five health problems associated with computer use.

Q2 What responsibilities does an employer have in protecting the health and safety of his or her employees?

Q3 What considerations should be made with regard to health and safety when designing new software?

Exam Questions

Q1 Explain what health-related design features should be considered when recommending and developing a new computer system for an experienced user. (3 marks)

Q2 What measures can a user take to protect their own health when using a computer system at home? (3 marks)

As long as you've got your health you're fine — but I'd rather be rich...

Take the money and run, so long as you can run. I know it's easy to joke when you're feeling fit and healthy, but before long you'll find yourself in a work situation where you're basically just sitting totally still for 8 hours a day, and then all this information will come back to you with a vengeance. Learn all this stuff well — not just for the exams, but because it's useful.

Word Processing and DTP

These pages are for AQA Unit 1 and OCR Unit 1.

Roll up roll up for the software-for-presentation-and-communication circus. Step right this way. First of all, ladies and gentlemen, come on a journey with me into the mysterious and frankly bizarre world of word processors and DTP.

Word Processing Packages Have Some Helpful Layout Features

1) **Standard formats / templates**
   Most word processors provide templates for standard documents, such as faxes, memos, letters, etc. These help you create documents with standardised formatting.
2) **Layout**
   Word processors also let you add more visual elements like graphics, tables and numbers. These can help make your document look more professional and readable.

DTP Software Has Lots of Features That Make Layout Easier

Desktop publishing software has specific features that will **help you design** all kinds of different publications, like leaflets, posters or newspapers. One of these features is that DTP software is usually **frame based**.

1) **Frame based software** means that the text or images are put on the pages in blocks, called **frames**.
2) The frames can be individually **moved** or **re-sized**. This means you can **easily edit** your DTP document by changing the size or position of the frames, as well as easily moving a frame from page to page.
3) Frame based software works a bit like a **noticeboard**. You have different pieces of information which you can move around until you're happy with the overall layout.
4) Word processors aren't usually frame-based, so the position of each object on the page depends on the position of everything else. If you move one thing, **everything else will move too**. This doesn't happen with frame based software (unless you want it to).

DTP packages have lots of **other clever features** too:

1) **Arrange / layers** — frames can be layered, e.g. you may want to put a frame containing text over the top of a frame containing a graphic.
2) **Grids / columns / guides** — these mean that frames can be positioned very accurately on the page.
3) **Rotate / flip** — these features allow frames to be easily manipulated (i.e. rotated or flipped in a certain direction).
4) Pages can be easily **added**, **deleted** or **moved**.
5) **Workspace** — this is the area around the page where images and text can be placed for later use. Nothing in the workspace will appear in the final document — it's a bit like having a notebook open. The workspace gives you the extra room to experiment with ideas and layouts.

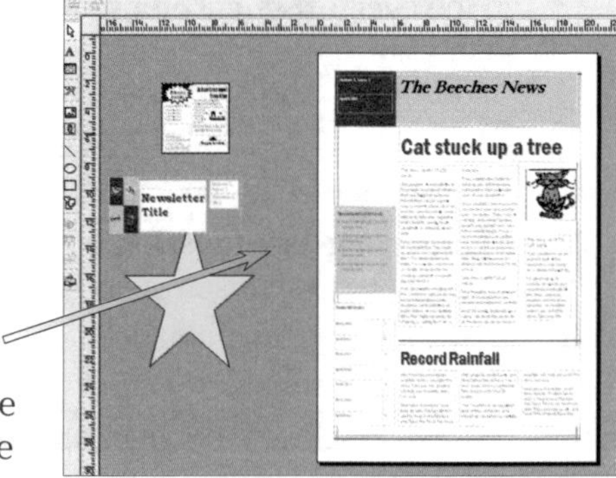

Word Processors Are More Suited To Text-Based Documents

1) As the layout can be changed more easily in a DTP package, it's **more suitable** for documents where this is important, e.g. newsletters which use lots of pictures.
2) Word processors are more useful for other documents that are largely **text-based**, like letters, memos, questionnaires, essays and reports.
3) Different users will use software in different ways. The box below shows examples of this for a word processor.

Scientific author —	technical dictionary, thesaurus, automatic section numbering and indexing, specialist clipart, template to automatically format into report style.
Secretary —	wide range of fonts, spelling and grammar check, templates for memos, letters and faxes, ability to create presentations.
Translator —	language specific dictionary, ability to insert specialist characters.

You could create your text in a word processor first, and then **import it** into the DTP package.

Word Processing and DTP

You Can Produce *Personalised Documents* Using *Mail Merge*

Mail merge is used to turn **standard letters** into **personalised ones** by "merging" a standard document with personal details from a database or spreadsheet — e.g. a mass-mailed letter about a change of address, a competition, a survey, etc. It can also be used simply to create **address labels** or to print envelopes.

Using Mail Merge

1) Create a spreadsheet / database containing the information to include in the letter (**data source**).
2) Create a standard letter using merge fields that match the fields in the data source. For example, Dear <<First_Name>> where "First_Name" is a field in the data source.
3) The letter and the data source are then **linked**. The software merges the data by inserting the appropriate fields from the data source into the letter. If there were 500 records in the data source, then the mail merge process would create 500 personalised letters, each greeting the reader by their first name.

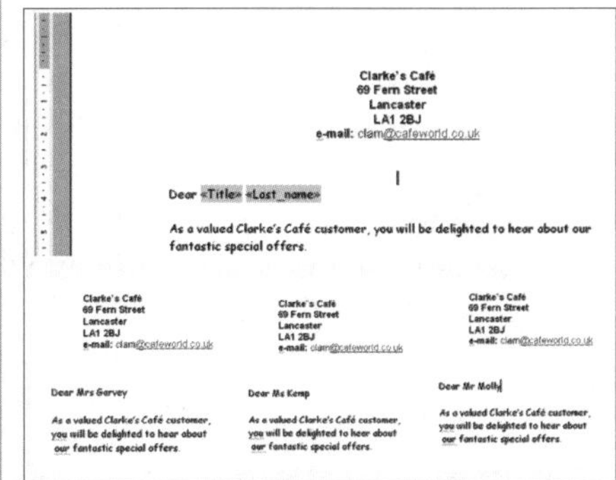

Using mail merge means:

1) You can produce **thousands** of letters **very quickly**.
2) You only need to **proofread** a single letter to know that all the others are correct.
3) You can use **word fields** to select the **exact** group of people to send documents to.

Word fields are extra commands (like Ask, Fill-in, If, and Next/Skip Record) which add extra information to the merged document and allow the user to **control** how the data is merged. Using word fields means data can be taken from other data sources, unwanted data can be filtered out and standard information can be inserted, e.g. date, time, etc.

ASK and FILL-IN — Both these functions prompt the user for information during the mail merge process. This is useful for variable information not available from the data source.

IF... THEN... ELSE — Sets conditions to limit which records are printed, e.g. IF somebody lives in Cumbria, THEN print the document, ELSE (i.e. if they don't), don't print it, or print something else.

NEXT RECORD — Merges the next data record into the current merged document instead of creating a new document. This is useful if lots of record details are to be included on one document, e.g. names and addresses.

SKIP RECORD IF — Misses (or skips) a record if a given condition is met. Two conditions are compared, and if the comparison is true, SKIP RECORD IF cancels the current merge document, moves to the next data record in the data source, and starts a new merge document. If the comparison is false, the current merge document is continued. This could be used to skip all records of recipients living in Lancashire.

Practice Questions

Q1 Name two features of DTP software that help with layout.

Q2 What is the difference between a word field and a merge field?

Exam Question

Q1 A newsagent uses mail merge to send letters to his customers about the balance on their paper bills.

a) Identify two examples of word fields the newsagent could use. (2 marks)

b) State two benefits to the newsagent of using word fields. (2 marks)

c) Describe two benefits to the newsagent of using mail merge to send letters to customers. (4 marks)

Word fields are where the matrix grows new words for us — like "schtoof"...

You've already gathered this, but keep in mind that it's not about which application is "better" or "worse" overall (we're not computer games journalists here) — examiners always want to know that you've thought carefully about what applications have to offer different kinds of users. The emphasis is on people here, not machines. What do YOU want from your software?

Word Processing and DTP

These pages are for AQA Unit 1 and OCR Unit 1.

You should already know most of the stuff on these two pages, but we have to recap it all some time, so make sure you don't skimp on any of the details. It's like sugar — cakes that skimp on sugar taste like cardboard. Be smart. Eat sugary detail.

Documents Have Various Standard **Layout Features**

Orientation, Margins and Page Size

1) You can choose the **orientation** of your document — this means choosing between landscape and portrait.
2) You can set the **margins** — you can either do this manually, or usually there will be a special dialogue box (like the one pictured here) that will help you to preview what the final page will look like.
3) You can also choose what **size** the page itself is.

Angry Cat Landscape

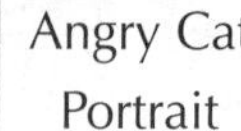

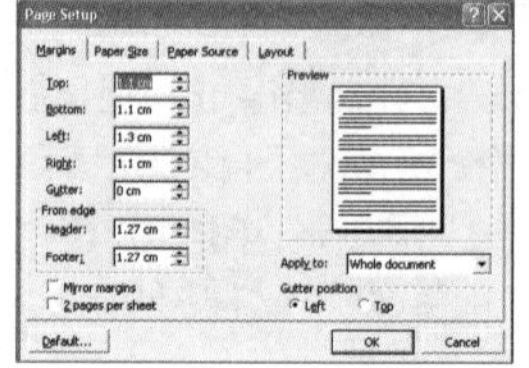

Paragraphs, Sections and Columns

1) These are all ways of dividing a document into sections, so that the **text can be formatted** either all together, column by column or else separately paragraph by paragraph. For example, you can choose the alignment (left, right, centre, justified), indentation, line spacing, bullets and numbering, and the font and size for each paragraph, section or column of text.

Jennifer's aunt was a dog-faced woman. There was no polite way around the subject. Jennifer had spent years plucking up the courage to talk to her aunt normally although nature was against it.

Her dad managed it though. Of course, he had had an extra couple of years to practise. "I wonder what would happen to me if I was a dog-faced woman?" thought Jennifer to herself one day.

And then, as if by magic Jennifer felt her face being whisked away and replaced by something altogether different. "Are those whiskers?" she said out loud, touching her new face with careful, delicate fingers.

"Yes, my dear," said a voice from above. "Those are indeed whiskers. And you are now a dog-faced woman, just as you were thinking. I am the thought fairy — I make all of your thoughts come true."

"Ah," thought jennifer. "why exactly did no one ever mention this before? I mean, Thank goodness I wasn't thinking about other things. blimey."

"Well, not to worry dear," said the thought fairy. "It'll wear off in a while and then you'll have:
- your own face back
- a guilty conscience

So grow up love, and stop daydreaming."

2) **Paragraph styles** can be set up — these are sets of rules for how the paragraphs are formatted (things like spacing, indentations, fonts, etc.). When you apply a paragraph style, all the text in the paragraph will obey the rules.
3) Pressing return ends the paragraph you're in and starts a new one, so this makes a **paragraph break**. You can also insert breaks into documents to start a new **column** or **page**.

Graphics

1) Word processors and DTP packages can both handle **graphics**.
2) You can either select a pre-drawn **AutoShape**, use a pre-existing **image**, or **create your own**.
3) You can then play with the graphic until you are **satisfied with its appearance** — e.g. by cropping, repositioning, wrapping text around it, etc.

Headers and **Footers** Make Documents More **Organised**

1) Headers and footers are descriptive **text** or **graphics** that can be added to the top or bottom margins of a document — headers go at the top, footers go at the bottom.
2) They usually contain **information** like page numbers, titles or the date, but could also include graphics.
3) You only have to add a header or footer once and the word processor will **automatically add it** to every page.
4) After adding the standard header or footer, you can also then **change them individually** in different parts of the document, e.g. you could use a unique header or footer on the title page or start the headers / footers on the following page.

Here's the header — the title, which is the same on every page.

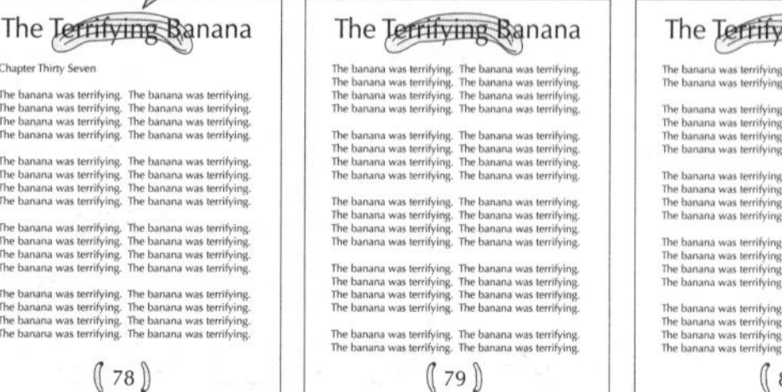

Here's the footer — the page number, which changes on every page.

Word Processing and DTP

Footnotes and *Endnotes* Help *Explain* Bits Of The Document

1) **Footnotes** and **endnotes** are very useful if you want to explain a word or phrase without having to do so in the main body of the text.
2) Instead, you can add a **reference number** to the relevant word or phrase, which will send the reader to the note it's referring to[1].
3) **Footnotes** come at the **foot of the page** the reference number is on. **Endnotes** come at the **very end** of the whole document.
4) You can choose how the notes are **presented**, e.g. whether they're separated from the main body text by a line, and what font and size etc.

Don't Forget To *Cater* For Your *Audience*

1) You always have to think about who's going to **read** your document when it's finished.
2) Make sure you've prepared something that is **appropriate** to their needs.
3) For example:
   - young children need clear, uncomplicated documents, e.g. using big fonts.
   - educational documents for older children or adults can have a more sophisticated layout, but still need all the information to be clearly explained.
   - you can use graphs and charts to present figures in a clear and interesting way.

WP or DTP — Which to Use...

Word processing and DTP packages have many similarities and often you could use either to produce the same type of document. But it'll usually be a lot easier to use one than the other.

WP	DTP
Letters	Flyers
Memos	Posters
Faxes	Brochures
Reports	Business cards

Practice Questions

Q1 Why might you want to adjust the margins of a document?

Q2 Explain what each of the following are: a) footnotes, b) endnotes, c) headers and d) footers.

Exam Questions

Q1 A company that sells mobility aids for senior citizens produces its own quarterly customer catalogue. Give two formatting techniques they could use to make the newsletter suitable for their customers. (2 marks)

Q2 Describe how paragraph styles can be helpful when a long document is produced by a team of people. (3 marks)

This is the funny top tip gag — on a loop[2]

It seems pretty obvious to say that you need to consider who's going to be reading the final document, but it's too easy to get so stuck in to what you're doing that you completely forget your readers will need everything to be clear and well explained in appropriate language. Non in Italiano per esempio... Mi capisci? Forse no. Forse Italiano non e proprio adatto a AS ICT.

[1] Just like this one did.

[2] Go to funny top tip gag.

Templates, Style Sheets and Wizards

These pages are for AQA Unit 1 and OCR Unit 1.

My mum's a witch. No really. A real life proper witch. She can fly. She has a black cat. She eats babies at halloween. She's really scary and doesn't have anything to do with AS ICT. Anyway, here's a couple of pages that mention wizards...

Creating Templates is Incredibly Easy

Templates are pre-made **outlines** of pages. You can add your own words and pictures in the places set aside on the template to quickly create professional looking documents.

Most word processing and DTP packages provide **standard documents** (letters, etc.) as default templates. However you can also create your own if you want a different look. This is usually pretty straightforward:

1) **Open** a new document.
2) **Edit** the new document so that it looks like the template you want. Design everything from text and graphics, margin sizes and page orientation to headers, footers and pages numbers.
3) When you're happy, **save** it as a template.

Now every time you want to use it you simply open your template and away you go.

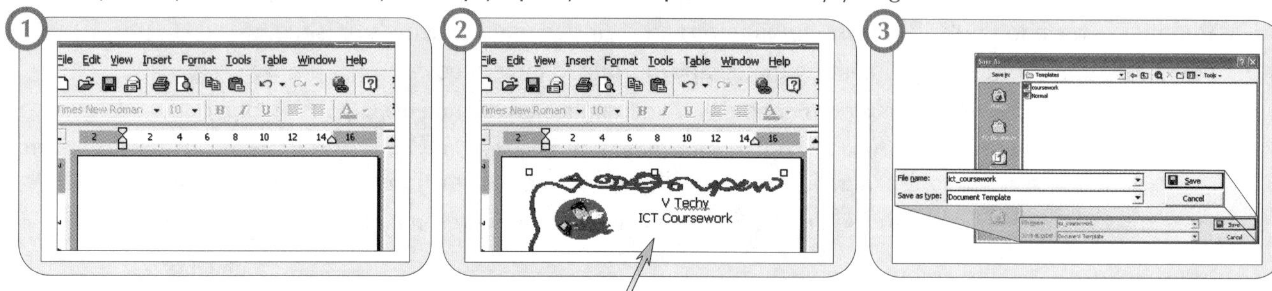

Handy hint — try not to make your coursework look like it's been done by a five year old...

Using Templates Has Advantages and Disadvantages

Good Stuff About Templates

1) Templates are already set-up, so users **don't have to waste time** formatting documents.
2) Templates make sure that documents have a **consistent style** and 'look'. This is especially useful in businesses that need employees to work in a **house style**.

Not-So-Good Stuff About Templates

1) If generic templates aren't satisfactory, then users need to **spend time** creating their own.
2) The **design is limited**, so if layout needs changing then this has to be done manually.
3) Documents can become **boring** as users don't bother thinking about new designs.

Style Sheets Are Templates For Desktop Publishing

1) Style sheets are a bit like word processing **templates**, but are used in **desktop publishing programs**.
2) They're used to set the **layout** and **format** of certain publications. They can also be called **master documents**.
3) Style sheets are **more complex** than word processing templates because the software is **more powerful** and has more functions.
4) When setting up your own style sheets, the **user has more control** over the details, e.g. they can drag the page number to wherever they want, or they can layer different objects and text together to form titles or headers.

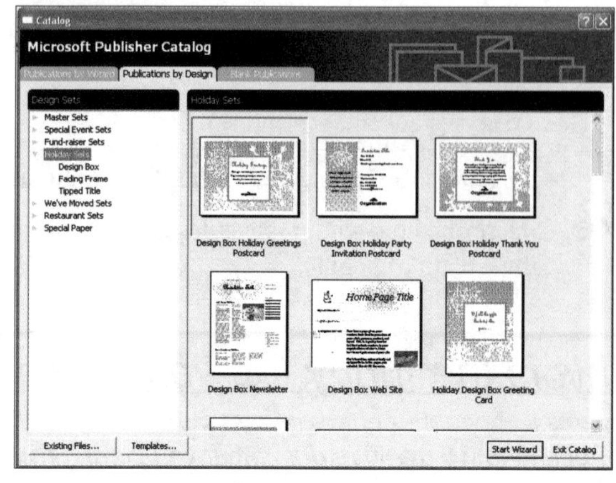

Templates, Style Sheets and Wizards

Using Style Sheets Has **Advantages** and (guess what) **Disadvantages**

Good Things About Style Sheets

1) They **save time** on designing pages.
2) They make sure that documents and publications can be produced in a **consistent house style**, even where they're being produced by lots of different members of staff.

Bad Things About Style Sheets

1) The documents and publications can end up all **looking the same**, making them less interesting and effective.
2) Someone must be **paid to develop the style**, and this will be money wasted if the style isn't followed.
3) It's hard for documents produced using style sheets to be **adapted** for different audiences.

A **Wizard** Can **Help** With **Tricky Tasks**

Lots of different programs have wizards which help you carry out certain tasks.

1) In word processors and DTP programs, wizards can help you with the **design** of your document or publication.

   Wizards have their own **preset layouts and styles** you can choose from. You just select the type and style you want, the colour scheme and details to include, and the wizard will **design and build it for you**, saving you time and effort.
2) Wizards can also be used to **create complex applications** or documents in very user-friendly ways.

   For example, a wizard can be used to build, search and design reports in a database package.
3) The down side is that you're **limited to the options available in the wizard**, and can't be original or creative.

   You also run the risk of your documents looking just like everyone else's.

Example — Using a Fax Wizard

1) Selecting the fax wizard opens up this dialogue box to guide you through creating a new fax.

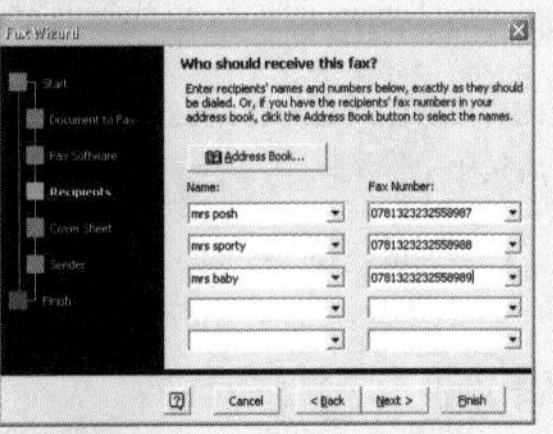

2) It asks you to fill in all the important information, e.g. sender / receiver details.

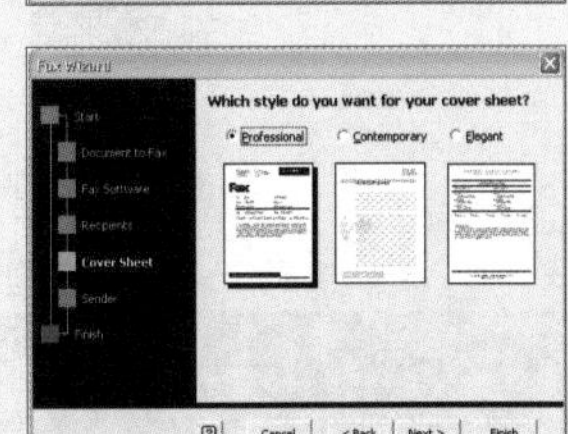

3) It even asks you to pick one of their pre-set templates, just to make life easy.

Practice Questions

Q1 Give one advantage and one disadvantage of each of these: templates, style sheets and wizards.

Q2 How do master documents, style sheets and templates help when working in a team?

Exam Questions

Q1 Give two advantages and two disadvantages of using a wizard to create a weekly publication in a desktop publishing package. (4 marks)

Q2 Clep Co is about to open offices across the UK as part of their expansion programme. Explain two features of generic software packages that could be used to ensure that all the company's documents have a consistent house style. (4 marks)

Anyone writing Harry Potter jokes will be gagged — with the help of a wizard...

It might seem as though templates, style sheets and wizards are all the same thing, but there are differences between them that you need to understand. So, don't go on to the next page 'til you're sure you know everything on this one. Then, you have to learn the rules of Quiddich. Then you have to find the one ring to rule them all — oh wait, that's the wrong book.

Clipart and Graphics Tools

These pages are for AQA Unit 1 and OCR Unit 1.

Ooh the joy of clipart. Why there's nothing I like better than relaxing on the sofa, sipping my brandy in front of the fire and leafing through my wonderful clipart libraries. My heart swells with pride and love, and occasionally a little trapped wind.

Clipart** is Usually **Free

1) Clipart is the name for graphics which have been created by someone for others to use. Often they're released into the **public domain** — this means that anyone can use them without having to pay for a licence.
2) The basic idea of clipart is that it's providing **non-artists** with a wide selection of graphics.
3) Clipart often comes **free** with software packages and is available on the Internet.
4) Clipart can also can also be bought in collections on **CD-ROM**. Although you have to pay for these, you normally get an enormous amount for your money, e.g. 120,000 images for a tenner. They'll normally also provide a **browser** so you can browse (surprisingly) the images or search for images using keywords.

*There Are **Pros** and **Cons** To Using **Clipart***

Good Things About Clipart

- Clipart is either **free** or very cheap.
- It's **quicker** than drawing your own graphics from scratch.
- You don't need to be a skilful **artist** to brighten up your document.
- You don't need special **training**.
- No special **equipment**, e.g. scanners or digital cameras, needs to be bought.
- The **cost** of the design process is reduced, e.g. when designing a logo as you don't need a designer.

Bad Things About Clipart

- You might not be able to find **exactly** the image you want.
- Because there are so many categories available it can take ages to **search** through them all just to find one image, especially with Internet clipart.
- The **quality** of clipart is very variable — some of it is way **out of date** and some is just plain pants.
- Other users will almost certainly have used that clipart before, so your documents can feel **unoriginal**.

***Browsers** Help you Find the Image You're After*

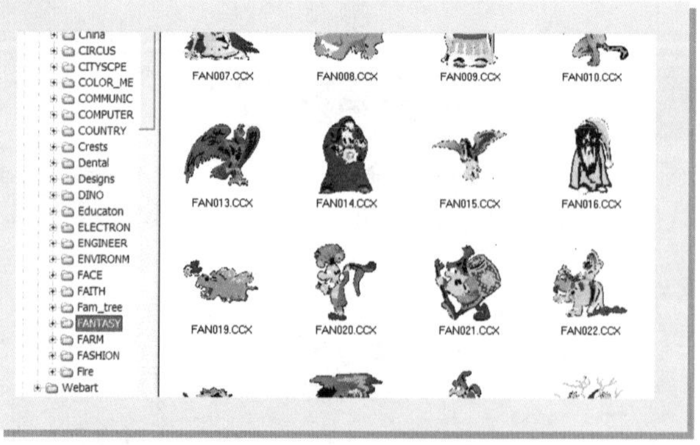

1) To help you find the graphic you want, clipart collections will usually come with a browser. This lets you look through the clipart images by choosing different **categories**, e.g. music, sport or animals.
2) The browser will also let you do **keyword searches** — each image in the collection will have a **description** or list of keywords associated with it so that you can find it through a search.
3) When browsing or searching, the clipart images will usually be displayed as **thumbnails** — these are small, lower-resolution versions of the actual graphics.
4) Using thumbnails means you can see **many images** on the screen at once, making it easy to display together all the images in a certain category or all the images matching a particular search.
5) Using thumbnails does have some **drawbacks** though — the **quality** of thumbnail images is often poor, making it hard to judge if the real image is going to be suitable. You also often can't tell what kind of quality and size the **actual image** is going to be. Another problem is that when there's lots of images to be displayed, it can take a **long time** to load all the thumbnails.

Clipart and Graphics Tools

*Images Are Stored Either As **Bitmap** or **Vector** Data*

Vector images are saved as a **geometric equation**, e.g. a red circle might be represented by its radius, the coordinates of its centre and a number for its colour. **Bitmap** (or **pixel**-based) images are stored as a series of coloured dots (pixels).

Vector Graphics	Bitmaps
Images are object-based, each object described by its features (length, colour, thickness etc).	Images are pixel-based, each pixel in the image saved individually.
The individual objects making up the image can be edited, e.g. moved, resized, coloured, independently.	Editing the image involves changing the properties of the pixels in the graphic as a whole or an area of it.
Mainly used for design purposes, e.g. technical diagrams, CAD, cartoons.	Used mainly for storing real images digitally, e.g. from a digital camera or scanner.
Can be resized or rescaled with no loss of quality.	When resized, image can become blurry and 'pixellated'.
File sizes are relative small.	File sizes large due to each pixel being saved individually.
The files cannot be compressed.	The files can be compressed.

*Graphics Libraries Provide **Standard Symbols** for Specific Uses*

Graphics software used for kitchen design, map-making (cartography) and network design include **libraries** of **standard symbols** and **graphical images** which have been developed with manufacturers and professional bodies.

1) A **kitchen design** software package will include symbols, e.g. for cupboards and kitchen appliances (cookers, dishwashers, etc.), used for planning and designing a kitchen.
2) **Network design** graphics libraries will contain industry-standard symbols for the main components needed in a network, e.g. servers, routers and cabling.
3) The graphics libraries used in **cartography** will include symbols for things like motorways, churches and schools. This means that all software used to produce maps use the **same symbols** with the **same meaning**.

So diagrams produced with graphics libraries follow an industry standard and will be recognisable in all parts of the world. The main problem with graphics libraries is keeping them up-to-date.

Practice Questions

Q1 Give three advantages and three disadvantages of using clipart.

Q2 Give two advantages and two disadvantages of using thumbnail images.

Q3 Describe two differences between vector graphics and bitmap graphics.

Exam Questions

Q1 A network design company uses a graphics library when designing the networks.
Describe one advantage and one disadvantage of using a graphic library. (4 marks)

Q2 A logo is to be created for a school snack bar.
Describe two advantages and one disadvantage of using a graphic library. (6 marks)

My bitmap cuts off everything east of Swindon...

If you've ever messed around with a drawing program, you probably know lots of this stuff already. Remember to revise though, and try the practice questions until you're sure you've got it all down. Especially the difference between bitmaps and vector graphics — watch out for that. Oh, and you can't really make a kitchen from a rolling pin. That's just silly.

Clipart and Graphics Tools

These pages are for AQA Unit 1 and OCR Unit 1.
Right. This page will at least pretend to be entertaining. And if not, then I'll tell you what — I can't give you your money back, but I can offer you a nice bag of slime from my auntie Maureen's biggest tub of lard. What do you say to that?

Vector Graphic Packages Help You Create and Manipulate Images

Graphics packages have lots of different features that are designed to make creating and manipulating images easier.

Lines
Straight lines and "freehand" lines can be drawn with a variety of brushes.

Shape tools
Regular pre-defined shapes, such as squares, circles and rectangles can be drawn with a special tool.

Fill
Objects can be filled in with a colour. Simply set the outlines and pick a colour, then everything within the outline will be coloured.

Size
You can change the size of the image itself, usually by selecting the graphic and dragging one of the "handles" outwards to make it bigger, and inwards to make it smaller. It's important to keep the proportions the same though, or the image gets distorted. Look at this poor goat.

Shade / Shadow
Some packages let you choose the position of a light source and work out the shadow created by objects, or create shading effects on objects.

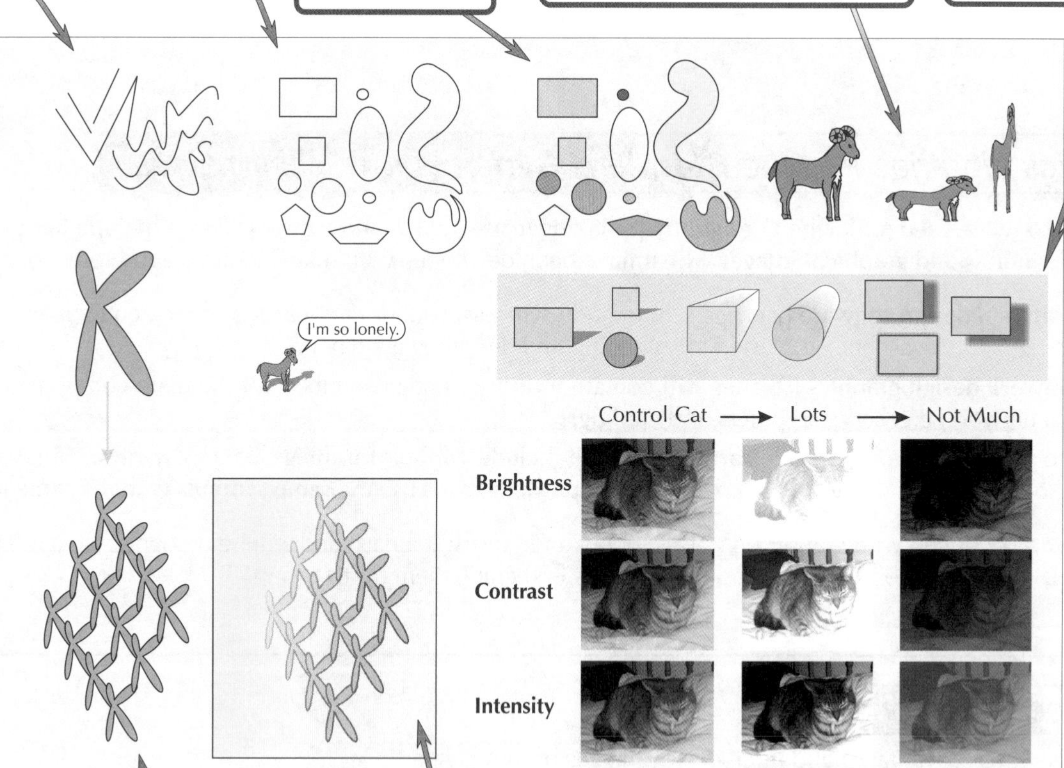

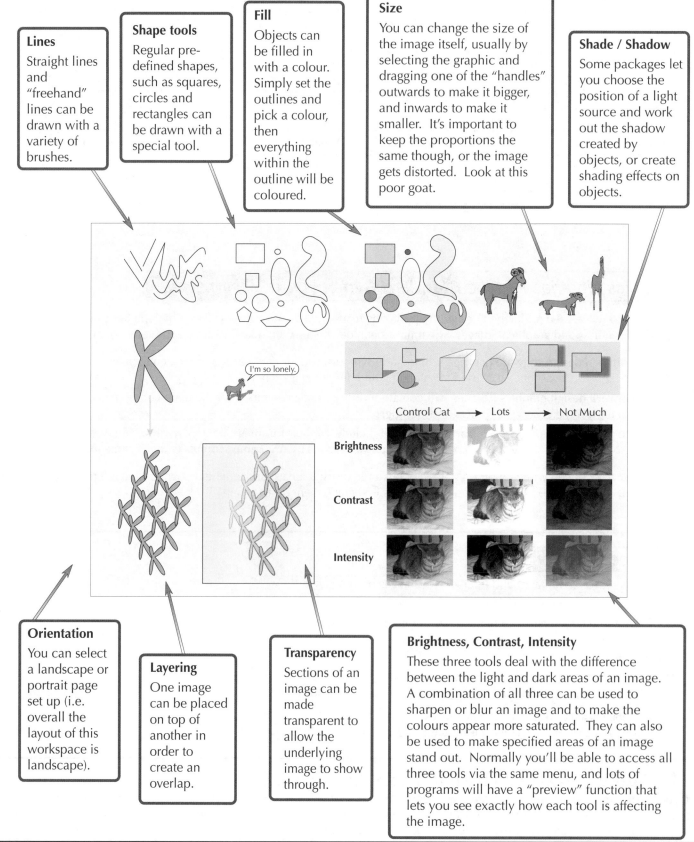

Orientation
You can select a landscape or portrait page set up (i.e. overall the layout of this workspace is landscape).

Layering
One image can be placed on top of another in order to create an overlap.

Transparency
Sections of an image can be made transparent to allow the underlying image to show through.

Brightness, Contrast, Intensity
These three tools deal with the difference between the light and dark areas of an image. A combination of all three can be used to sharpen or blur an image and to make the colours appear more saturated. They can also be used to make specified areas of an image stand out. Normally you'll be able to access all three tools via the same menu, and lots of programs will have a "preview" function that lets you see exactly how each tool is affecting the image.

Clipart and Graphics Tools

Sophisticated Graphics Packages Have Some Quite Fancy Effects

There are all sorts of crazy tools and effects you can apply if you have a sophisticated enough graphics package. These are just a few examples:

Control Cat

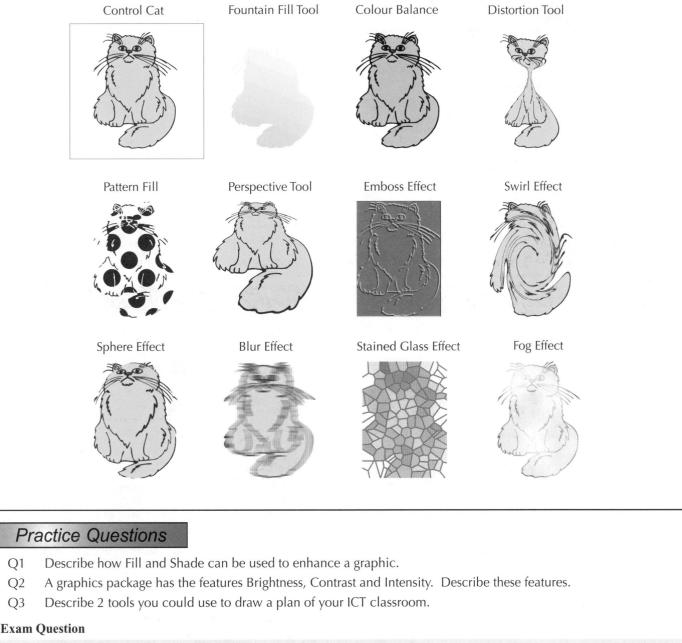

Fountain Fill Tool

Colour Balance

Distortion Tool

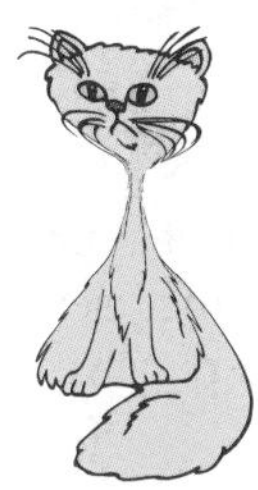

Pattern Fill

Perspective Tool

Emboss Effect

Swirl Effect

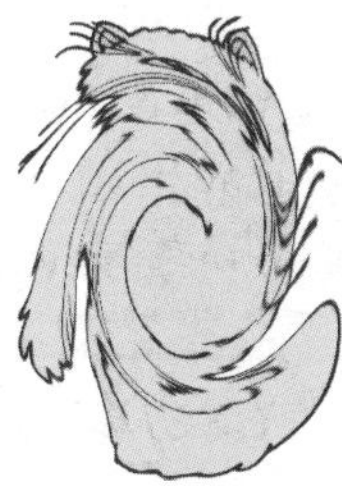

Sphere Effect

Blur Effect

Stained Glass Effect

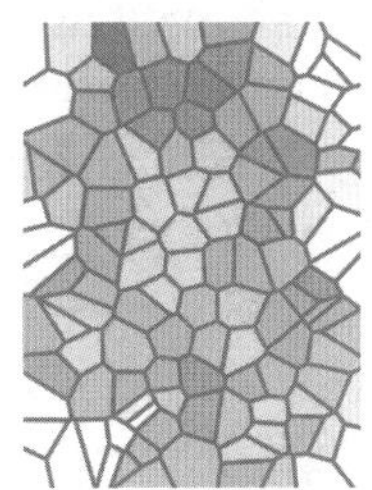

Fog Effect

Practice Questions

Q1 Describe how Fill and Shade can be used to enhance a graphic.

Q2 A graphics package has the features Brightness, Contrast and Intensity. Describe these features.

Q3 Describe 2 tools you could use to draw a plan of your ICT classroom.

Exam Question

Q1 Get16 is a popular culture magazine aimed at young teenagers. The publication's designers aim to engage their readers through imaginative graphics images and layout.
The pages include photos and vector graphic images.

a) Describe three ways that the publication's designers could use graphics software tools to create and manipulate vector graphics. (3 marks)

b) Describe three ways that the publication's designers could use graphics software tools to manipulate photographs to make them more visually appealing. (3 marks)

I have an interactive cat tool — it turns everything into cats which bite me...

Hard to say "learn all this" really... Just bear in mind that these tools exist, and that they're always really useful for livening up an image or even a whole page. And you don't have to use cats. I hear dogs are "in" this year. Or fish. Just don't use my friend Amanda's fish. They died. Horribly. In smelly water. But other than that, use whatever animals you like...

Multimedia Presentations

These pages are for AQA Unit 1 and OCR Unit 1.

Ah. A page with lots of text on it. I remember these. These are like the things your parents used to learn from. I'll bet they haven't got a clue what applications like PowerPoint® are though. "PowerPoint? Yes dear, it's where I plug the telly in."

OHPs Used To Be Used All The Time In Presentations

1) **Overhead projectors** (OHPs) used to be used to give presentations all the time (and often still are). They project information printed on transparent sheets (acetates) onto a wall or screen.
2) The acetates can be printed in black and white or in colour, and the person giving the presentation uses them one by one to illustrate important points.
3) You need to have a photocopier or printer linked to a computer in order to create acetates, but the actual presentations themselves use an **overhead projector**. This means you don't need to buy any fancy software or expensive multimedia projectors in order to use them.
4) However, they can look a bit **naff** and **old-fashioned** — there are lots of disadvantages to using them:

Disadvantages of Using OHPs

1) The speaker has to change each slide **by hand**.
2) Acetates can be **easily damaged**, e.g. by fingerprints, making them look unprofessional.
3) You can skip between slides with little trouble, but it's easy to muddle up the **order** of the slides.
4) The speaker may have to **cover** with their hands any information they don't want the audience to see yet.
5) Animation, sound and video can't be used, making the presentation potentially quite **boring**.

Multimedia Presentations Combine Text, Graphics, Video and Sound

You can use a software package to create a multimedia presentation. Multimedia presentations use a **combination** of **different media** elements — e.g. graphics, animations, videos and sound which all help to keep the audience **interested**.

They work by displaying electronic slides — you navigate by clicking buttons that link from one slide to another

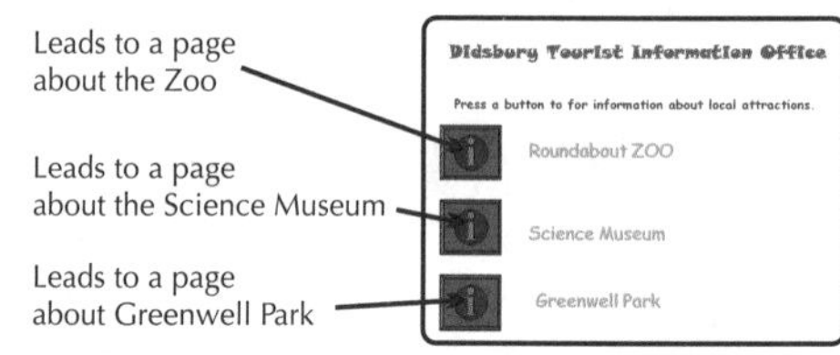

Different features of presentation software:

1) **Sound** can be used to liven up a presentation. It's much more effective to give audiences an audio element than just plodding on with boring silent visual images. The sound can be specially recorded or it could be an existing sound file, e.g. a company advertising jingle. The sound can be set to tie in with certain functions, e.g. skipping to the next section of a presentation, or it can play in the background or as part of a video.
2) **Video clips** can be inserted into the presentation, either specially recorded or from an existing file. Using a video can help break up the presentation and really emphasise certain parts that you want to get across. They can be set to play on a specified user action, usually a mouse click.
3) **Animation** effects are special sound or visual effects that are added to text or objects, e.g. charts, graphics. They can be used to change how items are displayed on a slide. For example, a bulleted list can be animated so that each bullet point will fly onto the slide separately. Or, you could set up an animation to compare different bar charts, so that you can watch the bars getting shorter or taller as you move to the next chart.
4) **Slide transition** sets how you move from one slide (or page) to another. Different effects can be applied so that you move to the next slide in an interesting way, e.g. one fading into another, one sweeping in from the side, etc. You can set the speed of the transition effect, and can choose if you want to apply the effect to just one slide or to a whole presentation.
5) **Buttons/Hyperlinks** can be inserted. Clicking on them takes you on to a different bit of the presentation.
6) **Hotspots** can be added to graphics — this is where different parts of the graphic act as hyperlinks. You usually need to get back to the page you started on through another hyperlink, so it's best not to use too many hotspots or the presentation gets too complicated.

This image has 3 hotspots, each taking you to a different slide or page. The hotspots are usually invisible, and the image gives the cues about where it should be clicked.

Multimedia Presentations

Presentations Should Have a Consistent Design

1) All the slides in a presentation should follow a similar kind of **design** and **colour scheme**. The software will have templates you can use, but making your own template will make your presentation look more original.
2) The software will also have some **auto-layouts** (a choice of pre-designed individual slide layouts). These suggest where the different elements of a slide could be positioned (i.e. the text, images, hotspots, etc).
3) A **master slide** could also be used. This is a bit like a style sheet in a desktop publisher, or a set of paragraph styles in a word processor (see page 70). It lets a team of people work on the presentation separately, and when their work is collated it's all in the same style. If any changes are then made on the master slide, then all the other slides will be changed automatically.
4) Fancy effects should be used carefully so they don't get distracting for the audience. The presentation needs to have a **consistent look** overall if you want it to feel professional.

Sometime You Don't Even Need to Present Presentations

1) Presentations are often given by a **speaker** who introduces the slides as they are projected on to a large screen.
2) Using presentation software, you can also create **self-running presentations**. One slide automatically moves to the next after a specified period of time, and the whole presentation can be set to re-start as soon as it has finished.
3) You can use these while a speaker gives the presentation, though it's **not really ideal** for verbal presentations because the speaker can easily be delayed and get out of time with the slides. Self-running presentations are more appropriate where **no speaker is involved**, e.g. a museum might want a self-running presentation to run constantly in the background of an exhibition, showing useful images and data about the exhibit.
4) Of course, whenever a presentation is left to run on its own, there's always the danger that something will **go wrong** with the program or the display hardware and no one will be on hand to fix it.

Advantages of Using Presentation Software

1) It produces **professional** looking presentations.
2) Using multimedia helps **hold people's attention.**
3) Presentations can be saved and **used again**, with or without a speaker being present.
4) It's easy to **edit** presentations and adapt them for different audiences.

Disadvantages of Using Presentation Software

1) It's very easy to **get carried away** by the technology and produce **badly designed** slides.
2) The software needs **expensive hardware** to run the presentation.

Practice Questions

Q1 What is an OHP presentation?

Q2 Explain the following features of multimedia presentations: i) hyperlinks, ii) hotspots and iii) animation.

Q3 Give one advantage and one disadvantage of a speaker using a self-running presentation.

Exam Questions

Q1 Mr Sharpe is a training consultant who frequently needs to give presentations to large groups from different companies. He currently uses an overhead projector with acetates but is considering switching to multimedia.

Give two advantages and two disadvantages to Mr Sharpe of continuing to use an OHP with acetates. (4 marks)

Q2 Mrs Jenkins is using a software package to design a multimedia slideshow presentation for use in work. Describe how she can use each of the following features to make an effective presentation:

a) slide transition b) buttons c) sound (6 marks)

I thought multimedia meant having more than one telly...

Okay, there's quite a lot on this double page. Although you need to learn it all for the exam, remember that most of it's really useful for when you're creating your own presentations. If I've said it once I've said it a hundred thousand million billion trillion quadrillion quintillion sextillion septillion octillion nonillion decillion times — think about your audience.

Multimedia Presentations

These pages are for AQA Unit 1 and OCR Unit 1.

Multimedia presentations are made up of lots of separate slides — screens or animations that tell the audience about a separate part of the subject. These slides can be organised in various ways.

Moving** from one slide to another is called **Transition

Transition can be either manual or automatic:

Manual transition — the speaker needs to perform some sort of action (e.g. a mouse or button click, or pointer) to move on to the next slide, e.g. a speech by a managing director analysing the performance of a company.

Automatic transition — no action is needed to move on to the next slide. The presentation can be set up to run automatically and display the next slide after a pre-specified period of time, e.g. a museum or open day display.

There are advantages and disadvantages to both:

	Advantages	Disadvantages
Manual	Can **control when** slides or individual items within slides appear. Can stop for **questions**.	Finding slides to answer audience questions can be tricky and may lead to important slides being **missed**. Speaker must know **how to navigate** the presentation.
Automatic	Run with **no intervention**. Can be set on a **loop** — as soon as one showing is over, it **starts again**.	**Timings** must be set — some people may struggle to **read a slide** before the next one appears. No **interaction** with audience possible.

*Most Presentations have a **Linear Structure**...*

1) Most presentations have a **linear structure** — they are designed so that the slides have a fixed order.
2) The person giving the presentation knows in advance **which slide will follow every other** in the presentation.

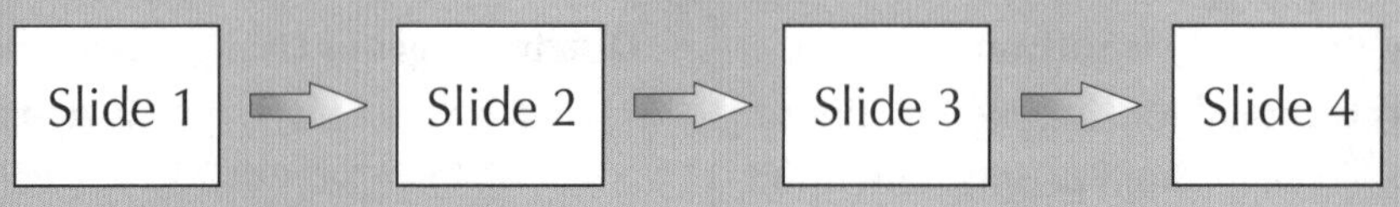

3) Presentations with linear structures are good for when you know **exactly** what you are going to need to say **in advance** — for example in speeches and lectures where the audience is unlikely to directly interrupt the prepared sequence of slides.

*...but Some have a **Nonlinear Structure**...*

1) If a presentation has a **nonlinear structure**, the slides have been set up so that they can be shown in **any order**.
2) For example, someone going to a **business meeting** might have to answer questions after making a presentation. They could prepare slides that help to **answer** some of the questions they **expect to be asked**. They'd then need to be able to jump through the answer slides in whatever order the questions arose.

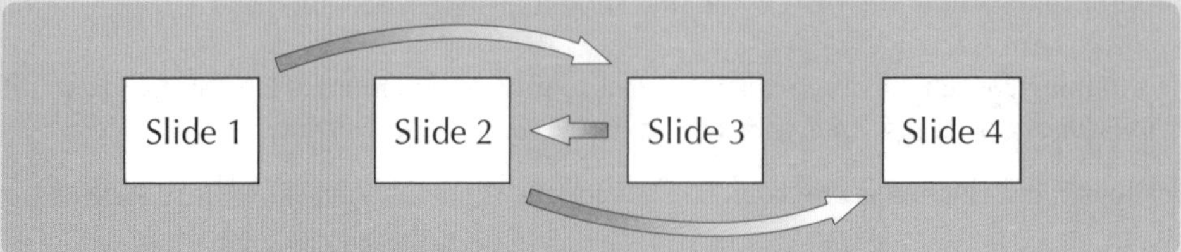

3) Slides can be set up so that they contain **hyperlinks**. After reading a particular slide, the presenter can click on different parts of the screen to pick which slide to go to next.
4) This sort of nonlinear structure can be a good choice if the presentation has been prepared so that it can be navigated by **someone else**, for their own use — for example to provide **interactive exhibits** at **museums** or **training courses** that people can use in their **own time** at **home**.
5) Another good structure for these uses would be a hierarchical approach — see up there...

Multimedia Presentations

...or a Hierarchical Structure

1) Some presentations operate a bit like the **menus** you get on things like **mobile phones**. You're offered a **set of options**, and when you pick one it takes you to part of the presentation.
2) When you're finished in that part of the presentation, you go **back to the original menu**.
3) It's also possible for a menu to give you options that take you to other menus. So if you draw out the entire presentation then it often looks a bit like this:

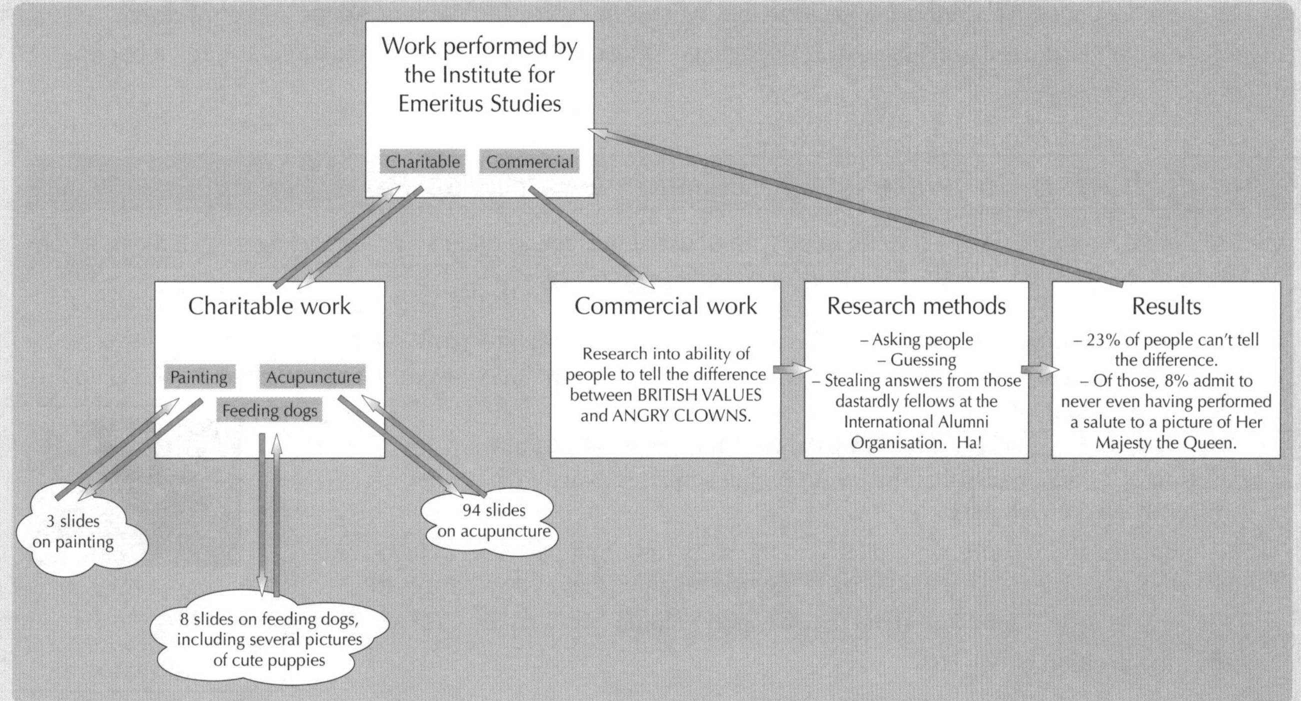

4) Hierarchical presentations combine some of the **best bits** of linear and nonlinear presentations — you have some choices about where to go next, but it's hard to get lost because you're **returned to where you started from** after each section.
5) Unfortunately hierarchical presentations are much **harder to set up** and can still be confusing if there are too many **menus within menus within menus**.

Practice Questions

Q1 Identify an appropriate situation where manual slide transition would be used.

Q2 Identify an appropriate situation where automatic slide transition would be used.

Q3 Describe the nonlinear presentation structure.

Exam Questions

Q1 Explain how a tourist information centre could use a hierarchical presentation to advertise local attractions. (4 marks)

Q2 A college is to show a presentation at its open day. The automatic transition method is to be used. Describe two advantages and one disadvantage to a college of using the automatic transition method. (6 marks)

I have a nonlinear memory...

I can always remember what happened to me in a day, I just sometimes repeat it in the wrong order. For example, earlier today I returned my shoes, woke up and got out of bed, went out to a midnight screening of my favourite film, had a quick break for lunch, bought some shoes that didn't quite fit and did a good morning's work. Or something.

Creating Stuff for the Web

These pages are for AQA Unit 1 and OCR Unit 1.

Of course the other way to present something to people is to stick it up on the old Internet. That way it's always there and people can look at it at their own leisure. Or else they'll ignore it entirely and go looking for more interesting sites...

You Can Build A Web Site Without Learning HTML

Web pages are written using **hypertext markup language** (HTML) and **cascading style sheets** (CSS). However, you don't normally have to learn them in order to build a website. There are two main methods of creating web pages:

1) Use a dedicated **web-authoring package**, e.g. Microsoft Expression® Web or Adobe® Dreamweaver®.
2) Use a standard **word processing** or **DTP** package. Most of these can convert documents into web format.

Web-authoring Software lets you Create Basic Web Pages Really Easily...

Web-authoring software usually has the same type of **user interface** as other software packages. But the functions and features included are specific to creating a website or web page.

1) Web pages are **visual representations** of code — normally HTML. However, if you're using a web-authoring package, you don't have to learn the code as the package will allow you to **drag and drop** objects onto the web page **template**.
2) Web-authoring packages use **WYSIWYG** (What You See Is What You Get) displays, which means that the **layout** on the screen is exactly what will appear on the web page.
3) **Templates and wizards** are available in the web-authoring packages to help create web pages. The package will usually include facilities that allow changes to:
   - text **style** and **font**, **line styles**, background **colours**
   - the **position** of objects
   - changes to **tables**, **columns** and **forms**.
4) Objects from **other software packages** can be used during the creation of the web pages. These might include **clip art**, **animation**, **video** and **sound clips**. In fact, everything that makes up a good, interesting web page.
5) Some packages include website **management tools**, e.g. tools to help the user upload and check pages.
6) Some packages will automatically check any **links** and alert users if they need updating.
7) With most authoring packages you can choose to **edit** your web page either by what appears on the final screen (WYSIWYG) or by editing the HTML and CSS directly. So they're suitable for both novices and experienced users who have a bit more technical knowledge.
8) If you want to create more impressive **effects** e.g. bits of the page that **change** depending on what the user does, then you'll need to integrate code samples written in a scripting language, e.g. JavaScript, using a companion program to the web-authoring package. This kind of thing is more advanced and **specialist training** is needed.

"Fat Ernie" McFatspider never noticed the irony in launching 'spinyourselfthin.com' until it was too late.

...But Also Has A Few Downsides...

1) Even though web-authoring packages have nice user interfaces, users still need **training** before they can use the software, especially the more **complex functions**.
2) In a company or organisation, the additional staff training would have **time** and **cost** implications.
3) The web-authoring packages and other associated applications can be very **expensive**.

Creating Stuff for the Web

You Can Make Really **Naff** Web Pages Using **Standard Applications Software**

1) You can create a web page using just standard applications like a **word processor** or **desktop publisher**.
2) It doesn't require any major **technical ability**, and (as you've probably already got the applications and the Internet connection), it's not going to **cost** you anything.
3) You simply design your page, select the "**save as web page**" option, then view the page in a browser.
4) Even a really inexperienced user could build a web page in this fashion, but there are disadvantages:

    1) It's really difficult to get the page to **look exactly how you want it**, as most standard applications software isn't very good at producing HTML or CSS — all sorts of graphics and other elements will **jump around** as the standard application converts your page.
    2) Because the standard application you'll use was primarily designed with other uses in mind, the code it creates is very **messy**. It's often a bit rubbish and might not be compatible with all browsers.

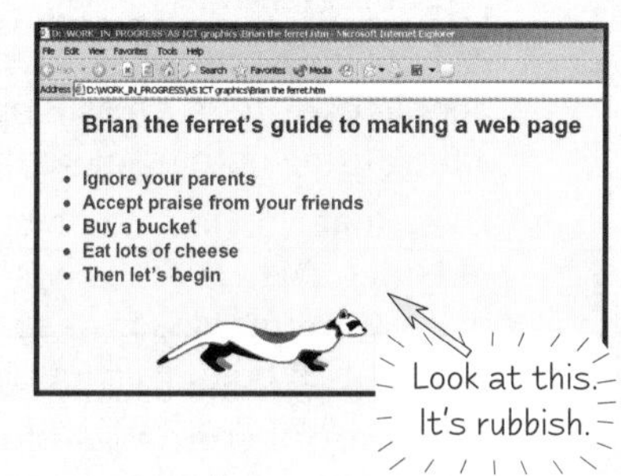
Brian the ferret's guide to making a web page
Ignore your parents
Accept praise from your friends
Buy a bucket
Eat lots of cheese
Then let's begin
Look at this.
It's rubbish.

Although in General, Web Pages Contain Some **Pretty Good Stuff**

HYPERLINKS

- Most web pages contain hyperlinks — these are links to **other web pages**, either within the website you're looking at, or to pages on other websites.
- When you click on a hyperlink, you're **automatically** taken to the page it links to.
- A web-authoring package will let the web page developer **create and add** hyperlinks to their web page.
- Hyperlinks can be added to **text** or **graphics**.

INTERACTIVE FORMS

- Many web pages contain interactive forms for the user to fill in — e.g. to **register** for a new e-mail address, or to **buy something online**.
- These normally need **CGI** (Common Gateway Interface) script but the web-authoring package can create forms without you needing to **write any code**.

Practice Questions

Q1 What are the two main methods of creating web pages?

Q2 What are hyperlinks?

Exam Questions

Q1 A school wants to develop a website. This can be done using web-authoring software or standard applications software and converting to HTML.

a) Explain the advantages of each of these methods. (6 marks)

b) Explain, with reasons, why the school should keep a similar layout on each of the web pages within the site. (4 marks)

Flash, Flash, I love you, but we've only got 14 hours to save the Internet...

I admit that creating a website is an excessive solution if you're a nervous speaker, but if you can find some web space to practise on, it's all useful stuff to know, not least for the exams. Web design scares me though. Once you've seen it for yourself — bah. Maybe I've watched the Matrix Trilogy too many times, making me as apathetic as a giraffe.

Creating Stuff for the Web

These pages are for AQA Unit 1 and OCR Unit 1.

So — you've got all the design skills of a potted plant. But don't panic, because if you can write well, or if you fancy trying your hand at a podcast, you can still get through to people on the Internet.

You can **Write a Blog** Using Just a **Web Browser**

1) Blogs are **web logs** — websites on which people **publish short articles**, often about their life or their thoughts. The articles are displayed so that newer articles are nearer to the top of the page. Most blogs move older articles into an 'archive' or list them on separate pages.
2) Although it's possible to create a blog in the same way as you'd make any other web page, most people use sites such as **Blogger** and **LiveJournal** — which are free to use and allow you to write a blog using nothing more than a **web browser**.
3) Every time you log in to one of these sites, you're given the chance to **create new posts** or **edit old ones**. When you're working on a post, you get a view in your web browser that looks a lot like a **word processor** — so you can do a lot of the usual text formatting operations, such as making text **bold**, *italic* or <u>underlined</u> and easily insert **pictures** or **videos**, or **links to other sites**.
4) When you're done, your blog page is **automatically updated** so that older posts are moved down and the new post is put at the top.
5) Blogs hosted by special blogging sites allow readers to leave **comments** — so other people can contribute their own opinions about your posts.

Some People follow Blogs through **Feeds**

1) One way to follow a blog is to visit its website regularly and check for new posts.
2) But many blogs also offer **feeds**. Feeds allow software to automatically check for new posts on a blog, and to get titles and summaries for all current posts.
3) The software that checks feeds is called an **aggregator**. Most of the recent browsers can detect when a page is offering a feed and either display the letters '**RSS**' (which stands for 'Really Simple Syndication', one of the technologies used by feeds) or show an icon like this:
4) If you click the icon then your aggregator will automatically **subscribe** to the feed. Nowadays, lots of the **browsers and e-mail programs act as aggregators**, so that doesn't necessarily mean that you'll be sent to a different piece of software.

Podcasts are **Audio Blogs**

1) Podcasts are like blogs, but people post **audio recordings** instead of **articles**. Each recording is known as an **episode** of the podcast.
2) Podcasts were originally just called **audioblogs**, but now most people call them podcasts because there is lots of software that makes it easy to download them to **MP3 players**.
2) Some **radio stations** use podcasts as an alternative way for people to listen to their shows — though for **legal reasons** they sometimes have to **remove songs** or other parts of the original programmes.

You can Subscribe Using an **Aggregator**, or through **Jukebox Software**

1) You can subscribe to podcasts using a **feed aggregator** just like any other blog. But now many **jukebox programs**, such as Apple's iTunes®, directly incorporate podcast support.
2) That means that you can click once to subscribe to a podcast, then the software will automatically **download new episodes** and **synchronise them** with your **MP3 player**.
3) So if there's a podcast you like which is always updated on a **Tuesday** and you're already in the habit of plugging in your MP3 player to charge **every evening** then the latest edition of the podcast should always be on your MP3 player for listening to on the way to work on a **Wednesday**.

When Hannah realised she'd bought an Apple with no jukebox software, she was furious.

Creating Stuff for the Web

You Can Also Produce A Blog On **Video**

Video blogs are also called **vlogs**. They can be one-offs or series of short **video recordings** featuring the blogger(s).

- The general idea is much the same as blogging and podcasting — other people can post comments and have discussions about the content of the vlog. It's also possible to **subscribe** to vlogs, just like blogs and podcasts.
- If you've got a **video camera** and a **fast internet connection**, you can upload a vlog.
- Once you've saved the video on your computer, it needs to be **compressed** and then **uploaded**.
- Some websites offer **free hosting** for vlogs, so most people use one of these to **publish their clips**.

If you've got a blog as well, you can post a **link** on the blog to the web page that contains your video so other users can access it **directly**.

Amateur Content — Everyone's At It Now...

1) Audio and video blogs are becoming more popular because **equipment** is generally **cheaper** than it used to be and you can find websites that will publish your video clips online for free.
2) Even if the videos are pretty **poor quality** they can be uploaded because there aren't really any restrictions — so clips from **digital cameras** or **mobile phones** can also be uploaded and posted online.
3) **MP3 players** now support video files (like .mp4) as well, so you can watch vlogs just as you would listen to podcasts.
4) Vlogs and blogs aren't really ever created to make the author/director any **money** — so because they're not very mainstream and unlikely to ever reach really massive audiences, they can be about **pretty much anything** the author wants them to be.
5) This is a big **attraction** to **amateur users**, who are now the biggest providers of this type of content on the Internet.

Obviously, logging is way more fun now than it used to be

Practice Questions

Q1 What does a feed aggregator do?

Q2 What is a podcast?

Q3 Suggest three suitable pieces of equipment for recording a video to be posted online.

Exam Questions

Sam posts a weekly blog through a website that enables him to use just his web browser to update and submit his writing.

Q1 a) What is a blog? (1mark)

b) Describe three advantages of using a website like this to post blogs online. (3 marks)

Q2 Why might you use jukebox software to subscribe to a podcast instead of a normal RSS aggregator? (4 marks)

Q3 Recently, amatuer video clips on websites like YouTube have become very popular.

Suggest four reasons why there is so much more vlogging and video content available on the Internet than before. (8 marks)

My blog is a free-association stream of consciousness...

... with occasional breaks for loosely structured poetry and scripted monologues in which I mostly discuss international political unrest and trade union organisation. It has won sixteen awards for its complete lack of interesting subject matter.

Customising Applications

These pages are for AQA Unit 1 and OCR Unit 1.

Whenever I think about what I'd like to customise in my life, it's normally things like hair, weight and complexion, not system interfaces. Then again, I guess my face is sort of a system interface for my brain. Then again, maybe not...

Generic Applications Can Be Customised

Generic applications can be **customised** using buttons, forms, menus and macros to make them **easier** and **faster** to use.

1) **Buttons** can be added to take the user to a **specified page** or **run an action** or **command**.
   - you can add a command button to the user interface of a database to run a search or to sort or edit data. A button can also display pictures or text. When the user clicks the button, the software runs that procedure.

2) **Forms** can be used to **input data** into a database or spreadsheet.
   Features like drop down menus and boxes that fill in automatically make things easier for the user.
   - E.g. when the user enters the postcode and town, the street and county automatically appear.

   Input forms can also include **validation code**.
   - E.g. the form will tell you if you've filled in an impossible date of birth or if you've not filled in one of the boxes.

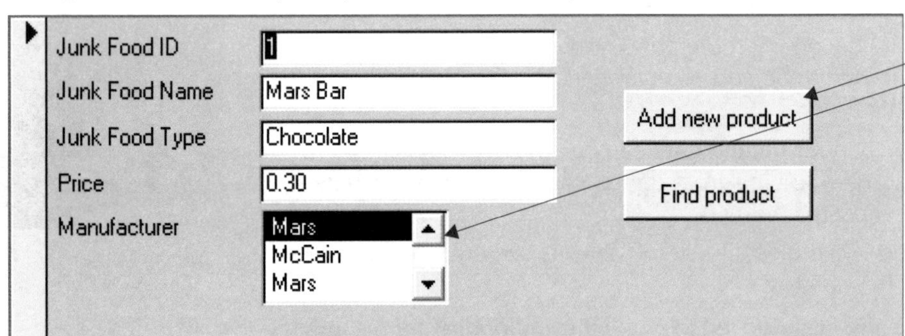

This database form uses buttons and a drop down list to make it quicker and easier to use

3) **Menus** can be used to **hide the inner workings** of the software from the user, and to make it more user-friendly. There are three main types:
   - full-screen
   - pop-ups
   - pull-down

   Each type of menu gives the user a **choice of actions**. Some options may not be available and these are usually 'greyed out'.

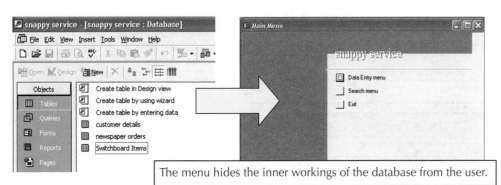

The menu hides the inner workings of the database from the user.

4) **Macros** let you **automate tasks** that you perform on a regular basis. This can be done by **recording a series of steps** that the computer will remember or using a scripting language.

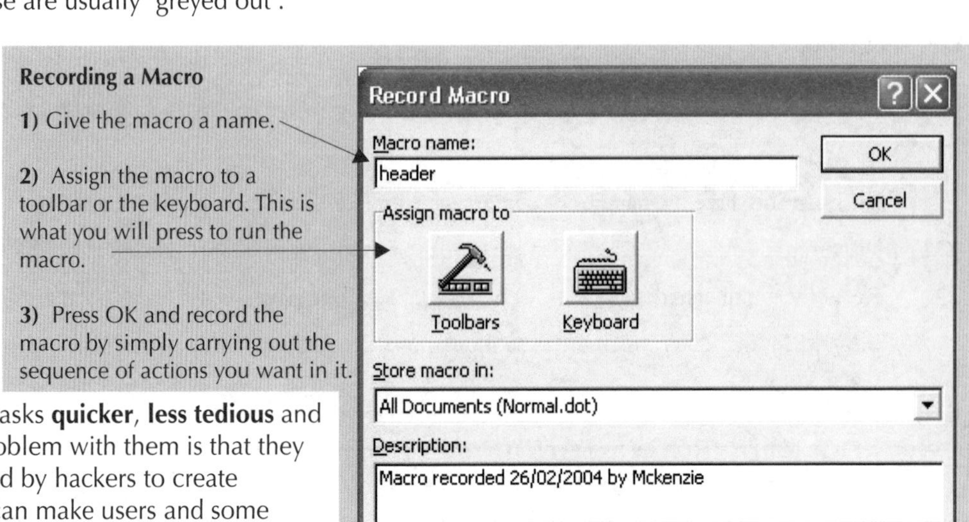

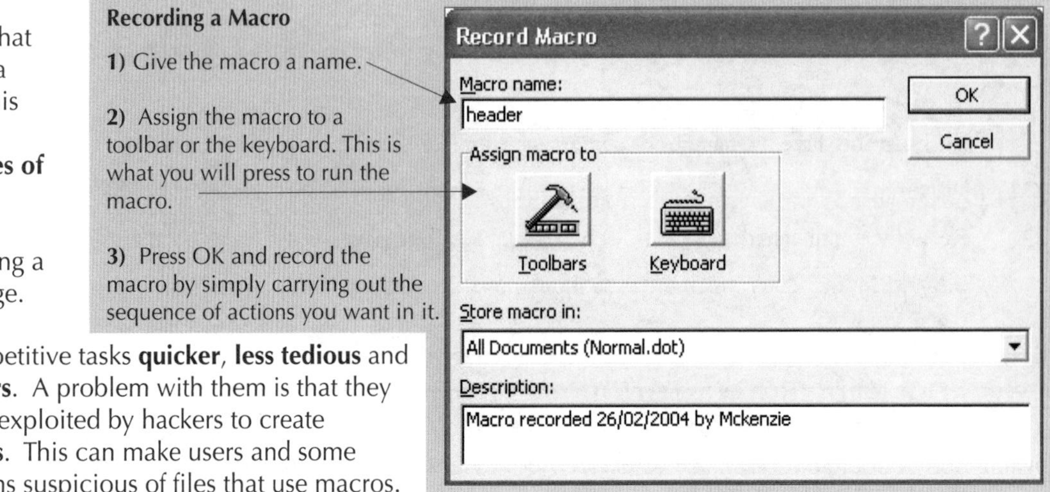

Macros make repetitive tasks **quicker**, **less tedious** and can **reduce errors**. A problem with them is that they have often been exploited by hackers to create computer **viruses**. This can make users and some software programs suspicious of files that use macros.

Customising Applications

Customised Interfaces — What's **Good** and What's **Not**...

Benefits of Having a Customised System Interface:

1) It makes it **faster** and easier to enter data, so users make fewer mistakes and are more productive.
2) The system is more **user-friendly** which makes it easier for inexperienced users.
3) The Interface can be set up so that data is **validated on entry**, reducing errors.
4) **Technical support** is easier as the complex interface is removed, making it easier to fix.

Disadvantages of Having a Customised System Interface:

1) If options have been **left off the interface** (due to poor planning) then users won't be able to do tasks that they could do with a generic interface.
2) A high level of **technical knowledge** is often required to create and test the interface.
3) If the software on which the interface is built is **upgraded** there are **no guarantees** it will still work as required.

Files may need **Converting** for use in **Different Applications**

When files are being transferred from one application to another, you need to make sure that the files are in a **format** that can be read by the target application. There are **two options** depending on what formats each application can cope with:

Package A can save the file in Package B's format	Package A cannot save to Package B's format
1) **Open** the file in Package A. 2) **Save as** or **export** to Package B format. 3) **Open** in Package B.	1) **Open** the file in Package A. 2) **Save as** or **export** to **Package C format.** 3) **Open** the file in Package C. 4) **Save as** or **export** to Package B format. 5) **Open** in Package B.

Practice Questions

Q1 How can tailoring generic applications software packages make them easier to use?

Q2 Give one advantage and one disadvantage of using a customised system interface.

Q3 Describe how to import / export a file if Package A can save the file in Package B's format.

Exam Questions

Q1 Describe three ways to customise the interface of a generic software package to make it more user-friendly. (6 marks)

Q2 A spreadsheet package has macro capabilities.

a) Explain what is meant by the term "macro capabilities". (2 marks)

b) Give two examples of situations where the use of macros would be appropriate. (2 marks)

Washing your socks regularly means a nicer interface for the feet...

Yes folks, you heard it here first — washing your socks means your feet will smell less. Unless you have naturally foul smelling body odours of course. In other news, AS ICT examiners have been found to cause 85% more boredom in pupils than Theatre Studies examiners. That's a statistic I just made up, but it feels true, doesn't it? Anyway, learn all this stuff, etc...

Using Spreadsheets

These pages are for AQA Unit 1 and OCR Unit 1.

Let's get into this spreadsheet thing a bit more seriously, shall we? It's like my old Great Uncle Bulgaria used to say, "Tobermory" he used to say to me, "Tobermory, stop pretending you're a womble. You don't even live in London."

Spreadsheets Are Made Up Of **Various Different Parts**

Cell

A cell is a data store that **holds a piece of data**.

They are known by their row and column address, a bit like **coordinates**, e.g. B5 is in column B, row 5.

Every cell in a spreadsheet has a unique address, and they can also be given **names** to identify them, e.g. RATE_VAT.

Each cell can be **formatted individually**. The formatting that can be applied to each cell includes font size and style, borders, alignment, conditional formatting and validation.

Conditional formatting means that the format of the cell is changed if the contents meet certain conditions, e.g. if a number is negative it can be set to turn red.

Cells can also be **protected** through using a password so they can only be changed by users who know the password.

Rows and Columns

A **row** runs horizontally **across** a spreadsheet. A **column** runs vertically **down** a spreadsheet.

Rows are normally identified by **numbers**, e.g. row 5. Columns are normally identified by **letters**, e.g. column B.

If a row or column is inserted or deleted they're renumbered / relettered **automatically**.

The **height** and **width** of rows and columns can be **altered** to ensure that all data and information held is visible.

Rows and columns can be **hidden** from the user, e.g. if rows or columns hold calculations that the user does not need to see.

Range

A range is a **group of cells** that can be identified by the cell references or given a name.

The range is usually given as the **top left cell** to the **bottom right cell**, e.g. B2:D6.

Ranges usually contain similar data and are often used in **formulas** and **functions**.

The same **formatting** can be applied to a range of cells. This is much easier than applying formatting to the cells one at a time.

Worksheet

A worksheet is basically like a **single page** of a spreadsheet. In MS Excel® 2007, worksheets can contain up to 16,384 columns and 1,048,576 rows. Individual worksheets can be given **meaningful names** to define the data that is held in them.

Workbook

A workbook is a **collection of worksheets** that make up one spreadsheet document.

The workbook contains **all the information**, whilst each worksheet would normally relate to a specific area.

For example: a business might have 4 sales regions, and each region's sales could be contained within a worksheet (4 in total) with the workbook containing all the information about the business. Data can be **linked** between worksheets, so if data is changed on 1 worksheet, the linked cells in the other worksheets **change automatically**.

Each worksheet held in a workbook can be **given different access rights**, e.g. if each worksheet contained information about a particular shop, it could be set so that only the manager of that shop could see that worksheet.

Using Spreadsheets

Formulas can have **Absolute** or **Relative Cell References**

It's very easy to **replicate data** in spreadsheets, e.g. by copying and pasting a range of cells from one column to a different column. When **formulas** are replicated like this, the cell references will be affected in one of two ways depending on whether the references are **relative** or **absolute**.

Relative Referencing Means the **Cell References Move**

When a formula is replicated, any relative cell references will change **in relation to the copy**.

If the formula is copied from one column to another, then the **column identifier** will **change automatically**.

If the formula is copied from row to row, then the **row identifier** will **change automatically**.

	A	B	C	D
1				
2	34	97	85	=A2+B2+C2
3	78	27	36	=A3+B3+C3
4	=A2+A3	=B2+B3	=C2+C3	

original (=A2+B2+C2) — copy (=A3+B3+C3)

original (=A2+A3) — copies (=B2+B3, =C2+C3)

Absolute Referencing Means **The Cell Reference Doesn't Change**

An **absolute** cell reference can be used if there is a single value you want to appear **in all the formulas**.

For example: a delivery charge of £2.50 is added to all orders. This is held in cell B1. The cell references for the total **changes** as it moves down the column, but the absolute reference **does not change**. The spreadsheet knows this cell is absolute because of the $ signs. Cell names can also be used as absolute cell references — you could call cell B1 "delivery charge".

The **main advantage** of using absolute cell referencing is that if that value changes it **only has to be changed once** as all the functions and formulas will automatically use the new value.

	A	B	C	D
1		2.5		
2				
3	Order	Total	Total+Delivery	
4	333	47.2	=B4+B$1	
5	334	89.8	=B5+B$1	
6	335	56.22	=B6+B$1	

Practice Questions

Q1 Give three examples of types of data that can be held in a cell.

Q2 What is conditional formatting?

Q3 How many cells are contained in the range E5:H8?

Exam Questions

Q1 Explain, giving an example, the purpose of each of the following in a spreadsheet:

a) worksheet b) workbook c) cell range. (6 marks)

Q2 Explain each of the following terms, giving an example of each:

a) absolute referencing (3 marks)

b) relative referencing (3 marks)

Wombles have cell references — they were caught stealing on the common...

Seriously though, wombles were just a bunch of thieving toerags weren't they? "Making good use of the things that we find?" Oh yes Tomsk, that's right. Just take Tobermory and Orinoco up to Wimbledon Common to "find" three wallets, a leather handbag and a confused looking bassett hound called Gerald. They should lock 'em up and throw away the key...

Using Spreadsheets

These pages are for AQA Unit 1 and OCR Unit 1.

Making charts and graphs is simple. You've probably been making them in class for zillions of years. But that doesn't mean you can skimp on your revision — learn these two pages properly and make sure you don't leave anything out.

Creating A **Chart** Is Dead **Easy**...

Spreadsheets show figures that can sometimes be **difficult to understand**. Graphs and charts show the figures in a **more user-friendly way**. All spreadsheets produce graphs and charts slightly differently, but the basic idea is always the same:

1) Get all the data you want to put into a graph into a single block. It's best if the data is arranged in columns.
2) Highlight the data you want to use — you might need to highlight column headings too.
3) Select the type of chart you want — be sensible and make sure it's suitable.
4) Choose a meaningful title for the chart that summarises its contents. Label any axes.
5) Decide if the chart needs a key (also called a legend).

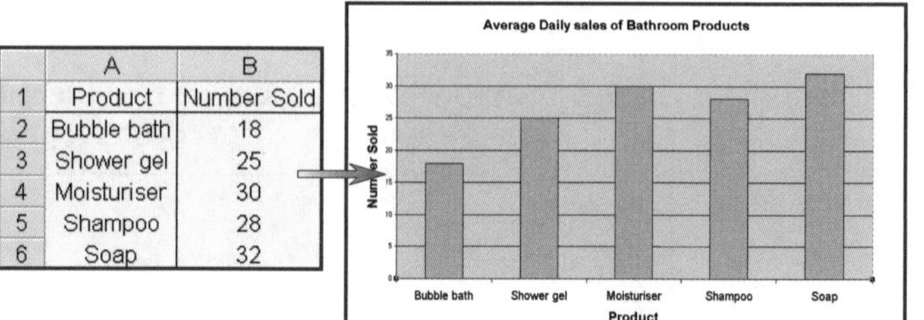

	A	B
1	Product	Number Sold
2	Bubble bath	18
3	Shower gel	25
4	Moisturiser	30
5	Shampoo	28
6	Soap	32

There Are Many **Different Types** Of **Graphs** And **Charts** you can use

1) There are many **different types** of graphs and charts that can be produced by spreadsheets.
2) It's important to choose the **most appropriate graph** for your data.

The most common types of graphs and charts are:

Bar / Column

Bar charts are useful when **comparing** two different sets of data. Each set of data must be **discrete** (separate from the others). The category is shown on the x-axis and the value/s are shown on the y-axis. The bars on the bar chart should be **clearly separated**. If the data is **continuous** then the bar chart is known as a **histogram**.

Bar charts could be used to show things like the number of sales of umbrellas each month, number of school absences for each day in the school week, etc.

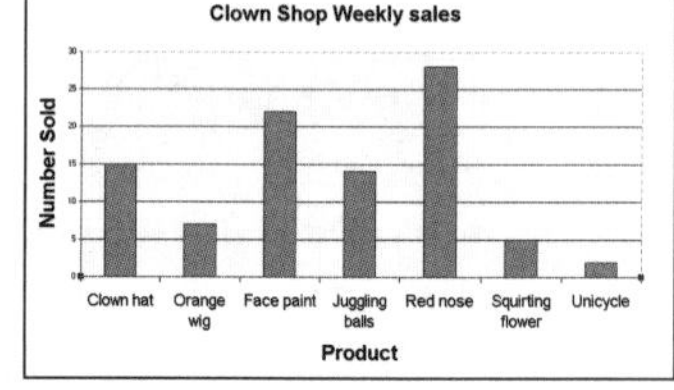

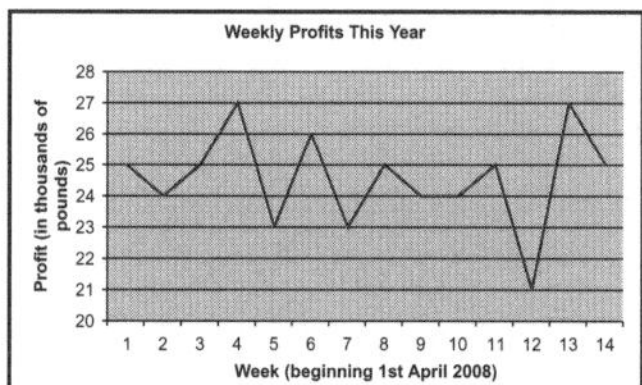

Line

Line graphs are used to show **changes over a given time period**. They're used when the x-axis **isn't in a category**, e.g. time. Line graphs can be used to show things like the amount of rainfall in Blackpool over a 30-day period, the total sales of a company over the period of a year, or the temperature of a room over a 24-hour period.

Scatter

Scatter graphs show the **relationship** (correlation) between two sets of data. One set is plotted along the x-axis with the other set plotted along the y-axis. A **trend line** can be used to show the relationship **more clearly**. Scatter graphs can be used to show things like the sales of umbrellas against the amount of rainfall, or the sales of deckchairs against the temperature.

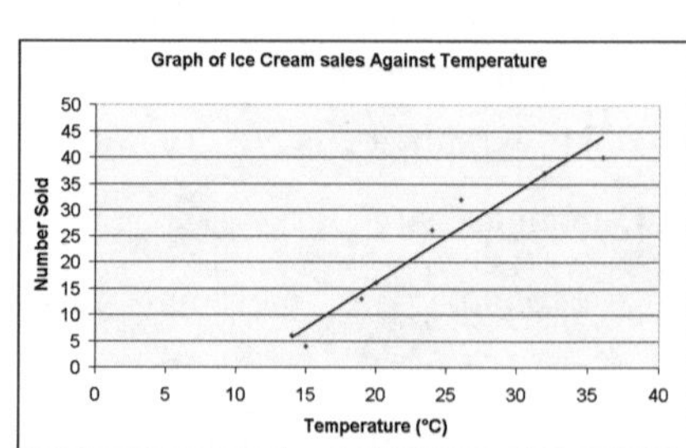

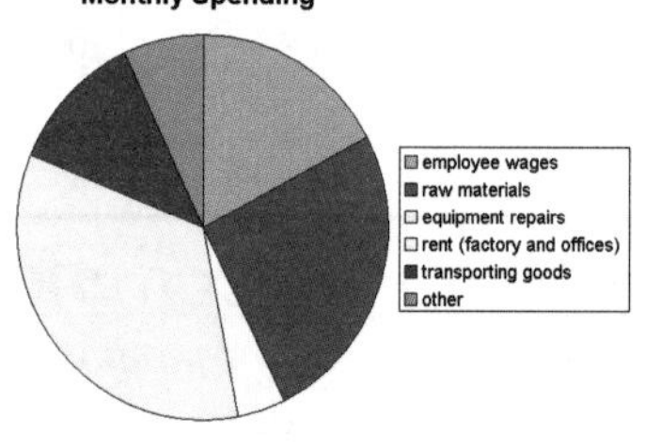

Pie

A pie chart is a circle divided into **segments**. It shows the **proportion** of individual categories of data to the total of all the data categories in a series. It displays the contribution of an individual value to a total. It's best not to have too many categories or the chart gets too cluttered. You can use pie charts to show things like the most popular colour of cars, or how a student spends their school day.

Using Spreadsheets

Form Controls Can Be Used To *Customise* A Worksheet

Form controls help the user to **input** the data and let them **add** more features to the spreadsheets. There are lots of form controls that can be used. The most popular ones are:

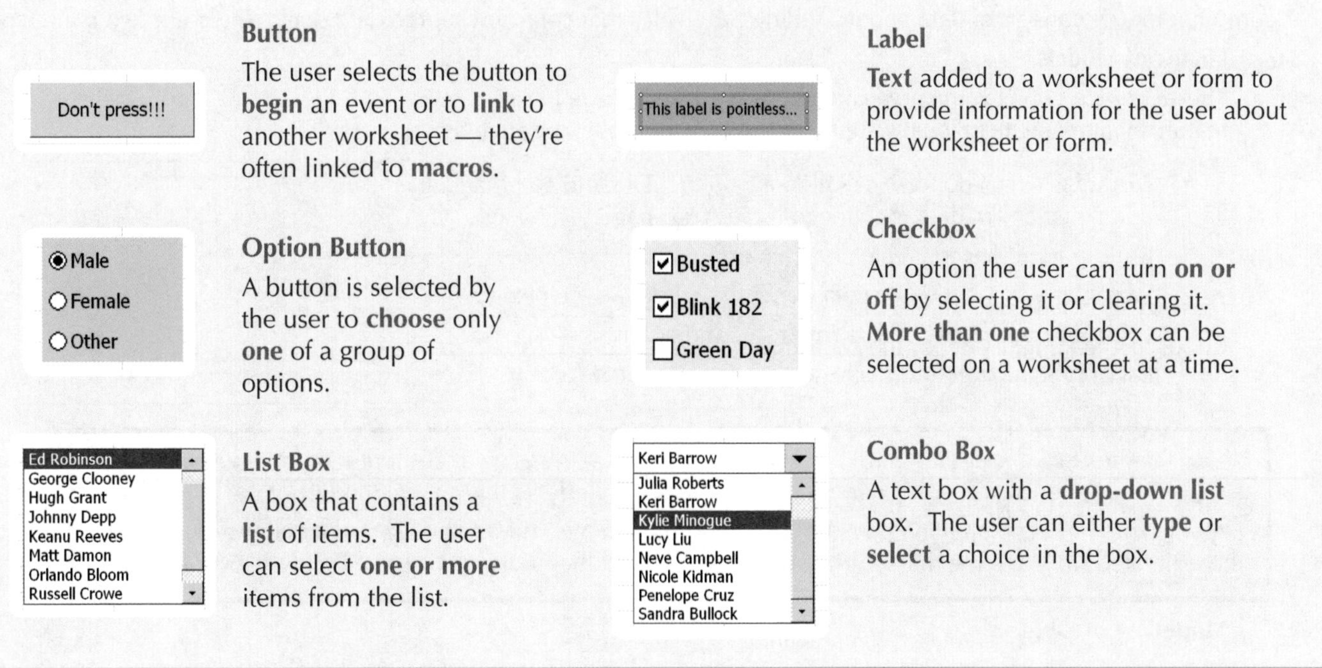

Button
The user selects the button to **begin** an event or to **link** to another worksheet — they're often linked to **macros**.

Label
Text added to a worksheet or form to provide information for the user about the worksheet or form.

Option Button
A button is selected by the user to **choose** only **one** of a group of options.

Checkbox
An option the user can turn **on or off** by selecting it or clearing it. **More than one** checkbox can be selected on a worksheet at a time.

List Box
A box that contains a **list** of items. The user can select **one or more** items from the list.

Combo Box
A text box with a **drop-down list** box. The user can either **type** or **select** a choice in the box.

Macros Can Also Be Used To *Customise A Worksheet*

1) Macros can be programmed to help users **perform tasks** when they are working on a worksheet.
2) A macro can be **linked to a button** so that when the button is selected by the user, a macro is run.
3) Macros can be used to **print** the worksheet, **open** a workbook, **move** to a different workbook or **perform a calculation**. A macro can also be used to **run an event**.

More on macros on p86.

Practice Questions

Q1 What are the four most commonly used charts and graphs?
Q2 Name three form controls that can be used to customise a worksheet.
Q3 Suggest three tasks you could use macros for in a spreadsheet.

Exam Questions

Q1 Say what the most suitable chart would be for displaying the following data about a car dealership.
a) The number of cars sold each month for a year. (1 mark)
b) The relationship between the age and mileage of all the cars. (1 mark)

Q2 Identify two methods of customising a spreadsheet worksheet and explain their advantages. (4 marks)

Well, I like bars and I like pies — shame about the rest of it...

Actually, these pages are a big improvement on the rest of the section in my opinion. No horrible formulas, functions or relative referencing — just nice ways to make your spreadsheets look pretty. If only everything in ICT was about making things pretty. E.g. "Q5) Add a nice coloured pattern to this database, then give it some matching accessories."

Modelling Software

These pages are for AQA Unit 1 and OCR Unit 1.

People used to tell me that I should do modelling on account of my perfectly-toned physique and striking features. So I took their advice and made a spreadsheet to help me with my finances.

There Are Two **Types Of Modelling** In ICT

A computer model consists of **data** about a "thing" and **rules** that control what the data does. There are two main types:

1) **Financial Models**

These are often done with **spreadsheets**. Spreadsheets have lots of features that make them ideally suited to this type of modelling such as:

- **Formulas** which perform calculations on the data and automatically update when the data is changed — see next page.
- Built-in **functions** to create complex and powerful formulas — see next page.
- **Variables** which hold key data about the model — see next page.
- Logical **arrangement** of data into rows and columns — see page 88.
- Easy **replication** of formulas and functions — see page 89.

These features make it easy to perform "**what-if**" analysis — this is what computer modelling is all about. The user changes certain **parameters** and sees what **effects** this has on the rest of the model.

E.g. in a spreadsheet modelling potential revenue from a new product, the user could change the price, the estimated sales and the marketing budget and see how these changes would affect the overall profit.

2) **Modelling of Objects**

This creates a **virtual representation**. It can be used to model large items like buildings, bridges and aeroplanes — designers can see how different events affect the model.

For example, a designer can see how an aeroplane will behave when flying in different conditions or how an earthquake affects a building. The model can also be used to **change** and **test** the design, and see how these changes affect the model. Modelling can also be set up to identify all the components that would be used to build the real object. **CAD** is a good example of this type of modelling. You can read more on CAD on p40.

Computer Models Have **Advantages...**

1) A computer-based model can be **used by different people** in different locations.
2) **No additional software is needed** if spreadsheets are used for financial modelling — spreadsheets are standard business software. Most people are able to use a spreadsheet, so **no specialist training** is needed.
3) The values held in the spreadsheet can be shown in a graph — the graph will **change automatically** as the value of the data is changed. This can be used to **show trends**.
4) Only **one** computer-based object model needs to be built, which can then be **changed**. If the real thing were built, then a new one would be needed for each change made. This takes **time** and can be **very expensive**.
5) They're **safer** than building the real thing, e.g. if a submarine was built and tested and something went wrong, lives could be lost.
6) Computer-based models can be **slowed down** or **speeded up** to see effects that are **difficult to see in real life**.

...And **Disadvantages**

1) It's **difficult** to create a good model. It usually takes **lots of time** and **lots of testing**.
2) If the model is complicated then it might need **expensive** computer hardware to be able to run effectively.
3) The model might still not be an **accurate** representation of the real world.
4) Some things are **really hard to model**, for example **human behaviour** or complicated mechanical systems with **lots and lots of variables**. These things may need to be simplified for modelling, leading to potential **inaccuracies** in the results.

Modelling Software

Learn these key **Modelling Features** of Spreadsheets...

Formulas

A formula is an **instruction** to the computer to **process data** held in **specific cells**. They use numbers, cell addresses (cell names such as "Week 1 Sales" or references such as E25) and **mathematical operators**. Formulas can be typed into the formula bar by the user — these are generally **simple calculations**.

SUM =C3+D3+E3

	A	B	C	D	E	F
1	Sales Team Performance					
2	First Name	Last name	Week 1 Sales	Week 2 Sales	Week 3 Sales	Total
3	Teresa	Wood	24	15	32	=C3+D3+E3
4	Tanya	Hide	33	30	41	
5	Colin	Moore	27	32	29	
6	Phillip	Farley	18	19	22	
7	Mia	Fernandez	35	33	26	

This simple formula adds the contents of cells C3, D3 and E3

Mathematical Operators:
* multiply   + add
– subtract   / divide

You can also create more **complicated** formulas using the software's built-in functions...

Functions

These are **standard routines** that are built into the spreadsheet. They can perform a variety of common routines and use reserved words. Functions have a help or wizard facility built into the spreadsheet to help the user. They can be nested within other functions in order to create more complicated ones.

Most Common Functions:

SUM: calculates the total of a range of cells.

IF: returns one value if the condition specified is true and a different value if it is false.

AVERAGE: returns the mean or average value from a range of cells.

Variables

A variable is an **identifier** (a cell reference like A3, or a cell name like "Week 1 Sales"). They appear in formulas and are important in "what-if" questions because they let you update many cells in the spreadsheet by just changing one variable. It's the value contained in the variable that is used. So if the variable named "RATE_VAT" contains the value 17.5%, this is the figure that the formulas containing the variable will use.

Practice Questions

Q1 Name a type of software that is used for modelling objects.
Q2 Explain the importance of "what-if" analysis to computer models.
Q3 What do formulas do in modelling?
Q4 Name three common functions.
Q5 What is a variable?

Exam Questions

Q1 Explain three advantages of using a spreadsheet for financial modelling. (6 marks)

Q2 Describe what functions and formulas are, as used in a spreadsheet, giving an example of each. (6 marks)

But more importantly, what-if I actually don't give a monkeys...

... well tough because you still have to learn it. CAD and spreadsheets are good examples of modelling software but you also need to be able to talk about the features of modelling software in a more general way. So remember, you need a set of data, rules that control how the data is used and the capability to do what-if analysis. That's models in a shellnut.

Databases

These pages are for AQA Unit 1 and OCR Unit 1.

Now it's getting really exciting. If there's one ICT topic that's 100% guaranteed to get your pulse racing, surely that subject is... databases. As Dr Johnson said, "A man who is tired of databases is tired of life". Or words to that effect.

Databases are Used to Store Information

1) A database is a collection of **related data**.
2) Databases can **store** vast amounts of data without taking up too much space.
3) Users can **search**, **sort** and **combine** data very quickly.
4) Databases can be used to produce **reports**.

There are Lots of Database Terms You Need to Know

When you're **designing** a database, you have to think about the entities and attributes.

1) An **entity** is a name given to anything that data is stored about. All the data held in an entity refers to that entity. For example, the entity "Customer" will **only** hold data about customers.
2) Every entity has **attributes**. The attributes describe the properties of the entity. For example, the attributes of the entity "Customer" might be: Forename, Surname, Address 1, Town, County, Postcode.
3) When you create a database, the entities become **table names** and the attributes become **fields**.
4) **Tables** contain data about a particular entity, e.g. students, suppliers, customers, etc. The data is organised into rows (records) and columns (fields). The simplest databases consist of a single table and are called **flat-files**. Databases with more than one table are **relational databases**.
5) A **record** is a collection of data about a single item, e.g. a particular supplier, customer, student. Each row in a database table is a separate record. Each record in a table must be **unique**.
6) **Fields** break the records into separate pieces of data. Each field must have a unique name and contain a single data item. Fields can have different data types and have their **own validation**.

A **table** is made up of **records**, records are made up of **fields**.

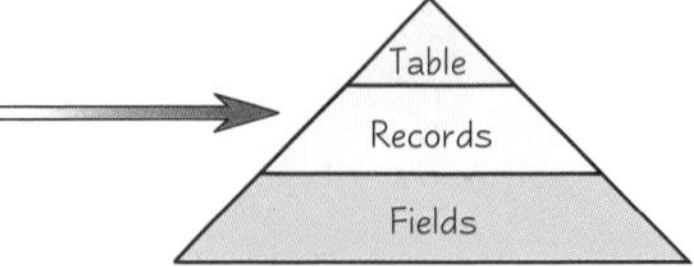

There are Two Main Types of Key

This bit is just for the OCR course.

There are two main types of key that can be used in a relational database — **primary key** and **foreign key**.

The **primary key** is the most important one.

The primary key is a field in a table that allows each record to be uniquely identified.

Every value in the primary key field must be **different**.

Forename	Surname
Fred	Stuart
Henry	Brown
Fred	Spencer
Eric	Brown

There is repeating data in both these fields so they cannot be used as a primary key.

ID	Forename	Surname
1	Fred	Stuart
2	Henry	Brown
3	Fred	Spencer
4	Eric	Brown

This field can be used as the primary key as each value is unique.

The **foreign key** is used to link tables together to form relationships.

A foreign key is a primary key in one table that is linked to a field in another table.

The data types of the fields that are linked must be the **same**.

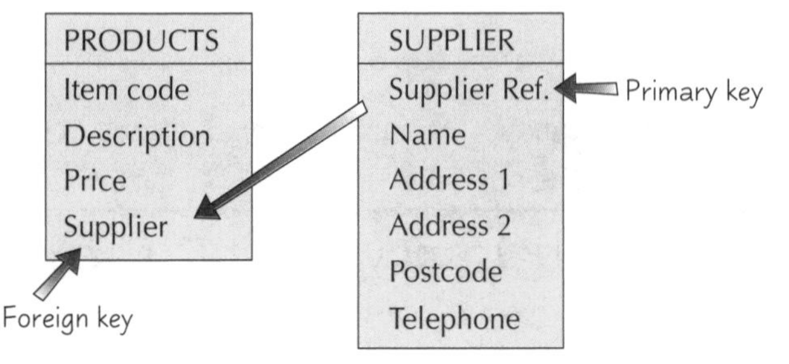

Use these conventions for writing data structures:
- Write the table name in CAPITAL LETTERS.
- Put the attributes (field names) in brackets, separated by commas.
- <u>Underline</u> the primary key and overline the foreign key.

For example, the products table shown to the right would be written PRODUCTS (<u>Item code</u>, Description, Price, $\overline{\text{Supplier}}$).

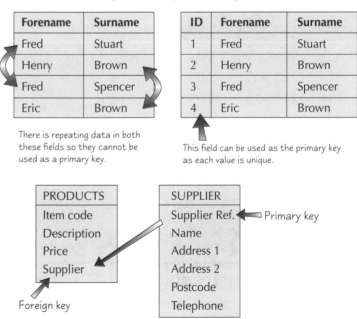

Databases

Tables are Linked by Relationships

The tables in a relational database have to be linked through **relationships**.
There are three main kinds of relationship that can be used:

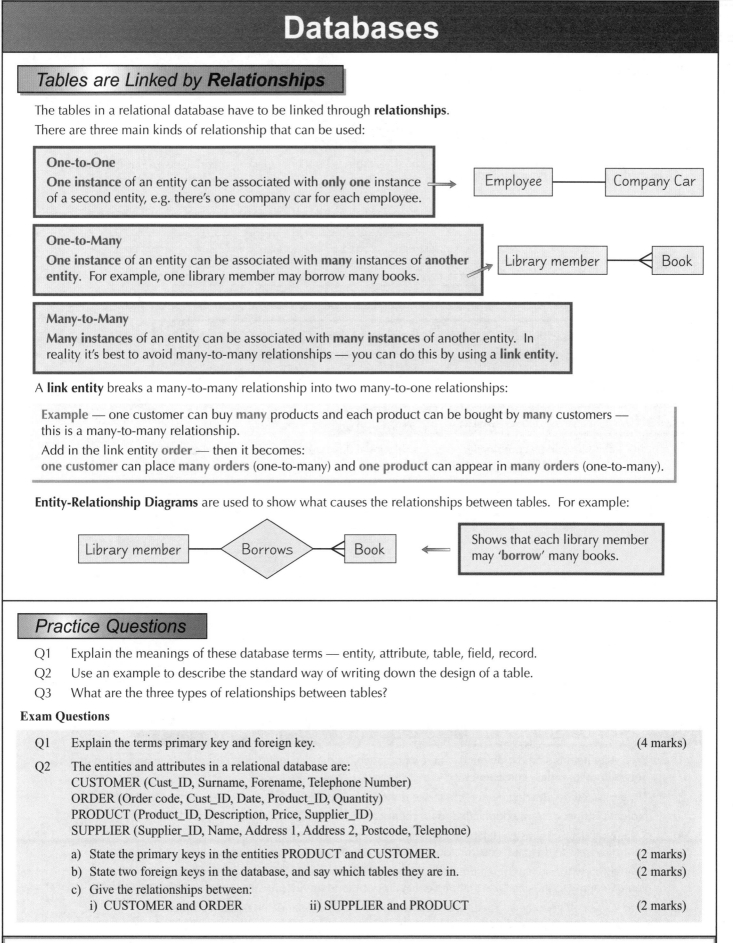

One-to-One
One instance of an entity can be associated with **only one** instance of a second entity, e.g. there's one company car for each employee.

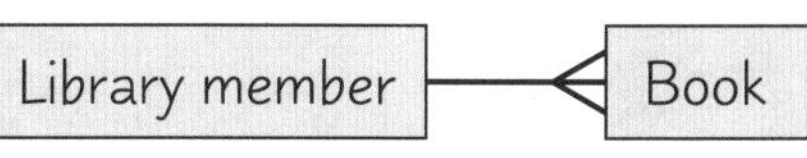

One-to-Many
One instance of an entity can be associated with **many** instances of **another entity**. For example, one library member may borrow many books.

Library member — Book

Many-to-Many
Many instances of an entity can be associated with **many instances** of another entity. In reality it's best to avoid many-to-many relationships — you can do this by using a **link entity**.

A **link entity** breaks a many-to-many relationship into two many-to-one relationships:

Example — one customer can buy **many** products and each product can be bought by **many** customers — this is a many-to-many relationship.
Add in the link entity **order** — then it becomes:
one customer can place **many orders** (one-to-many) and **one product** can appear in **many orders** (one-to-many).

Entity-Relationship Diagrams are used to show what causes the relationships between tables. For example:

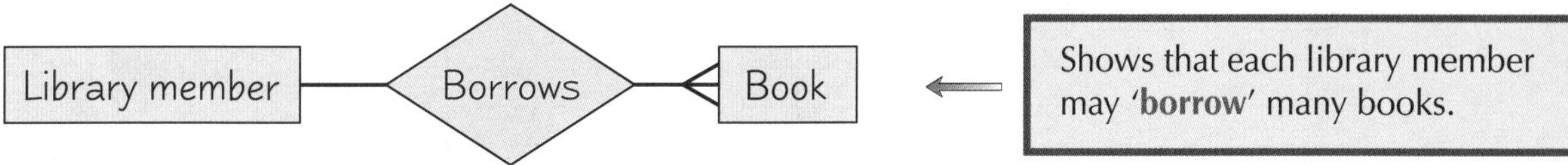

Shows that each library member may '**borrow**' many books.

Practice Questions

Q1 Explain the meanings of these database terms — entity, attribute, table, field, record.

Q2 Use an example to describe the standard way of writing down the design of a table.

Q3 What are the three types of relationships between tables?

Exam Questions

Q1 Explain the terms primary key and foreign key. (4 marks)

Q2 The entities and attributes in a relational database are:
CUSTOMER (Cust_ID, Surname, Forename, Telephone Number)
ORDER (Order code, Cust_ID, Date, Product_ID, Quantity)
PRODUCT (Product_ID, Description, Price, Supplier_ID)
SUPPLIER (Supplier_ID, Name, Address 1, Address 2, Postcode, Telephone)

a) State the primary keys in the entities PRODUCT and CUSTOMER. (2 marks)
b) State two foreign keys in the database, and say which tables they are in. (2 marks)
c) Give the relationships between:
i) CUSTOMER and ORDER ii) SUPPLIER and PRODUCT (2 marks)

Just in case that was all too easy, here's an extra complication...

In addition to normal primary keys, you can also have ***composite*** *primary keys. This is where two (or more) fields work together as the primary key. So you can uniquely identify every record in the table through different combinations of these fields. You'll need to know this for later on where everything gets a wee bit tricky...*

Databases

These pages are for AQA Unit 1 and OCR Unit 1.

You really need to concentrate for the rest of this section. Databases are simple at first, but they do get trickier and trickier. And yet fear ye not gentle students! Stick with me and I'll get you through it — TO THE ICTMOBILE!

Flat Files are the Simplest Kind of Database

A **flat file** database consists of a **single table** of data. This table is not connected to anything else. Flat-file databases are often used to store lists and are very easy to create. But they tend to contain a lot of duplicate data.

The example below shows DVDs owned by a rental shop.

Primary Key Field — each item is unique

Each column is a different field

Member M0025's details appear twice because she has taken out 2 videos.

Each row is a separate record

Item of data

Code	Name	Type	Certificate	Cost of Hire	Membership No	Member Name	Member Address	Postcode	Telephone	Date
V0001	Gullivers Travels	Drama	U	£1.50	M0001	Heather Palin	The Haven, Skelly Crag	BS4 7RL	0117 4332957	22/11/2003
V0002	The Princess Bride	Drama	PG	£2.50						
V0003	Matrix	Action	15	£2.50	M0025	Barbara Millward	27 Crescent Drive	BS4 6PT	0117 3445817	22/11/2003
D0001	Human Traffic	Drama	18	£2.50						
D0002	American Pie	Comedy	15	£2.00	M0025	Barbara Millward	27 Crescent Drive	BS4 6PT	0117 3445817	22/11/2003

The main **problem with flat-file databases** is the duplicate data which means:

- file sizes are large, storage space is wasted and it's **slow** to retrieve data.
- it's easy to create **errors** or **inconsistencies** when you're entering data or updating it.

Relational Databases Combine Flat Files

Two or more flat files can be combined to create a **relational database**. The different tables are linked using **foreign keys** and **relationships**. Here's a better database for the rental shop example above:

DVDS

Code	Name	Type	Certificate	Cost of Hire	Membership number	Date
V0001	Gullivers Travels	Drama	U	£1.50	M0001	22/11/2003
V0002	The Princess Bride	Drama	PG	£2.50		
V0003	Matrix	Action	15	£2.50	M0025	22/11/2003
D0001	Human Traffic	Drama	18	£2.50		
D0002	American Pie	Comedy	15	£2.00	M0025	22/11/2003

MEMBERS

Membership Number	Name	Address	Postcode	Telephone
M0024	John Williamson	35 Priory Avenue	BS4 3AJ	0117 9754412
M0025	Barbara Millward	27 Crescent Drive	BS4 6PT	0117 3445817
M0026	Sanjeev Patel	43 Albert Street	BS4 8UB	0117 9423184

This database uses two tables — DVDS stores details of all the shop's DVDs, MEMBERS stores the contact details of all the members. The membership number field links the two tables — it's the **primary key** of the MEMBERS table and appears as a **foreign key** in the DVDS table.

It's a many-to-one relationship between DVDS and MEMBERS because each membership number can appear many times in the DVDS table, but only once in the MEMBERS table.

Relational Databases are More Efficient than flat file databases

1) Each data item is stored only once. There's no danger of data being updated in one place and not in another. This is known as **data consistency**.
2) Time is saved on entering data — it's **faster** if the same data doesn't have to be entered repeatedly.
3) No data is unnecessarily duplicated (**data redundancy**) so no storage space is wasted.
4) Relational databases use a database management system (**DBMS**) which can control access to the data, ensuring only authorised users can see certain bits.
5) The DBMS will also have a feature called **referential integrity** — this is a set of rules you can apply to the database that prevents you from entering inconsistent data.
6) Still, it's not all good news. Setting up and maintaining relational databases is **complex** and **time-consuming**, and if the database fails, all applications using the data are affected.

For example, in a database, if Table A has a foreign key field that links to Table X, referential integrity would make sure that when you change any fields in Table X, the records in Table A that link to it will be updated too.

The main **problems with relational databases** are:

- **complex software** is required to set up and maintain the database
- **expertise** is needed to carry out effective design, creation and maintenance.

Databases

Hierarchical Databases are a *Special Kind* of *Database*

1) In a **hierarchical database** the records are linked together in a **tree data structure**. Each record below the top level is a **child**. Each child has only one **parent**, but can be parent to many children of its own. It's a bit like how folders work in Windows Explorer.
2) Users need to know how the tree is **structured** to find data within it (like finding files hidden at the end of a long path of folders in Windows Explorer).
3) Hierarchical databases used to be widely used on mainframe computers, but they're far less common today because of their **restrictive nature**.

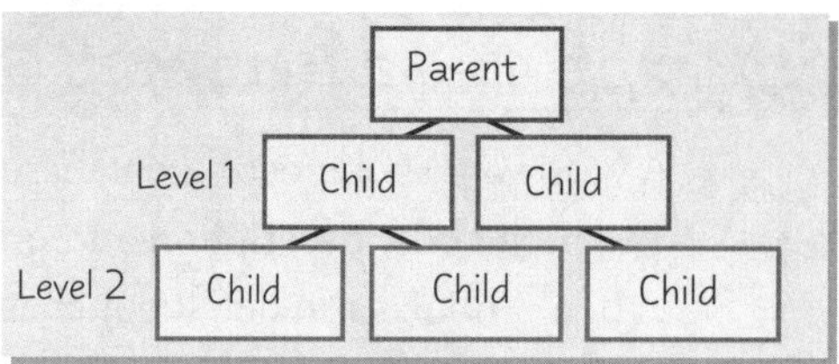

You Can *Run Queries* to *Search Databases*

1) You **search** databases by looking for items that meet certain criteria — this is called **querying**.
2) Most modern database programs use a **special language** to query their databases.
3) **SQL** (structured query language) lets you **choose** the data to extract and from what tables.
4) If you know what you're doing, SQL is a very powerful tool for extracting information from complex databases. But it's pretty complicated to learn, so an easier way is to use **QBE** (query by example). With QBE, a **grid** enables you to **select fields** from the tables you wish to query, and **specify search criteria** in a visual manner.
5) Queries can be performed by the DBMS itself or by **other software** which uses the database.

For example, when you do a mail merge, the word processor queries the database to extract the data it needs. Websites often link to a database to create dynamic content (it is updated as soon as a change is made), e.g. online stores and booking systems.

This query will find all the PG DVDs which cost more than £1.50 to rent. The name and cost of the DVDs will be displayed.

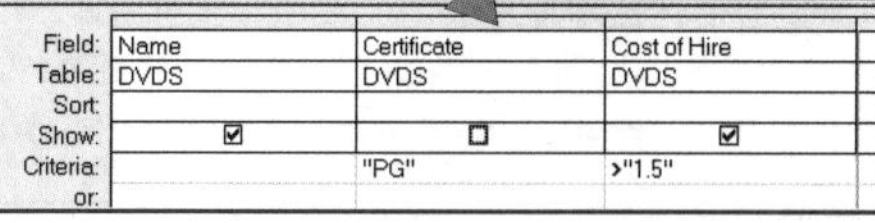

Field:	Name	Certificate	Cost of Hire
Table:	DVDS	DVDS	DVDS
Sort:			
Show:	☑	☐	☑
Criteria:		"PG"	>"1.5"
or:			

Reports *Make Sense* of *Queries*

1) Query results look just like tables — they're not formatted.
2) **Reports** are used to format the data from queries to make it easier to understand by **grouping** and **summarising** data.
3) **Graphs** are often used because they present results in a very accessible, visual way.

New DVDs (January)

Romantic Comedy, Action, Thriller, Science Fiction, Drama

Practice Questions

Q1 What are the problems associated with flat file databases?

Q2 Explain the structure of a hierarchical database.

Q3 What do the following terms stand for: 'DBMS', 'SQL' and 'QBE'?

Exam Questions

Q1 Give four advantages of using a relational database instead of a flat file system. (4 marks)

Q2 An electricity company has a relational database containing information about all the work it does. Suggest three tables that are likely to be in its database. (3 marks)

Q3 A school has a table in its database which holds details of all its pupils. The table is named PUPIL. Name 5 fields that this table might contain and state which of them would be the primary key. (6 marks)

I used to retrieve data from Madonna's rubbish bins — 'til the court order...

Phew, there's quite a lot on these two pages. Some of it's straightforward stuff you just need to memorise, but some of the more involved relational database stuff will need a bit more brain power. I recommend some chocolate, a cup of tea, and a brisk slide down the pole that goes into the batcave, so you can go for a holy-concentration-inducing ride in the ICTMOBILE.

Examples of Databases

These pages are for AQA Unit 1 and OCR Unit 1.

Here's a couple of case studies of relational databases. The one on this page is pretty easy, but the next one's a bit trickier. Don't worry though — read it all through carefully and answer the questions, and you'll be laughing... Ho. Ho. Ho.

Example 1 — a Hardware Shop Database

- A hardware shop needs a database for the products it sells.
- The **item code**, **description** and **price** are needed for each product.
- When products run out, the manager needs to be able to order more from the **supplier**.
- This means that **contact details** for the supplier are needed. Some suppliers supply more than one product.

The simplest solution for the hardware shop would be a **flat file database.**

Item code	Description	Price	Supplier Ref	Supplier Name	Supplier Address 1	Supplier Address 2	Supplier Postcode	Supplier Telephone
501432	Hanging Solutions	1.99	12	Wallis	Bridgend Business Park	Bridgend	BG21 6EQ	01376 812371
601433	Light bulbs (2 pack)	1.65	34	Kellaway	21 Finsbury Crescent	Gosforth	GF45 6TR	0452 897543
841562	Light bulbs (3 pack)	3.99	34	Kellaway	21 Finsbury Crescent	Gosforth	GF45 6TR	0452 897543
104992	Stanley screwdriver set	6.99	35	Tools Are Us	3 The Buildings	St. Andrews	SA6 6YH	0904 876931

This supplier's details are entered twice.

BUT this is not a very efficient solution because:

- Some of the data is **repeated**, which takes up **more memory**.
- If a supplier **changes**, the new supplier's details will have to be **re-entered** for every single product that will come from them.

It would be **better** to have a **relational database** with two tables:

1) PRODUCTS (Item Code, Description, Price, Supplier_Ref)
2) SUPPLIERS (Supplier_Ref, Name, Address 1, Address 2, Postcode, Telephone)

PRODUCTS

Item code	Description	Price	Supplier
501432	Hanging Solutions	1.99	12
601433	Light bulbs (2 pack)	1.65	34
841562	Light bulbs (3 pack)	3.99	34
104992	Stanley screwdriver set	6.99	35

The foreign key in the products table...

SUPPLIERS

Supplier Ref	Name	Address 1	Address 2	Postcode	Telephone
33	Bolton's	33 Carnarvon Road	Lestor	LS1 2AW	0131 9345671
34	Kellaway	21 Finsbury Crescent	Gosforth	GF45 6TR	0452 897543
35	Tools Are Us	3 The Buildings	St. Andrew's	SA6 6YH	0904 876931
36	H&P	121 Johan Street	Gothenbury	GT11 4RF	09871 654382

...is the primary key in the supplier table

This is a **many-to-one** relationship — lots of products can come from one supplier.

Examples of Databases

Example 2 — a Hospital Database

- A hospital is organised into a **number of wards.**
- Each ward has a **number** and a **name** recorded, along with the **number of beds** in that ward.
- Nurses have their **nurse number** and name recorded, and are assigned to **a single ward.**
- Each patient in the hospital has a **patient number** and their name, address and date of birth recorded. Each patient is under the care of a **single consultant** and is assigned to a **single ward.**
- Each consultant has **a number of patients.** Their **consultant number**, name and specialism are recorded.
- When a patient goes to the hospital they always go to the **same ward** and are treated by the **same consultant.**

You couldn't use a flat file database because it's just too complicated. This example calls for another **relational database**. There are four different entities — wards, nurses, patients and consultants. This means there will be four different tables in the relational database:

1) WARD (Ward Number, Name, Beds)
2) NURSES (Nurse Number, First Name, Surname, Ward Number)
3) PATIENTS (Patient Number, First name, Surname, Address1, Address2, Postcode, Date of Birth, Consultant Number, Ward number)
4) CONSULTANTS (Consultant Number, First Name, Surname, Specialism)

There is more than one foreign key in table 3.

CONSULTANTS

Consultant Number	First name	Surname	Specialism
C001	James	Gibson	Gynaecology
C002	Mary	Somerville	Oncology
C003	David	Clarke	Pediatrics
C004	Malcolm	Hughes	Plastic surgery

Many-to-one / One-to-many relationship.
Many patients have the same consultant / One consultant has many patients.

PATIENTS

Patient Number	First name	Surname	Address1	Address2	Postcode	Date of Birth	Consultant Number	Ward Number
P0001	Charlotte	Ireland	29 Royal Albert Road	Thornbury	BS23 3AD	12/03/1945	C004	W002
P0002	Megan	Gibbs	21 Etloe Road	Frenchay	BS12 7GG	23/05/1939	C004	W010
P0003	Timothy	Long	30 Bayston Road	Little Nailsea	BS10 8HC	30/10/1984	C011	W001
P0004	Robert	Zimmerman	5 Victoria Street	Rosettenville	BS6 8YP	01/04/1943	C020	W001

Many-to-one / One-to-many relationship.
Many patients are on the same ward / One ward has many patients on it.

WARD

Ward Number	Name	Beds
W001	Cotswold	12
W002	Brecon	6
W003	Mendips	9
W004	Chilterns	14

Many-to-one / One-to-many relationship.
Many nurses work on the same ward /
One ward has many nurses on it.

NURSES

Nurse Number	First Name	Surname	Ward Number
N001	Mary	Williamson	W007
N002	Jenny	Sunley	W004
N003	Rosemary	Barnes	W001
N004	Stephen	Simpson	W001

Practice Questions

Q1 Give two reasons why relational databases are better than flat file databases.

Q2 A vet wants to create a relational database of his work. Suggest three tables it would have.

Exam Question

Q1 Cotswold Coaches runs a very comprehensive coach service. Coach routes are divided into different fare stages. All coaches have just 44 passenger seats arranged in two pairs across the bus to a length of 11. The seats are labelled A1, B1, C1, D1 -------- A11, B11, C11, D11. All seats on every coach must be booked in advance. The seat booking system is ICT based and includes the use of spreadsheet and relational database software that can communicate with each other.

Describe THREE tables you would expect to find in the company's booking system. (5 marks)

I relate to databases — but they always give me socks for Christmas...

I know it might take a while to sort out how relational databases work, but here's a tip. If you're struggling to follow the hospital diagram above, try sketching it out for yourself. It will all fall in to place as you start to trace the links between the tables yourself. It's really quite straightforward — just get all the vocab down so that you know what bit is what.

Entering and Retrieving Data

These pages are for AQA Unit 1 and OCR Unit 1.

Do you remember that episode of Star Trek where it turns out Commander Data's got an evil brother? Well that has no relevance at all to these pages — although it is a more entertaining topic.

Data-entry Screens need to be Tailored

Tailored data entry screens are specific screens that have been designed to make it **easier to input data** into a database.

Data-entry screens should be designed through the use of **forms**. If you present the user with the table in a database they will find it difficult to use — providing them with a form with **instructions**, **buttons** and **sensible error messages** helps them. There are **two main factors** to consider when designing and creating data-entry screens:

Consistency

1) The **screens** should look as similar as possible.
2) **Buttons** used should be in the same place.
3) Data that has to be entered on several screens should have the **same format** on each screen.
4) If the data being entered comes from a paper form the screen must match the **layout**.

Relevance

1) The screen should only ask for **relevant data** — it shouldn't show too much unhelpful information.
2) The information must be **concise** and **useful**.
3) **Graphics** and **animation** should be kept to a minimum.

Select Queries Retrieve Data From the Database

1) **Select queries** return data from one or more tables, displaying the results in a single table, e.g. a simple select query might involve selecting two or three fields from a table to be displayed.
2) **Parameter queries** are a more interesting type of select query where you search for **particular values** in a field. The **parameter** is the value used to select records. Parameter queries can be **static** or **dynamic.**
   - A **static** parameter query **cannot be changed** — the query has been hard coded. Each time it is run, it will **only search** for the parameters set when the query was made. This may cause some problems, e.g. over time records will be added, edited or deleted from the database and the static parameter query may no longer be suitable to search all of the records.
   - A **dynamic** parameter query **asks the user** for the parameter value to search for. This is normally done through a dialogue box.
3) **Complex queries** are parameter queries that search using **more than one** parameter value or field. The parameters or fields are often searched using **logic functions** like AND, OR and NOT.
4) **Cross-tab queries** collate and summarise data together in a **grid**. This makes the data more compact and easier to analyse. To create one, you need to specify which **field's values** you want as **column headings** and which you want as **row headings**.

Surname	Department	Amount Spent
McDonald	Lingerie	£533.19
McDonald	Cosmetics	£564.28
McDonald	Soft Furnishings	£24.53
Von Kotze	Lingerie	£169.99
Von Kotze	Cosmetics	£253.32
Von Kotze	Soft Furnishings	£65.99
Data-Paulin	Lingerie	£56.98
Data-Paulin	Cosmetics	£17.99
Data-Paulin	Soft Furnishings	£2.99

Results of a standard select query to see three customers' purchases in a department store.

Surname	Lingerie	Cosmetics	Soft Furnishings	Total Spent
McDonald	£533.19	£564.28	£24.53	**£1122.00**
Von Kotze	£169.99	£253.32	£65.99	**£489.30**
Data-Paulin	£56.98	£17.99	£2.99	**£77.96**

The same results as a crosstab query. Note — this layout makes it easier to compare and look at totals.

Entering and Retrieving Data

Action Queries **Change** the Data Source

Action queries are different from select queries which simply retrieve data because they actually **modify** the data source. There are **four main** types of action query:

1) **Delete queries** delete records from a table.
2) **Update queries** change specified values within existing records.
3) **Append queries** add new records to a table.
4) **Make table queries** create new tables. They could be used when, for example, data is to be archived.

Reports should be Tailored for the User

1) **Reports** are usually printed as the **product of a query**.
2) Reports must be "**fit for purpose**" and **easily understood**. How the information is **presented** should also be considered — this could be through the use of text, graphics, numbers or a combination of these.
3) When you're designing reports, screens and queries you also need to think about:

- **titles** and **colour** to identify the screen, report or query.
- **drop down** and **list boxes** to restrict input and provide validation.
- **option buttons**.
- **default values** for speed of entry.
- **buttons**, **icons** and **menu items** that relate to the application only.
- useful and user-friendly **help** and **error messages** and context sensitive help.
- **dynamic updates**, e.g. selecting "Miss" in the title field automatically updates gender to female.
- use of **white space**.
- **font**, font size and colour.
- the **house-style** of the organisation.

Graham loved the way the report had been tailored to his needs.

Practice Questions

Q1 What's the difference between parameter and cross-tab queries?

Q2 Explain the terms static query and dynamic query.

Q3 Identify two types of action query.

Exam Questions

Q1 Describe four features that should be taken into account when designing a data entry screen. (4 marks)

Q2 Parameter queries and complex queries are used by a publishing company to search a database.
Describe and give an example of: a) a parameter query, b) a complex query. (6 marks)

Q3 Describe the difference between a simple and complex query. (2 marks)

Do you like my report? Do you, sir? Oooh, suits you...

That was a small tribute to the old BBC sketch show, 'The Fast Show', which also had a very funny vegetable game sketch. Do you know the vegetable game? It's great fun. It goes something like this... Aubergine make carrot sure parsnip you radish learn beetroot everything sweetcorn on turnip this onion page. Hmm I remember it being funnier than that.

Data Verification and Validation

These pages are for AQA Unit 1 and OCR Unit 1.

Validation and verification are long words for very easy ideas, so don't be scared off. It's not as if you're being chased around your house by a seven foot big-toothed slobbering monster with bad breath now is it? No. It's not. It's just ICT.

Data Always Needs To Be **Verified And Validated**

A problem with computer systems is that it's very easy to put incorrect data into them. Data **needs to be checked**.

VALIDATION means CHECKING THE DATA ENTERED IS REASONABLE
VERIFICATION means CHECKING THE FINAL DATA ENTRY MATCHES THE DATA CAPTURED

Incorrect Data Can Enter the System **at Different Stages**

1 At **Data Capture** Stage

Errors are unlikely to enter the system if the data is entered automatically, e.g. barcodes. However the following errors could occur when data is captured manually, e.g. from forms:

- The form could be filled in wrongly.
- A form could get lost before the data has been entered.
- A form could be illegible, e.g. damaged, messy handwriting etc.

An old-fashioned approach to capturing data.

2 At **Transcription** Stage

- When the data is keyed in (transcribed), human error can cause mistakes e.g. misreading a name, adding too many zeroes to a price etc.
- A form could be entered twice by mistake.

3 At **Transmission** Stage

- When data is sent down a transmission medium, e.g. a telephone line, it can become corrupted.

4 At **Processing** Stage

- Problems with hardware or software might lead to data being corrupted.

There Are **Five Different Types of Data**

1) **Integer numbers** store positive and negative whole numbers, such as –1, 0, 23 or 48.
2) **Real numbers** store numbers with decimals like 8.23 and -12.351.
3) **Strings** are blocks of text. They're useful for data that it **isn't helpful to turn into numbers**, such as addresses.
4) **Booleans** can only store one of **two values** — either '**true**' or '**false**'. So they're used to store things like whether a customer has agreed to be on a certain mailing list.
5) **Date/Time structures** store the data and time in a standard way that allows the computer to **compare** different dates and times.

Different **Validation Checks** Test For **Different Things**

We can use computers to check data with a variety of different validation checks:

1) **Presence check**: this makes sure that important information has been entered. For example, a contacts database might require a full postal address. If the postcode field is empty, the software will ask for it to be filled in.
2) **Range check**: this checks that the data is within a specified range. For example, a date of birth entered as 13/13/2000 is impossible. The software will ask for the month to be re-entered.
3) **Type check**: this checks to see whether the data that was entered is the right type, e.g. the software won't accept a number with a decimal point in a field that is meant to take an integer.
4) **Length check:** this makes sure that entered data is the right length. For example, a phone number area code that is only three digits long is invalid.

Data Verification and Validation

Sometimes **More Sophisticated Checks** Are Used

1) **Lookup Tables**
The program checks whether entered values match one of a set of pre-defined inputs. Sometimes the user is restricted to the pre-defined inputs using a drop-down list.

	A	B	C	D
1	**First Name**	**Surname**	**Age group**	**Addres**
2	Megan	Gibbs	15 to 17	
3	Peter	Sweatman		
4	Malcolm	Bristow	12 and under	
5	Lucy	Hughes	13 and 14	
6			15 to 17	
7				

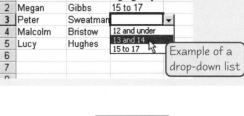

Example of a drop-down list

2) **Picture/Format Checks**
Data is rejected if it doesn't "look like" it's meant to. For example, if the computer expects a date in the format DD/MM/YYYY then it might reject an attempt to enter 12/031/997.

3) **Check digit**
This checks that numerical data has been entered accurately. The final digit of a number is determined by a formula using all the previous digits. For example, when a barcode is scanned, the software will reject the data if the check digit it calculates is different from the check digit it reads.

Check digit

Verification Means **Checking For Accurate Input**

Data verification checks to see whether **the data which has been input** is the same as **the original**.

1) **Proofreading** is when input is verified by comparing the data in a system with the original — a human goes through the entered data and reads it, comparing it to the original. Data that doesn't match up is re-entered.

2) **Double entry** is when data is entered twice by two different people. The computer compares the two versions and highlights any differences between them, showing where the errors are.

Even **After** Validation and Verification, You **Can't Be 100% Sure**

Problems with validation:

- Error trapping is only as good as the software designed to trap the errors.
- Validation only makes sure the data is reasonable, not that it is correct.

Problems with verification:

- Both double entry and proofreading are time consuming and expensive.
- Verification only makes sure that the data entered matches that in the input form, not that it is correct.
- Human error is still possible.

Practice Questions

Q1 Explain the difference between data validation and data verification.

Q2 Explain how a check digit works.

Q3 Describe how three data validation checks work.

Exam Question

Q1 An electricity supply company needs to arrange for householders' meters to be read regularly. Meter readers visit each house and record the current meter reading for each account on a paper data capture document. At the end of the day all the data is directly captured by the computer system to avoid transcription errors.

a) State two items of data that should be printed on the data capture document before it is given to the meter reader. (2 marks)

b) Describe two validation checks that should be performed when the data is captured by the computer system. (4 marks)

c) How is it still possible for incorrect data to be stored in the computer system? (2 marks)

I want the TRUTH but I can't handle it — because it's not an object...

I had an awful lot of fun on this page, didn't you? I know data validation and verification might seem a bit confusing at first, but it's only cos they both start with "v". Validation checks make sure the data is of the correct type, range and that type of thing. Verification is about checking the data is actually correct and uses methods like proofreading and double entry.

Normalisation

These pages are for OCR Unit 1 only.

This is where it gets a mite tricky. ***Skip these two pages if you're taking AQA.***

Normalisation Breaks Down Tables into the **Smallest** Possible Units

Normalisation is completed during the **design stage** of a relational database.

1) It creates a **logical structure** of related tables and helps to create a flexible, efficient and easy-to-query database.
2) Normalisation ensures **data consistency** and **integrity** and gets rid of repeated data (**data redundancy**).
3) Normalisation is a **staged** process consisting of first (**1NF**), second (**2NF**) and third (**3NF**) normal form.

You've got to know the **rules of normalisation** and be able to identify and explain which normal form data is in.

Before a table gets to 1NF, it is in **unnormalised** form — **0NF**.

A table is in **1NF** if:
- every data value in a field is **atomic** — i.e. the data cannot be broken down any further.
- there is a **primary key**.
- there are no **repeating fields** within a table.

A table is in **2NF** if:
- the table follows the rules of **1NF**.
- each table has a **single** primary or composite key.
- there are no **partial key dependencies** — every non-key field must be directly related to the whole primary key (see below for an example).

A table is in **3NF** if:
- the table is in **2NF** (and therefore 1NF)
- there are no **non-key** field **dependencies** — there should be no non-key fields dependent upon any other non-key fields (see below for an example).

Note — you only get partial key dependencies if the table uses a composite key.

Here's an **Example**

Each student in a school takes 3 AS level courses. The database is structured like this:

STUDENT (StudentID, Forename, Surname, AS_ID, AS_Title, TeacherID, Teacher_Name, AS_ID, AS_Title, TeacherID, Teacher_Name, AS_ID, AS_Title, TeacherID, Teacher_Name)

Before → After

This is not in 1NF form because there are **repeating fields** — AS_ID, AS_Title, Teacher_Name and TeacherID are all repeated 3 times.

1NF
STUDENT (StudentID, Forename, Surname, AS_ID)
COURSE (AS_ID, AS_Title, TeacherID, Teacher_Name)

There are no repeating fields or groups of fields, so it's in 1NF form now. Each student will have 3 records, 1 for each AS they are taking.

The fields StudentID and AS_ID form a composite primary key for the STUDENT table — each record can be uniquely identified from these two fields combined.

But there are partial key dependencies — forename and surname are dependent on the StudentID field but are not uniquely linked to AS_ID. So they're only dependent on part of the primary key (which is StudentID and AS_ID combined, remember).

2NF
STUDENT (StudentID, Forename, Surname)
COURSE (AS_ID, AS_Title, TeacherID, Teacher_Name)
ENROLLED (StudentID, AS_ID)

The tables are now in 2NF as there are no partial key dependencies. But there is still a non-key dependency as the Teacher_Name field is dependent upon TeacherID (which is "non-key") rather than AS_ID.

3NF
STUDENT (StudentID, Forename, Surname)
COURSE (AS_ID, AS_Title, TeacherID)
ENROLLED (StudentID, AS_ID)
TEACHER (TeacherID, Teacher_Name)

The tables are now in 3NF and provide a logical basis for the database structure.

The database structure can be shown as:

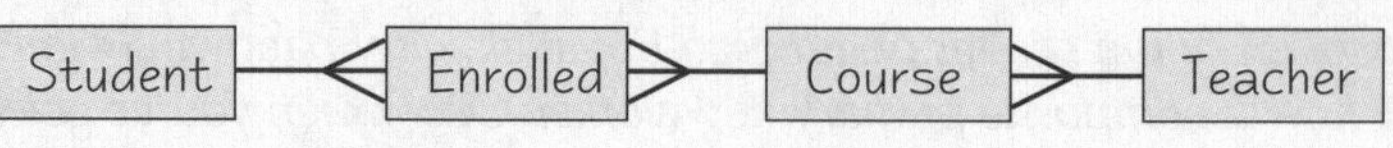

Data Dictionaries

A Data Dictionary Holds Data about a Database

All databases have associated data dictionaries. They're either produced **manually** by the database developer or developed by the database software **automatically** when the database has been created.

1) The main purpose of data dictionaries is to ensure **consistent data usage** within a relational database.
2) If the database needs to be **modified** then the data dictionaries will give all the details about each table and field.
3) Each table contained within the database will have an **associated data dictionary**, so a 3 table relational database would have 3 data dictionaries.

The basic **components** of a data dictionary are:

- **table name** — a unique name for each table in the database.
- **table security** — who has access to write, update, edit or delete values to or from the table.
- **keys** — primary keys are identified.
- **relationships** — the relationships between the tables are identified — one-to-many etc.
- **field name** — each field is identified.
- **field data type** — the data type given to each field — text/string/date/Boolean etc.
- **field length** — the number of characters allocated for the contents of the field.
- **field default value** — if a field has a default value that automatically appears on the creation of a new record.
- **field validation** — any validation applied to the field, i.e. drop down lists, look-ups, presence checks.
- **indexes** — any field that is indexed.

Each data dictionary would give **specific details** about the fields held within the table.
The data dictionary can also be used to identify **different names** used for the **same pieces of data**.

Practice Questions

Q1 Why should a database be in 3NF?

Q2 What are the rules of 2NF?

Q3 Give three items that would be found in a data dictionary that relate to tables.

Q4 Give three items that would be found in a data dictionary that relate to fields.

Exam Questions

Q1 A data dictionary holds information about the data held in a database. Give five items of information that could be held about data in a data dictionary.
(5 marks)

Q2 Explain why the table shown is not normalised.
(4 marks)

Customer Name	Customer Address	Regular Order
Henry Stuart	Fugg House Dog Lane Catshire CT4 4LG	3 pints milk 2 pots cream 5 pints orange juice
George Spencer	The Old House Moggie Court Catshire CT4 3FK	1 pint milk 1 pot cream 3 pints orange juice

Normalisation — it's not big and it's not clever...

Normalisation really is a stinker of a topic. But stick with it and you'll get the hang of it in the end. Make sure you understand how a composite primary key works. Only when you've got that figured will you be able to understand partial key dependencies. And don't forget the reasons for doing it in the first place — you could easily get asked that in an exam.

More Uses of Applications Software

These pages are for AQA Unit 1 and OCR Unit 1.

One more page on applications software, this time looking at some common applications for more specific purposes. Try to keep awake at the back, I know it's been a long day.

Stock Control Systems Control Stock

1) **Stock control systems** are used by companies such as supermarkets and shops to **keep track of their products**.
2) They keep a count of **how many** of each product is **in stock**. When new stock is **delivered** workers scan a barcode on the packaging and the computer **automatically increases stock levels**. When stock is **sold**, a signal is sent from the till to the main computer and the computer **automatically decreases stock levels**.
3) If stock falls **below a certain level** then the computer can automatically **order more** from the manufacturer, provided it is shown how to contact the manufacturers itself.
4) Some systems also keep track of **patterns in demand**. For example, they might deliberately start ordering **more products** in the run-up to **Christmas**.

Route Finding Software... Finds Routes

1) **Route finding software** is used to plan **how to get from one place to another**.
2) Lots of big companies, including **Microsoft**® and **Google**™, offer access to route planning software for free via the Internet.
3) It's also installed directly onto things like **in-car satellite navigation devices** — which also include fancy satellite tracking technology to work out exactly **where you are** on the map and show you live updates on your progress.

Route planning software needs...

1) **maps** of everywhere that you might want to drive through.
2) **an index of postcodes** so that you can easily describe where you want to start and go to.
3) records about approximately **how long it takes to drive along each road**, allowing for average congestion, road surface quality and so on, so it can work out the **fastest route**.
4) to **stop calling me** at all hours, telling me how lonely it feels now. **I've moved on**.

Booking Systems, Ummm...

1) **Booking systems** are used for **booking stuff**. Like travel tickets, theatre tickets, health appointments, etc, etc.
2) So booking systems need to maintain a **database of availability**, e.g. a list of which seats are available for which films, and to **update it** based on what users book.
3) They also often do nice comforting things like send out **confirmation e-mails** and some can even send you **text reminders** about the thing you've booked so that you don't forget to go to it.
4) Many booking systems include some sort of **secure payment area**, so that people can pay for the things they're trying to book.

Online Training Could Help if you Can't Work Out What Booking Systems do

1) **Online training systems** do things like offer **training over the Internet** (or an intranet).
2) So, for example, a college or university might offer a chance to **learn from home** using the web. Each user is given a **unique username and password**, and they can then login to the system.
3) When they login they might get a **list of the courses they are taking**, the latest **lecture slides** available for those courses, details of any **assessments** they've been set and any **deadlines** that are pending, and a **history of their marks** for previous assessments. Some even include **online assessments** to that students can test themselves.
4) The software **automatically updates** all of these details by tracking the actions of students and allowing people giving courses to add new material, such as new lecture notes or new online assessments.

More Uses of Applications Software

Companies use **Customer Record Systems**

1) **Customer Record Systems** help businesses to **keep track of their customers**, including their **contact information**, details of **what they've ordered**, whether they've been **invoiced** for it yet, whether they've **paid** for it yet and whether it's been **dispatched** to them.
2) Customer Record Systems have to comply with the provisions of the **Data Protection Act 1998**. That makes a lot of companies more willing to buy outside software, since it's already guaranteed to work in a way that allows the company to **comply with the law**.

Online Banking Saves You a Trip to the Bank

1) **Online Banking** is a bit like a **Customer Record System** used by a bank, but customers are given access as well.
2) When you log onto your bank's website, you can do things like **check the balances on your accounts**, **move money from one account to another**, **pay bills**, **order statements** and all the other things you'd usually do at a bank.
3) So an online banking application has to **keep track of lots of different accounts at once**, know how to **talk to the banking applications at other banks**, be extra careful to make sure that it doesn't do anything silly like take money from one account and then forget to put it in another and be **secure** enough to make sure that nobody can take control of anybody else's accounts.

Schools use **Administration Software**

School administration software does three important things.

1) It holds a database that links each student's **Unique Pupil Number** (**UPN**) to their personal details, including things like their **address** and who to contact in case of **emergency**. A student's UPN is kept with them throughout their academic career.
2) It records the **marks** students have received for exams. Most school administration software can **automatically prepare reports** based on a student's results, for sending to parents or just to monitor a student's progress.
3) It can monitor the **attendance** of individual students. Results can be used to build attendance statistics for the entire school and to pursue students that often have unexplained absences.

Practice Questions

Q1 Briefly describe how online training works.

Q2 Describe the two different methods that can be used to access a route-finding system.

Q3 Explain the main features of booking systems.

Q4 Give three things that you can do with online banking.

Exam Questions

Q1 Describe four things that a Stock Control System might do. (4 marks)

Q2 Describe the characteristics of a software-based route-finding system. (8 marks)

Q3 Explain three features commonly found in school administration software. (6 marks)

Application software usually does exactly what the name says...

Cover the page and see if you can remember what each of the following types of application software does: stock control systems, route finding software, booking systems, online training, customer record systems, online banking, and school administration software. Then keep the page covered and see if you can remember how each of them does it. Then relax.

Analysis — Problem Identification

This section is based around the AQA unit 1 "Practical Problem Solving in the Digital World". If you're doing OCR, you should find it helpful for unit 2 "Structured ICT tasks".

This section covers the systems life cycle — the analysis, design and implemention of an ICT solution to a problem.

Find a **Good Problem** to Solve

Some situations are suitable for ICT solutions and some aren't. Pick a situation which **needs improving** — if it's already working well then you won't have anything to talk about. Here are some examples of **suitable situations**:

- **boring** or **repetitive** tasks
- jobs which have to be done **quickly**
- jobs where **data** needs to be **better organised**
- jobs that need **more security**, e.g. passwords
- jobs where there is a **shortage of labour**
- jobs where **more information is needed** in order to **make decisions**
- jobs where there needs to be **better presentation**, e.g. a newsletter, not a dog
- jobs that need to be **accessed remotely**

You Should Pick **Task-Related Projects**

1) A **task related project** is related to **one specific problem** — it's not meant to be about an entire system.
2) Don't **invent** the problem — it's much better to solve a problem with a **real client** and **real end users**.
3) The **client** is the person / company that you're producing the solution for.
4) The **end users** are the people who will actually be **using** the new system on a regular basis, e.g. to change or update the content.
5) For some solutions, such as presentations or web pages, you might have an **audience** as well as an end user. The audience are people who just **view the content**, e.g. a presentation, without actually changing the data.

Example Problem — Penny Bridge Cricket Club

Penny Bridge village has a thriving cricket club with over 100 members. It has a new pavilion and an attached social club. It has three teams, including a junior one, which each play 20 games a year. Fixtures are played all over South Cumbria.

You could base a project on this cricket club because:

- the events that require organisation are **mainly repetitive**,
- they need to be done **speedily**,
- they require a **professional output** that is easily produced using ICT.

Penny Bridge Cricket Club

Look at the scenario and see if this fits into any of the three strands — data handling, presentation or multimedia. The table below shows possible uses of databases and spreadsheets that you could use to solve this problem.

Strand	Application	Possible uses
Data handling	Database	Database of members Database of fixtures and teams
	Spreadsheet	Members subs payments League tables and statistics
Presentation		Website for cricket club An electronic photo album of the last match The cricket club blog
Multimedia		A set of podcasts for the cricket club, giving a commentary and video of the matches. A rolling multimedia presentation for the club.

Analysis — Problem Identification

Once You've Chosen, You Need To **Start Researching**

Here are the main research tasks you'll need to carry out for the business / end user you've chosen:

1) **Collecting documentation** used by the business — invoices, bills, price lists, photographs.
   - How were they produced?
   - Do they need updating?
   - Could their use be automated?

   You can get lots of points by including **relevant** examples of real documentation you've thought about.

2) Carrying out a **structured interview**.
   - Produce the questions beforehand and check them with your ICT tutor.
   - Make sure the questions are not all "closed" questions (i.e. questions that can only be answered by one word answers). You need the end user to tell you what their requirements are.

3) **Using questionnaires.**
   - Produce questionnaires for other end users that you will not be interviewing, e.g. cricket team members, or other employees if using a small company as your end user.
   - Think how you can prompt and focus useful responses.

4) **Observing the processes** undertaken by end users. This is rarely done or documented in projects, so doing so is likely to get you a few extra marks.
   - Arrange to visit your end user and sit back and observe the various stages and processes that the task you are studying involves.
   - For example, how does the cricket club secretary manage the subs, mail merging, team selection sheets, keeping the league table up to date?

5) **Researching similar businesses / situations** to see what similarities there are and what ideas they have to offer.
   - Use the Yellow Pages™ or Internet search engines to find similar firms or organisations.
   - Thompson's Local Directory or trade journals at the local library are other good sources.

Now you have carried out the research you should have a great deal of information which you will need to sift through. At the end of the sifting you should have everything you need to proceed. Break the task into small chunks and then solve each of these chunks separately.

You are now ready to produce the **problem identification**. This is a description of the problem that you are going to solve; it identifies who the client is (the person you are producing it for), who will use the solution, what the users' ICT skills are, and any further intended audience.

Ted identified his problem as lack of motivation.

Practice Questions

Q1 List five examples of suitable situations for an ICT solution.

Q2 Explain what a task-related project is.

Q3 Explain the difference between a client, user and audience.

Q4 List the five main tasks to carry out when researching a project.

Q5 Do you like cricket? Do you love it? Do you, Sir? How much?

Houston, we have a problem. Your records just aren't selling anymore...

I remember Whitney in her glory 80s days. Especially her massive barnet in the "I Wanna Dance with Somebody" video. That was a thing of true beauty. Classic tracks too, "saving all my love for you", "how will I know", "I'm your baby tonight". Don't know how I got onto Whitney, but that's not important right now. You just need to learn all the stuff on this page.

Analysis — Client's Requirements

These pages are for AQA Unit 1.

OK, so you've done lots of research and know all about how the business works. Now you need to pull all of this together and work out exactly what you need to do. Cheer up, it's not that bad. This page has fat squirrels, so how bad can it be...

You Need to Know What the **Client** Wants

As part of the analysis stage, you need to:

1) Identify the **client** — the person / company needing the ICT solution.
2) Identify the **users** — the people who'll use the ICT system, and describe their current skills.
3) Describe the **problem** and **client requirements** — what they want to achieve with the new system.
4) Explain what **your solution** is going to do.
5) Compare what **you can produce** to the client's requirements.

You Need to Identify Clear **Aims and Objectives**

1) **Aims** are **general** points, while **objectives** are **specific** ones. Your **objectives** should explain **how** you intend to **achieve your aims**.

> Example **Aim:** to increase the number of people attending Penny Bridge Cricket Club.
> **Objective:** to make the fixtures available 24/7 on the Internet so the number of spectators will increase.

2) Objectives can be **quantitative** or **qualitative**. **Quantitative** means they are objective, and therefore can be easily measured. **Qualitative** means they are subjective — i.e. open to personal opinion and not easily measurable. **Quantitative** objectives are best.
3) Remember to **number your objectives** so that you can track them through the project and refer to them easily.

Examples of objectives for a web design project:

1) To ensure the Home Page downloads within 10 seconds (quantitative).
2) To ensure that navigation is intuitive and consistent (qualitative).
3) To ensure that the pages can be read in the 4 most commonly used browsers (quantitative).
4) To ensure that forms submit all their contents in full (quantitative).

Indicators Help You **Measure Your Success**

Performance indicators say how you're going to fulfil the performance criteria — so they tell you if your objectives have been met. Here are some examples to match the website objectives above:

1) The Home Page should be no more than 200 Kilobytes in size with graphics which are in a compressed format such as gifs or jpegs.
2) Navigation buttons on each page must be in the same area of the page. Buttons must be consistent in shape, have consistent lettering and have consistent actions.
3) The pages must be correctly coded with opening and closing tabs for each element. They are then viewed in four browsers, Internet Explorer®, Netscape®, Mozilla Firefox® and Safari to check that they can be read properly.
4) Data input into forms should reach the intended recipient in the expected format. I shall input some names and addresses into the form then post it to myself in order to check the truth of the contents.

Analysis — Inputs, Processes and Outputs

You Need to List Your Inputs, Processes and Outputs

1) The next step is to work out the inputs, processes and outputs you need to **match** the client's requirements.
2) You need to identify what your solution **needs to do** (processes), what **data is needed** to do it (input) and what **comes out** at the end (output). If you don't understand this, you won't be able to produce a good solution.
3) You should **list** your inputs, processes and outputs and then **explain them** in greater detail.

The table below shows the inputs, processes and outputs to match two client requirements.

Client Requirement	Input	Process	Output
List of all the players for a cricket match.	Date of match. Level of match, e.g. seniors	Search database using info about date and level.	Header stating date of match and opposition team. Tabulated list of players sorted by playing position, containing the following details: Playing position, first name, surname, contact telephone no.
Podcast of weekend cricket match with photos and voice commentary and interviews.	Voice input for the commentary and interviews. Digital photographs.	Record audio tracks and take photos. Import audio and images. Edit data using suitable software to create a finished media file. Convert file to mp4 format. Upload file to website as a podcast.	Completed podcast of weekend's match available for download on website.

Processes — what Actually Happens to the Data

Processes tends to be the hardest of the three to get your head round.
These tables show you the kind of processes you can expect for different types of software...

Type of software	Example Process
Database	Sorting Searching Calculations Merging text and data
DTP	Manipulating the text or graphics Formatting text
Web pages	Linking pages to other pages Formatting text

Type of software	Example process
Spreadsheet	Sorting Searching Calculations
Presentation	Linking pages Manipulating the slides Formatting text
Podcasting	Editing the audio / video Converting file formats e.g. to mp3 / mp4 Uploading file to website as a podcast

Practice Questions

Q1 List five things to mention during the analysis stage.

Q2 What's the difference between aims, objectives and performance indicators?

Q3 What's the difference between quantitative and qualitative objectives?

Q4 Give two examples of processes you might do with each of the following:
a) databases b) DTP c) web pages d) spreadsheets e) presentations f) podcasts.

What a lovely, lovely page... shame about the fat squirrel... *(It's actually a groundhog)*

Wow, this is the real thing, isn't it? I have to admit, I was a bit worried that this section was going to be a bit dull. But nothing of the sort — this is the real stuff. This is where it's at. I'm really feeling this ICT vibe, and I think you are too. This is all hugely important stuff by the way. If you don't set clear objectives at the start, you'll get lost later on.

Design — Data Capture and Validation

These pages are for AQA Unit 1 and OCR Unit 2.

As part of the design process you need to think about how to get the data you want onto the system and how to stop errors creeping in at the input stage. That's what these two lovely pages are all about.

Decide how to **Capture** your Data

1) The methods of data capture you use will depend on your **solution**.
2) The most obvious method is to use an **electronic data capture form**, so that the user can **manually** type in the data. You'd probably use this for a spreadsheet or database solution, for example.
3) For other solutions, you might need to input **video** or **audio** data into your system, e.g. for an electronic photo album or to create podcasts.
4) To input video data, you might use a digital camera or camcorder to capture the video. You could then **input** it onto the system by connecting the device to the computer, e.g. with a USB cable or Bluetooth connection, and using suitable software to **transfer** the data.
5) To select the most **appropriate** method of data capture you need to think about:

Look — it's a dog in funny glasses pretending to use a camera! We're having fun, aren't we.

- **speed** of input and processing required
- **quantity** of data being processed
- **ease** of entry and processing
- **environmental conditions** under which the entry and processing takes place

You need to produce **Designs** for all your **Data Entry**

You need to **think carefully** about the design of your entry forms and screens, spreadsheet worksheets, web pages and any paper-based documentation for data collection.

Five Tips for Producing Great Designs

1) Your designs should be detailed enough for **another person** to pick them up and create the solution that you were going to produce.
2) Designs are not static things, they will probably **change** when the solution is being developed. This is fine — just include the **changes** with your original designs and explain the reasons for them.
3) Keep **checking** your designs as you go along to make sure you're producing what you intended to do.
4) **Presentation** of the design is important — it needs to be neat and easy to follow.
5) Designs should be produced on paper or word processing software, **not** on the software application you're going to do your solution on.

Penny Bridge Cricket Club
League Table Recording System
Please enter the result from the last match

Opponents [ ]

Home or Away Match [ ]

Details of match

Penny Bridge: Runs [ ] Wickets [ ] Overs [ ]
Opponents: Runs [ ] Wickets [ ] Overs [ ]

Date of match dd/mm/yyyy [ ]/[ ]/[ ]

Design of a data screen for Penny Bridge Cricket Club.

And here's a bonus 6th tip for good luck...

6) The **user interfaces** you design and implement need to be appropriate for the **client** — don't have lots of features that'll confuse them or use language they won't understand.

Design — Data Capture and Validation

You'll have to set up *Validation Checks* for Data Entry

Validation makes sure that the data entered is **reasonable**. But — it doesn't check whether it is correct.

Spreadsheet validation methods:

Validation of spreadsheets involves checking data as it is input into individual cells.

Validation	Explanation
Text length	Only accepts text up to a set max. no. of characters.
Whole number	Only accepts whole numbers within a given range.
Decimal	Only accepts decimal numbers within a given range.
List	Restricts input to a list which the user selects from.
LookUp	"Looks up" values from a data table in the spreadsheet.

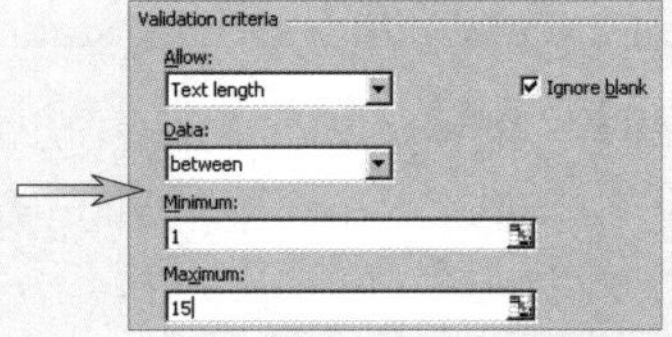

Setting up data validation in a spreadsheet — this will only accept text of up to 15 characters.

Database validation methods:

Database validation should be at table and form level, e.g. your forms can have check boxes, drop downs and "combo boxes", offering limited choices and ensuring the input of reasonable data.

Validation	Explanation
Presence check	Checks data has been entered when it is required e.g. date of birth or credit card expiry date.
Format check	Data entered must fit a preset format such as class being named after its teacher using a three character code.
Range check	Checks data entered is within a range e.g. "date of birth" is between 1986 and 1991.
Look up check	Data is checked against an acceptable list of values.
Check digit	An extra digit on a data code, e.g. ISBN number. The data code is checked on input by performing a standard calculation which should give the check digit.

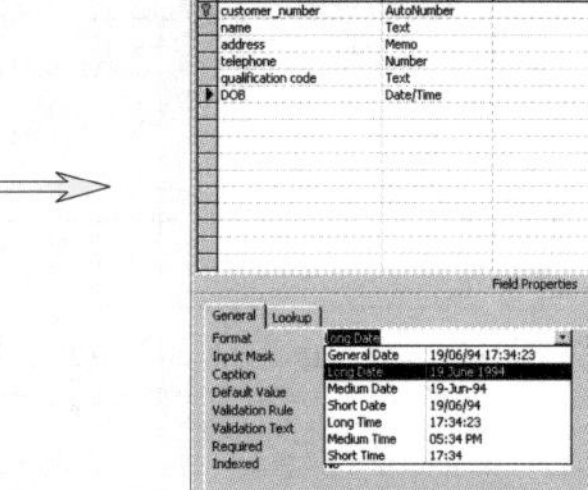

The format property controls how fields are displayed. In this example, DOB is formatted to "long date".

Web page validation methods:

If you do a web project you'll need to include some data submission forms. Here are the main validation checks you'd use on these...

Validation	Explanation
Presence check	Checks that all required fields have data entered.
Format check	Checks the correct type of data is input into a field.
Drop down lists	Restricts the user to choosing from a list of preset choices, e.g. Title (Mr/Mrs/Ms) or Gender (M/F).

Error message generated when a required field is blank.

DTP program validation methods:

It's hard to validate data in a DTP package, because they're more concerned with manipulating things you bring into them, e.g. graphics. So you'll have to work on validating things in other applications before importing them in.

Practice Questions

Q1 Name three different ways of capturing data that you could use.

Q2 Name three things that will affect which means of data capture you choose for your project.

Q3 Give three specific examples of validation for: a) spreadsheets b) databases c) web pages.

What do you call a dog with a camera? Sparky...

That's what I called my dog anyway. Doesn't have much to do with cameras, so not much of a punchline, really. Oh well, this is AS ICT, not AS Hilarious Gags. It's not meant to be fun. Besides, I can't be funny all the time. Just get off my case, alright? Anyway, it's not just input screens that you need to do designs for, you need designs for processes and outputs too...

Design — Hardware and Software

These pages are for AQA Unit 1 and are a useful reference for OCR Unit 2.
As part of the design process, you need to think about what software and hardware you're going to use. I'm sure you know the difference by now, but just in case — hardware is the bits that are tough and leathery, software is the squishy bits.

Give **Details** About The **Hardware**

This part of the design should be **more** than just a list of hardware — lots of detail is needed with **reasons** to explain the hardware choices. Here are the main things to think about...

1) **computer specifications** — laptop or desktop, processor make and speed, memory available.
2) **the screen** — size, resolution and quality (the larger the screen, the better for DTP solutions).
3) **printers** — type, quality of print and paper, the size of paper they can print to (A3 might be useful with spreadsheets), whether they support colour or not, printable area, and the cost of cartridges, special papers and labels.
4) **other peripherals** — including scanners, digital cameras, CD-ROMs, CD-rewriters, DVD players and writers, speakers and plotters.

The table below shows you the kind of things to consider for each hardware element.

Hardware Element	**Example**	**Comment**
Processor type and speed	E.g. Intel® Core™ 2 Duo , 2.4 Gigahertz	Most modern computers will happily run any generic software package, but some applications can still slow the computer down if you don't have a fast enough processor, e.g. graphics / multimedia programs, large databases.
RAM available	2 Gb	The more RAM the better, especially for multimedia.
Monitor/VDU	22" TFT LCD flat screen	Again, the larger the better (and pricier). With a DTP project a screen that can show an A4 sheet in full is best. Other things to think about include what resolution it can display and standard versus widescreen.
Printer	Laser or inkjet, black and white or colour	Lasers give better quality but can be expensive. Inkjets are cheap to buy but expensive to maintain. Also consider the cost of special papers to print colour photos from an inkjet.
Scanner	Most scan up to 1200×2400 dots per inch and can scan in 48 bit colour	Resolution, colour depth and speed are important.
Digital camera	7 Megapixels, 3× optical zoom, high quality video capture	Factors to consider include size, resolution, lens quality, zoom capabilities, quality of video and audio capture.
Mouse, Keyboard	Wired, wireless	A wireless keyboard and mouse increases flexibility, but may need to be plugged in frequently for charging.
Backup device	Tape streamer, DVD writer	Tape streamers are more expensive and less flexible, but individual tapes are cheaper and more reliable.

Make **Full** And **Effective Use** Of Your **Software**

1) As well as describing the major applications packages you are going to use, you should also describe **other packages** you might use to solve the problem.

   For example — in a website based project you might use a WYSIWYG editor like Dreamweaver®, but you'd probably also use an HTML editor, like Arachnophilia or Notepad, scanning software, a photo editor (such as Photoshop), a word-processor, several Internet browsers and, of course, Operating System software. In this case, you'd need to give full details of all the additional bits of software you're using.

2) You also need to think about the **constraints** imposed by having different versions of the same program running on different machines, e.g. MS Access™ 2002/XP at school, MS Access™ 2003 at the end user and MS Access™ 2007 at home. There's more about this on the next page...
3) Where a database seems to be the only solution, you should discuss the pros and cons of using **different database packages**, e.g. you could compare the key features of MS Access with those of Filemaker® Pro.

Design — Hardware and Software

*Example — **Constraints** On The **Hardware** and **Software***

Here is an example discussion of the **hardware constraints**:

1) This section deals with the **hardware** that I have at school and that owned by my client, Mr Jones, who is the secretary of the Swarkestone Tennis Club.
2) He uses a desktop computer with a 19″ flat screen monitor, which is a decent size. It shows more of the spreadsheet than a standard monitor, which cuts down on the amount of scrolling he has to do. As the spreadsheet is not viewed for long periods of time, a **screen filter** will not be necessary.
3) The desktop computer has a high specification and includes a hard disk that holds 500 gigabytes of data which is more than adequate. It has an **Intel® 2 Core™ Duo processor and 2 GB of RAM** which is enough to run the spreadsheet and other applications he might need to use. The computer is also equipped with a CD/DVD drive which is useful for backing up and externally storing files. Mr Jones also has an A3 inkjet colour printer which is great for printing out large spreadsheets. He has an **ADSL modem** and **Internet account** which allows him to link quickly to the Internet. This facility also allows him to easily transfer files amongst Tennis Club officials.
4) Mr Jones also owns a **laptop** which has 512Mb of RAM, an AMD Athlon processor and a 20Gb hard drive. This is sufficient to run a program such as Excel. The 17″ laptop screen is useful as it gives him a wide view of each worksheet. The main improvement he could make to his laptop would be to add a larger hard disk.
5) At school the equipment is rather old. Students use Intel® Celerons® made by Research Machines. These have slow processors (333 MHz) and have only 256Mb of RAM. The storage space allocated to my files is limited to 15Mb on the network so I have a constant battle keeping inside my space limits.

Introduce the subject.

Even though this screen filter is **not** being used, it's good to mention as it shows you're thinking about what is needed.

Good to give specific details like this.

Oh goody more detail.

Be sure to mention all available bits of hardware, even if he does most of his work on his desktop computer.

Don't forget to talk about your own hardware constraints, and not just the end user's.

Here is an example of how you could **discuss software constraints**:

1) The software available to Mr Jones both at home and on his laptop is Microsoft Excel®. Unfortunately they are different versions of Excel® and there is some incompatibility due to different macro languages being used. Mr Jones will have to be very careful that he saves his files in a format that allows him to transfer data easily.
2) His two machines run different operating systems; the laptop has Windows® XP and the desktop has Windows® Vista. The machines I am using at school run Windows NT® which causes problems as it doesn't support the latest versions of the Microsoft® Office suite.

Make sure you explain exactly what the problems are.

Don't forget that in the objectives section you'll have to say how you plan to overcome these problems.

Practice Questions

Q1 Name five common "peripherals".

Q2 What type of project benefits the most from having a large monitor?

Q3 What features are important in a scanner?

Q4 Describe the hardware and software you would need to produce a multimedia website project.

Q5 What problems might you have using different versions of the same software on several different machines?

My personal hardware is constrained by time, space, gravity and burgers...

To do a good job with this part of the design, you really need to understand what options are available for each type of hardware or software. Have a look on t'Internet to compare what's available, e.g. have a look at what digital cameras you can get now and how their specs and prices compare. Careful though, you're just looking, not buying, 'kay?

Design Advice

These pages are for AQA Unit 1 and are a useful reference for OCR Unit 2.

Ooh designs eh? Remember that designs don't automatically mean diagrams. You could use a spreadsheet, or a listy type thing, or a goat, or maybe a cow with brown spots and a big long tail instead. Huh. How did I get onto farms, suddenly?

The **Designs** must Explain how to **Implement** your Solution

Things you need designs for:
inputs, processes, outputs
testing
backup / security systems
validation (spreadsheet / databases / web pages)
user interface (help screens and user guide)

1) Whatever the project, your designs will show how you're going **to solve the problem**.
2) The designs need to be good enough for a **third party** to be able to pick them up and **implement** your solution.
3) This means you need to use a lot of **detail**, and you need to present it in a very **straightforward** way.
4) Remember — designs are **not static**.
   As you create your solution, they will **change** — this shows that you're thinking about how well the system is working and trying to improve it.
   Changes may be needed as a result of **testing** the system, or in response to **feedback** from your client.
   Your final design should include the original design, plus all the changes that have occurred.
5) Your designs should produce a system that is **easy to use**.

Your **Designs** Need To **Avoid Certain Things**

There are certain things you need to avoid like the plague when doing your designs:

- **a poor level of detail** — e.g. too little or no annotation.
- **poor presentation** — e.g. scruffy diagrams, diagrams in poor quality pen (use colouring pencils).
- **processes that aren't designed** — e.g. macros in spreadsheets, queries in databases, backup systems, password systems, form submissions in web design projects, the scanning and manipulation of graphics for DTP, presentation and web projects.
- **poor design of outputs** — e.g. database reports, mail-merged documents.
- **lots of pages of input designs** — e.g. spreadsheet forms or database tables and nothing else.
- designs produced **very obviously during the implementation stage** of the project.
- **not amending your designs** after making changes in the implementation section.

Make sure it's Suitable for the **Client and User**

1) Remember, there's a difference between the **user** and the **client**. The client is the person that **asked you** to produce the solution. The user is the person that actual uses the finished system.
2) Don't make your designs too **complicated** for the end user.

   Think carefully about how to make the designs user-friendly — e.g. navigation around database and spreadsheet forms and web pages, careful use of colour, consistency in the use of objects such as buttons on switchboards and other menus, etc.

3) Make sure you have catered for the client's **needs and abilities**.

   Use templates that the end user can amend as much as possible and make it clear where the data goes by a set of instructions on the template. In database projects, the end user should input the data into the tables through a clearly labelled form. With spreadsheets, you should provide the end user with forms to input data. With presentation projects you need to "shield" the end user from typing directly into a text frame. With website projects, don't expect the end user to update their web pages using HTML. If you are creating a blog then users must add data to clearly defined templates. If you are creating a podcast or a webcast the system must be very simple to use.

Design Advice

Example — Designing a **Spreadsheet**

The secretary of Penny Bridge Cricket Club wants a computerised system to produce tickets for each match. The admission prices are £10 per adult and £5 for juniors or senior citizens. Members get a 10% discount on the total ticket cost. A family ticket is £25 and consists of 2 adults and 3 juniors max.

- The **input** is the details about the persons on the ticket.
- The **process** is **calculating** the **total cost** of the ticket (by using **formulae** — see below.)
- The **output** is the printed ticket.

Here is an example spreadsheet design:

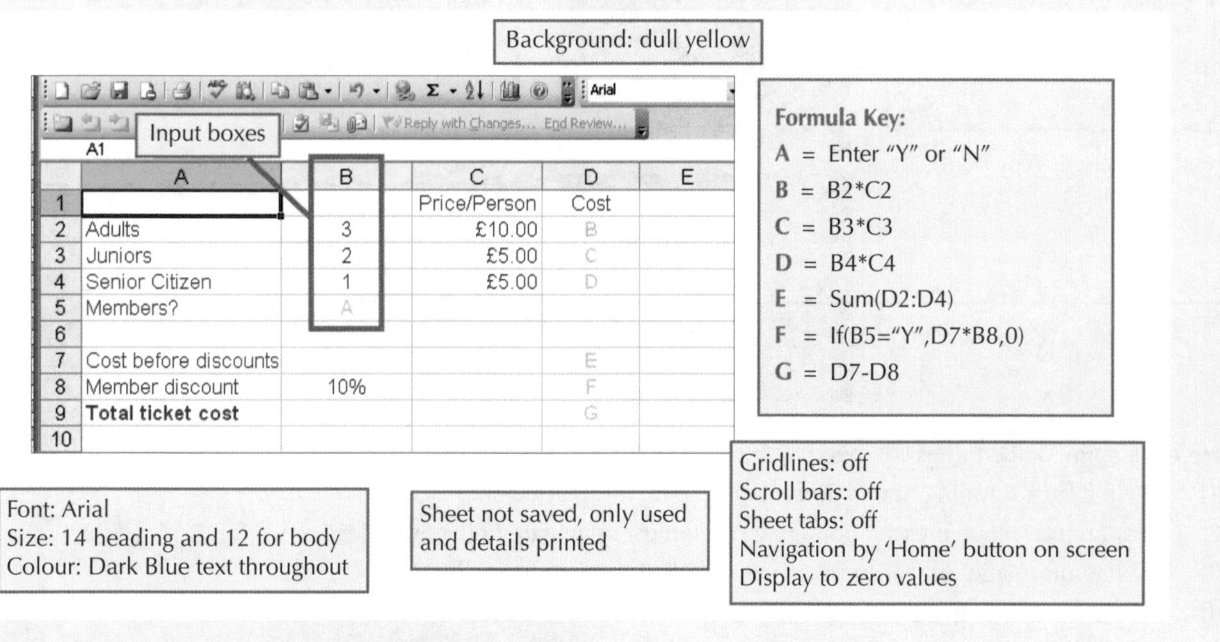

Remember to Include **Plenty of Details**

Remember that a design needs to give enough detail so that someone else could pick up your design and produce the same solution. Here are the details given in the spreadsheet design above:

1) **Markers**, i.e. the orange boxes — this makes the design uncluttered.
2) All the **formulae** to be used
3) **Labelling / naming** cells
4) **Example** data
5) Any **formatting** required
6) Highlight the cells for **inputting** data
7) Page **orientation** — landscape or portrait
8) **Saving** details — when to save, filename
9) Any **special features**

You also need to give details of any **macros** used. In the spreadsheet above, the "Home" button will use a macro to return to the main sheet. As part of the design, you should **list** all the **steps** of the macro (in simple English, not code).

Practice Questions

Q1 At what point in a project should you do your designs?

Q2 Name five general things you should avoid when creating your designs.

Q3 List eight details to include with the design of a spreadsheet.

What's brown and comes out of cows — the Isle of Wight ferry...

Hm. That joke doesn't really work on paper, does it? Because you'd need to write "Cowes" the place, not "cows" the beast. Also, someone's just told me the Isle of Wight ferry isn't brown. Oh well. Scratch that one up to experience I suppose. I didn't mean to compare the ferry to cow pats either. I'm sure it's very nice really. Sorry, Isle of Wight ferry.

Design Advice

These pages are for AQA Unit 1 and are a useful reference for OCR Unit 2.

Another two lovely pages of lovely design tips to help you with your own lovely ICT designing. Lovely...

Example — Designing a **Presentation**

Penny Bridge Cricket Club need a way to publicise their new social facilities.
Your client has decided to have this created using presentation software.

Here is a basic **slide layout** design for the presentation:

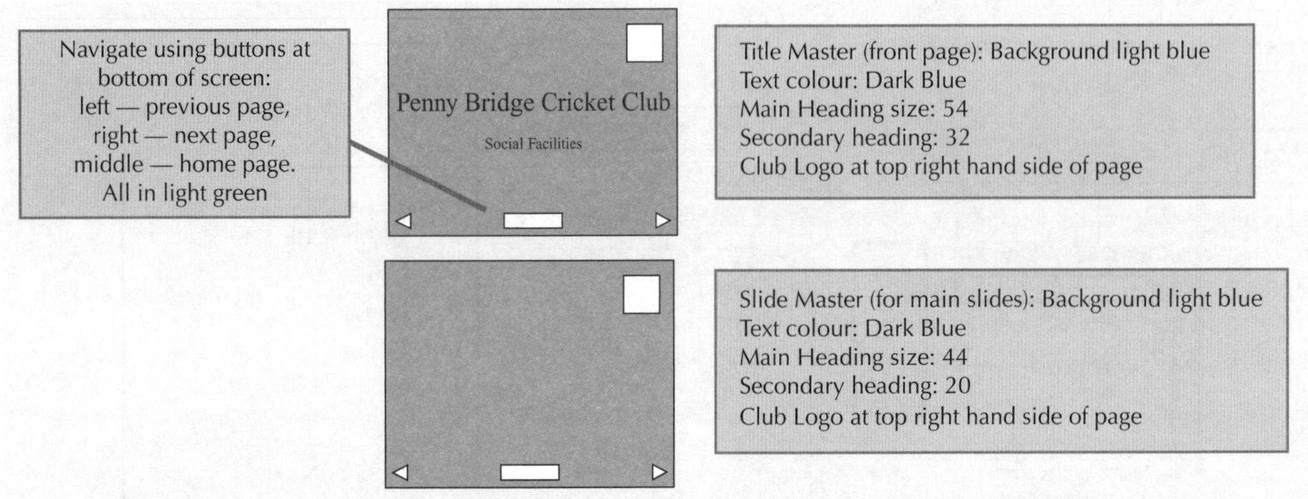

Here are some of the things you need to think about for a presentation design...

1) Will it be a scrolling, **timed** presentation or an **interactive** one?
2) For an interactive presentation, how will the user **navigate** between slides?
3) What information needs to be on every slide (for the **master slide**)?
4) What kind of **outputs** are required? Graphics / Audio / Video?
5) What kind of visual / transition **effects** would be appropriate?
6) How does the **client** insert, change or remove slides?

Example — **Database** Designs

1) For a database solution, you need to produce a nice grid like this for each table in the database.

Fieldname	Field Type	Field length	Example data	Validation
Last name	Text	15	Smith	
First name	Text	15	Jacob	
Age	Number		56	>120
Start date	Date	N/A	01/01/1996	>02/02/1992

2) For a relational database, you should produce a **diagram** to show how all the tables are **linked** together by **relationships**.
3) You'll need to identify:
   – the **primary keys**
   – the **foreign keys**
   – the **relationships** between tables.
4) The inputs, processes and outputs are fairly obvious for a database solution, but they all need designing...
   – **data entry forms** needs to be designed for data **input**.
   – **queries** and **sorts** need to be designed — these are the **processes**.
   – queries and sorts are used to produce **reports** — these will be the **outputs** from the system.

Design Advice

Tables are good for Describing Processes

It's not always so obvious how you're supposed to design some processes, e.g. manipulation of graphics for a web page. Listing the main steps involved is often a good way.

Here's an **example** of how you could design the processes of **scanning a photograph** and then **manipulating it**.

Process description	Scanning and preparing a photograph for a web page
Stage1	Select graphic and place on scanner
Stage2	Select area to be scanned
Stage3	Select output
Stage4	Save as jpg or GIF
Stage5	Import into Adobe Photoshop and adjust size
Stage6	Crop back to the area needed
Stage7	Resize image to x by x pixels
Stage8	etc.
Stage9	etc.

Web Projects — Blogs

Blogs are a fairly recent addition to ICT courses, but all the same principles apply — you've got to design something that matches the needs of the **client**.

A blog is a web page where new **entries** are added on a regular basis and are usually displayed in **chronological order**. They're useful for keeping **online diaries**, but they can and are used to cover virtually **any** topic.

Blogs can contain:

- **text** and **images**
- **audio files** or **movie clips**
- links to other **web pages** or **media**
- **interactive** elements, e.g. allowing users to **post messages** or **subscribe** to receive automatic updates.

You'll need to design a **layout template** for the blog, work out how your **client** will use it, e.g. how they'll add new entries, and consider any **other features** you might want it to have, e.g. message-posting facilities. Before you get stuck into your design, spend some time **blog surfing** on the web to get a feel for what works well and what doesn't.

Web Projects — Podcasts

A podcast is a collection of media files made available through a web page. Users can usually **subscribe** to a particular podcast, so that when a new file is added, their computer **automatically downloads** the update.

Here are some things you might want to cover in the design of a podcast:

- **layout** of the main web page.
- podcast **directory structure**.
- **content** (what's actually in them? Is this what the client wants?)
- **frequency** of updates, e.g. new one added every week?
- what the **client needs to do**, e.g. to add new files.
- details of **subscription** facilities.

See p.84 for more on blogs and podcasts.

Practice Questions

Q1 List five details to include on the slide layout design of a presentation.

Q2 Write down five questions you should consider when designing a presentation.

Q3 List four different elements that might need designing as part of a database project.

Q4 What is a blog? What would the design of a blog contain?

Q5 What is a podcast? What would you put in the design of a podcast?

OK OK, nuff about designs already...

Your designs don't need to be a work of art — they just need to be clear, neat and give lots of detail of how it will look and work. And remember, you need to be thinking about the client and users the whole time. Don't get those two mixed up. Anyway good sentiment expressed in large text at the top of this box. Bored of designs now, let's move on...

Implementation Advice

These pages are for AQA Unit 1 and are a useful reference for OCR Unit 2.

Implementation is where you actually make the system you've spent all this time designing — also known as the fun bit. But remember — you've got to document what you do, otherwise no one will believe you ever did it...

You Need Good Generic and Package-Specific Skills

You should be displaying a high level of **generic** and **package-specific** skills in your solution.

Generic Process Skills = general skills you can apply to almost any software package.
Package Specific Skills = skills needed to use the special features of a particular software package.

Here are some **generic process skills** you should be happy using:

- Efficient **navigation** of packages using **menus** and other relevant **features.**
- Showing you know how to use **help files** and **online tutorials** to use the program effectively.
- Effective use of **predefined elements** like templates, styles, glossaries, etc.
- Effective use of **macros** — macros found in libraries as well as ones you've produced yourself.
- Appreciation of the benefits of **OLE** (Object Linking and Embedding — allowing an object in one document to become part of another).
- Selection of **suitable formats** for the presentation of output.

Use Some Advanced Package-Specific Features

You need to use some **advanced features** of the software. Don't go crazy though — use them when they help, not just for the sake of it. Remember, the main thing is to produce something that meets the **needs of the client**.

Website Advanced Features

- Use of tables to position text and graphics.
- Ability to alter HTML code.
- Use of CSS — cascaded style sheets.
- Use of Metatags (keywords and descriptions used by search engines).
- Graphics manipulation (in a package such as Adobe® Photoshop®).
- Installation of a bulletin board, form or guestbook.
- Installation of visitor counters.
- Use of Javascript™, e.g. for a menu system.
- Browser recognition feature (loading alternative pages for different browsers).
- Buttons with "rollovers", hotspots, anchors, forms.

Spreadsheet Advanced Features

- Linked mult-sheets.
- Formulae.
- Charts and graphs.
- Filters.
- Macros to automate common processes such as sorting and printing set areas.
- User forms, combo boxes, dialogue boxes and drop-down lists.
- Pivot tables.
- Named ranges.
- Lookups and IF functions.

DTP Advanced Features

- Master page templates.
- Text frames, columns, wrapping text around images, fitting text to complex paths.
- Consideration of margins, gutters, white space, leading, kerning, tracking.
- Image manipulation — colouring, cropping, resizing, skewing, flipping, rotating, splicing, extrusion, colour washes, separation, gradient fills.
- Long document support — indexing, tables of contents, links.
- Consideration of how the end user will input data into documents.

Try to avoid using built-in features of the software like wizards or templates — you're supposed to be producing your own unique solution. If you have to use a wizard, then customise it, e.g. change the defaults.

Implementation Advice

Provide Evidence to Show What You've Done

1) As part of the implementation stage, you need to **provide evidence** to show that you have created the solution.
2) Remember — the implementation must reflect the **designs** and your **client's requirements**, as well as making **full** and **effective** use of the software.
3) You need to explain **what you did**, what **problems** you encountered, and how you **solved** them.
4) Take **screenshots** and **annotate** them. Annotations should show:
   - the key features of the documents that you've made
   - brief comments explaining why you've done things a certain way.
5) You **don't** need to produce reams of paper, just enough to show that you've actually made the solution. Try to make it sufficiently detailed for someone else to reproduce the solution from your notes.

Plan Your Time Wisely....

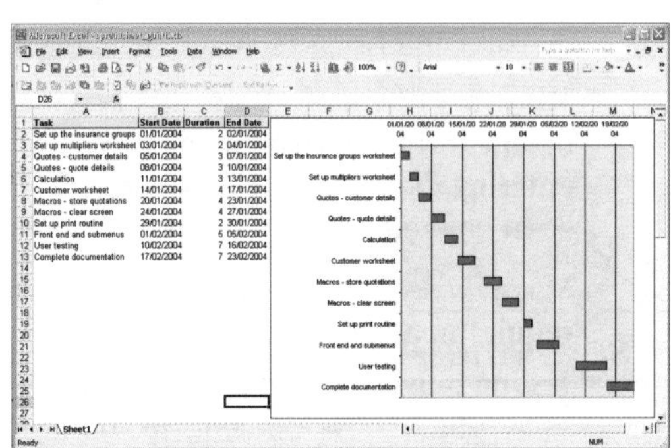

1) To produce a working solution before the deadline date, you need to **plan** out your work and **set targets** to pace yourself. Things beyond your control can go wrong later in the project, so be **prepared**.
2) A good way to schedule your work is using a **Gantt chart** like this, where everything is broken down into small tasks.
3) If you're stuck, don't be scared of getting **advice** from your teacher — they'll be able to put you back on the right track and save you hours of wasted time.

Keep Files Well-Organised and Safe

1) Use a **logical system** for labelling files and objects, e.g. forms, tables etc. — **don't** use default names like table1 or query1 and query2. Give everything meaningful and consistent names, e.g. qryVacanciesAugust for August vacancies in a lettings database for holiday cottages.
2) Keep a **separate folder** in your user area at school and at home for your coursework project. Create sub-folders inside this folder so that you have some order to your work. Everything's easier if you do this at the start.
3) Constantly **back up** your work. Save your work regularly with a different file name e.g. AnalysisVer1, AnalysisVer2, AnalysisVer3 etc., when you have made some significant changes to it. This will make it easier to keep track of your progress.

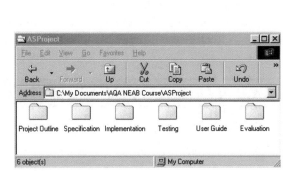

Practice Questions

Q1 What's the difference between generic and package-specific skills?

Q2 List six advanced features you could use in each of these solutions:
a) a website b) a spreadsheet c) DTP.

Q3 What should you do to any screenshots you include with your implementation?

Q4 How can Gantt charts be useful in your project?

Q5 List three good pieces of advice for keeping your files well-organised.

I find time keeping so hard, I don't know why — I just gantt do it...

Organisation, people. That's the dish of the day. Organisation, organisation, organisation. A well-organised project just feels different. It means that you'll be more confident with your work. Everything will be methodical and in its place, and there's less room for things to go wrong. And the birds will sing in the trees, and happiness will fill the air...

Testing

These pages are for AQA Unit 1 and OCR Unit 2.

Testing, testing... one, two, one, two... testing? Check, check, one, two, one, two, one, one, one, one, one... Is anyone out there? You're reading this so you must be there. So why can't I hear anything? Hm... testing, testing... is this thing on?

Make a **Test Strategy** During the **Design Stage**

Testing is designed to prove that the solution you have created does what it is supposed to do in the way that it is supposed to do it. The best place to start is to make a basic **test strategy**.
For this, you just basically have to decide:

- **what** you're going to test and **how** you'll test it
- **when** and in what **order** you'll do the tests
- the **expected outcomes** (i.e. what you expect to happen)

1) Testing needs to happen **throughout** implementation — you can't just do it all at the end.
2) The order of your tests needs some thinking about, e.g. in a database or spreadsheet program, data validation should be tested while you're **entering** the main data. You can't do the queries until all the data's been entered. So validation has to be tested before **queries**.
3) Make cross-references back to the **performance indicators** and **client requirements** in the analysis section.
4) Testing **must not be static** — just like your designs may have to change as a result of developments in your implementation, you may also have to produce new tests along the way. If you change part of the solution, following a test, the new part will probably need testing too.
5) The solution should be fully tested **yourself** and then tested by the **client** — this equates to alpha and beta testing.

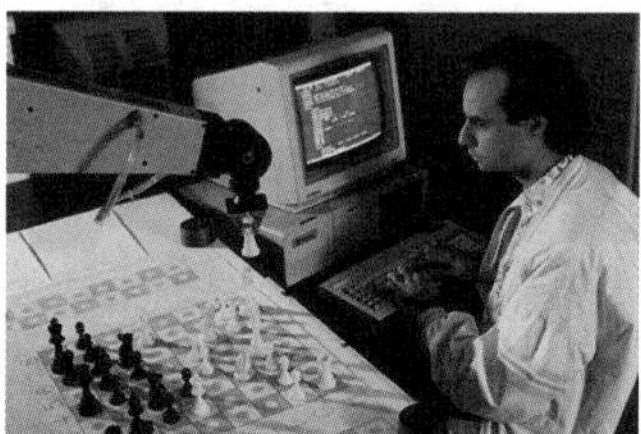

All good test strategies will involve at least one game of chess.

You Have to **Design** a **Test Plan**

For each type of test you'll also need to make a test plan — these are usually done as **tables**.

Test no	Purpose of test	Test data used	Expected outcome	Actual outcome	Evidence
1	Test password	Soll Niederau Pamporovo	All fail except Pamporovo		
2	Test Main Menu Options		Correct sub menus open each time. Application closes when Exit button pressed		
3	Test Option button (sex)	Click on male/female	Returns 1 or 2 in E15		
4	Test Combo box (age)	70+	Returns 10 in E22		

Example test plan for a website project (to go in the design section)

You could also produce screenshots to go with some of your tests and annotate them to show how you've corrected any mistakes.

Test no	Purpose of test	Test data used	Expected outcome	Actual outcome	Evidence
1	Test password	Soll Niederau Pamporovo	All fail except Pamporovo	Only Pamporovo succeeds	See printout 1 on p67
2	Test Main Menu Options		Correct sub menus open each time. Application closes when Exit button pressed	All buttons when clicked opened submenus except Exit macro which failed. Corrective action required.	See printouts 2 to 6 on pp67-68 for successful opening of submenus. See page 69 for alterations of VB code. Retest Test 31.
3	Test Option button (sex)	Click on male/female	Returns 1 or 2 in E15	Returns 1 or 2 in E15	See printout 7 p69
4	Test Combo box (age)	70+	Returns 10 in E22	Returns 10 in E22	See printout 8 p69

Completed test plan (to go in the testing section)

Make sure your screen shots are large enough to read — remember not everyone's eyesight will be as good as yours.

Testing

Choose Your Test Data Carefully

You should declare your test data in your test plan, which forms part of the design of the solution. You should include a good range of data that tests the solution; this must include normal data, extreme data and incorrect data.

Normal data

This is data **your system should cope with.** This type of data is expected to work correctly in the task.

Extreme data

This is data **at the boundary of acceptance**, e.g. a spreadsheet allows an entry in the range of 1 to 10; the extreme data to use to test this would be 1 or 10.

Out of range (erroneous) data

This is data **outside of the acceptable range**, e.g. a spreadsheet allows an entry in the range of 1 to 10; the incorrect data to use to test this could be 0 or 15.

The easiest way to display the test data you're going to use is in a **table**.

This table shows a set of data to be used for testing a database.

Remember — the aim of the testing game is to try and make your system **fail**.

Field	Comment	Normal data	Extreme data	Out of range
Membership ID	Integer — not negative and less than 1000	54	999	1003
First name	Text (max 10)	James	James Troy	James Troyes
Surname	Text (max 10)	Green	Greenhough	Greenhough-Smythe
Subscription	Currency (max £50.00)	£10.00	£50.00	£100.00
Address 1	Text (15 max)	8 Field Road	8 Fielding Road	8 Field Road, Ticknall Derby
Postcode	Text — format check	DE1 2LF	DE217FE	DEE731ZZZ
DOB	Date > 01/01/82	01/01/90	02/01/82	20/03/55

And Finally — Some Testing Dos and Don'ts

DO

- Do your testing as you go along.
- Re-use any screenshots you made in the implementation section.
- Reprint the table you produced in the design section showing the extra columns filled in.
- Show a range of tests and test data.
- Provide evidence that your end user has tested your system and user guide.
- An average number of tests for a solution should be in the range of 100 tests.

DON'T

- Produce a test plan with ticks or phrases such as "OK", "failed", or "as expected".
- Have identical tests.
- Provide no client involvement.
- Produce printouts without annotations, titles or cross-referencing to the test plan.
- Make the screen shots too small.
- Make anything up...

Practice Questions

Q1 What's the difference between a test strategy and a test plan.

Q2 When setting up a test plan table, what column headings could you use?

Q3 What are the three main categories of test data?

Q4 Write down three project testing 'do's and three 'don't's.

It doesn't work, the USELESS bloomin' — oh I see, there's an "on" switch...

Don't get confused with all the similar sounding terms on this page — the test strategy gives an overview of the testing, and the test plans are tables describing the individual tests you'll do... And remember to use the three types of test data during your tests — it's no good just using nice, regular data that wouldn't harm a fly.

Evaluation

These pages are for AQA Unit 1.

Evaluation already? How can we have reached the evaluation stage already?! Is it going as quickly for you as it is for me? Why I feel just delightful... like cherry blossom dancing over the hills on a warm spring day. Or maybe a small pile of mud.

Evaluation Is Ludicrously Important

1) Evaluation is a very important part of the solution, but unfortunately it often gets left too late and is rushed. Try to give yourself **enough time** to do it justice.
2) Lots of evaluations are only a couple of pages long. If you can make yours **longer** than this, you'll be off to a good start. And I mean properly longer, not just increasing the font size by a few points...
3) Your evaluation section needs to provide evidence that you've **understood** what the solution was meant to do and **assessed** it effectively, and also that you know what **mistakes** you made and have made efforts to **correct** them.

There Are Four Key Elements To A Successful Evaluation

A **successful evaluation** of the project hinges on having four things:

- a suitable **client**
- a good list of **client requirements**
- a good list of **performance indicators**
- a rigorous and efficient **testing strategy**

There Are Some Things You Have To Comment On...

To give an effective evaluation, you need to talk about these things in detail:

- How **successful** you were at hitting the client's requirements.
- How **successful** you were at hitting the performance indicators.
- What **shortcomings** there were with your solution.

...and Some Things You Have To Avoid Mentioning

In order to make your evaluation direct and professional, it's a good idea to avoid mentioning these:

- Your **package specific** skills — you've already discussed this earlier in the project.
- Your **time management** skills — you've already discussed this.
- The amount of **help** you have received from your ICT tutor.
- What you have **learned** from producing your solution — this is not relevant.

Write Up Your Evaluation Carefully

1) Go back to your original **objectives** and **performance indicators / criteria**.
   Handy hint — cut and paste them into your evaluation document then add your comments under each one.
2) **Consider** each of the criteria in turn and **discuss** how successful you were in meeting them.
3) Show **evidence** from the testing to **support** your statements. This could take the form of a screenshot of a test or a photocopy of a comment from the client.
4) **Discuss** the **limitations** and **failures of your solution**.
5) Describe what **improvements** you'd like to make to meet the performance indicators if you had the opportunity to do the project again (or had more time to develop it).

Evaluation

Example 1 — **Evaluating Your Objectives**

1) You need to evaluate your objectives **one by one**.
2) The example below shows what you might put for a website project.
(The text in italics has been copied and pasted from the analysis section of the project.)

Objective 1: To ensure that the Home Page downloads rapidly within 10 seconds.

Performance criteria: The Home Page should be no more than 200Kb in size with graphics which are in a compressed format such as gifs or jpegs.

I managed to fulfil this. I kept the main graphics on the Home Page to 30Kb. The original files were much bigger but I compressed them to a smaller size by using the 'save to the web' option in Adobe® Photoshop®. My end user was impressed by the fact that the graphics, though tiny in kilobytes, were still sharp. I did this by using the "sharpen" filter. Other objects such as buttons were also compressed to minimise download times.

Objective 2: To ensure that navigation is intuitive and consistent.

Performance criteria: Navigation buttons on each page must be in the same area of the page. Buttons must be consistent in shape, have consistent lettering and have consistent actions.

I based all pages on a template with the buttons in the non-editable area of the template. All buttons worked on each page and were tested by my end user. However, initially some of them didn't find the correct page. I sorted this out by altering the html code. The buttons to external links opened pages in a new window as I wanted them to do.

Example 2 — **Evaluating Your Limitations**

The Guestbook was hosted on some web space that was beyond my control. I would prefer to have the script running from my own website.

I didn't manage to get the JavaScript™ code working for the visitor counter and had to link to one supplied by a company called Nedstat which unfortunately included some advertising on the Home page.

The end user wants to update the website herself. I haven't completely worked out how to do this easily for her.

Example 3 — **Evaluating Possible Improvements**

My end user, after working through my solution, asked if she could have an online database of products which could be updated daily if required.

I will investigate how to use the program Macromedia Contribute so that my end user can update parts of the site easily.

My end user would like me to investigate how to install an online booking system for visitors. Initially this might be through e-mail or a form. Eventually I hope that this could run in almost real time on the web site.

Practice Questions

Q1 What are the four key elements to writing a successful evaluation?

Q2 Should you mention any shortcomings in your project?

Q3 How would you involve your end user in the evaluation of your project?

Objective: turn cheese into gold — evaluation: didn't work for some reason...

Evaluation is really where it all comes together. You need to be clear, precise and honest. Admit your mistakes, and explain exactly what happened. Don't pretend that everything just went precisely to plan. It's much better to admit to problems and say how you tried to fix them. And it's good to think about how your solution could have been even better too.

Documentation

These pages are for OCR Unit 2 but are useful background info for AQA unit 1.

There's no point producing a Super-Fancy-Pants ICT system if you don't tell people how to work it. That's what user guides, helpsheets and technical documentation are all for.

User Guides Are There To Help Your End User

A good comprehensive user guide should contain these sections:

1) **Contents page** – including the page numbers of each section so the user can quickly find what they want.
2) **Introduction / overview** – briefly explaining the purpose of the guide and what the system does.
3) **Hardware requirements** – all the hardware needed to run the application should be listed, including minimum hardware specifications.
4) **Software requirements** – listing the applications software needed, stating the earliest version that will work, e.g. Microsoft Excel® 2000 or later. It should also list the operating system(s) it is compatible with.
5) **Instructions** – the main part of the guide which gives the user clear guidance on how to use the system. All the main tasks the user will need to do should be included as well as any other sub-tasks.
6) **Glossary** – a list of technical words used in the user guide with definitions. The glossary should only contain words that have been used in the user guide.
7) **Troubleshooting help** – containing a list of likely error messages or problems that the user might have with the system. For each problem or error, there should be a clear description of how to fix it. This section must only relate to the new system and not to any general problems that could occur with the computer system itself.

A Help Sheet Gives Instructions for One Particular Task

1) A **help sheet**, or instruction guide, is a small document (1 or 2 pages) that assists the user with **one specific task** and any **sub-tasks** that this will involve.
2) It is usually a set of **step-by-step** instructions that the user can work through systematically to complete a certain function within the system.

Percy decided the breakdancing instruction guide was actually a bit useless.

The Format is Important

1) The **language** used in user guides and help sheets must be **jargon-free** and appropriate to the user.
2) **Screenshots and pictures** give the user a reference point for each step rather than trying to understand a **huge chunk** of text.

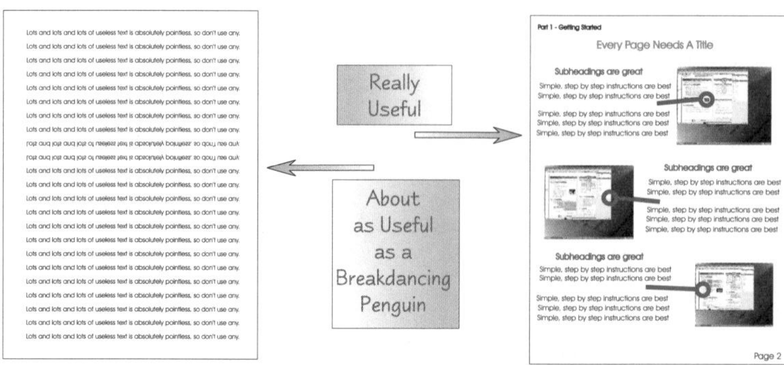

3) The **layout** of each page should be **clear and not cluttered**. This means that pages should have **titles** and **subheadings** to break up the sections. The steps or checks should be broken down in **bullet points** or **numbered lists**. A good user guide will use these features consistently so the pages are all of a **similar style**.
4) **General instructions** such as opening and closing the application and saving work should be included. A good user guide will contain the **file name** and the **location** of any files or folders also needed to run the application.

Documentation

Electronic Documentation *is Accessed from Within an Application*

Electronic documentation enables the user to access help from **within an application** without referring to a paper-based document. The user can access it by clicking on a **hyperlink** or **button** or through a **shortcut key**.

Electronic documentation should contain:

1) A **contents page** that should include a clearly labelled set of hyperlinks or buttons to take the user **directly** to each section.
2) Hyperlinks/buttons within each page to access **related topics**, go back to the contents page or to exit.
3) **Screenshots** so the user can **visualise** what to do.
4) **Sound and video** to explain and offer **demonstrations** of tasks to the user. They can be set up to run **automatically** or as an **extra resource** started by the user.

Most of the icons used in documentation are pretty **standard**, so that even if people aren't familiar with the application, they know what will happen if they click on the button. You're probably familiar with the following:

Sound Icon

Video Icon

Exit Icon

Technical Documentation *can Help the User in the Future*

Technical documentation is written for people who will be responsible for **maintaining** and **upgrading** the application. It should contain the following sections, similar to a user guide:

1) **Contents page**
2) An **introduction / overview**
3) The **hardware requirements**
4) The **software requirements**
5) It should also include a section on **Configurations and Settings**. Technical documentation needs to show how the application was **developed** and the configurations and settings that were used. The section could include data structures, annotated program code, validation routines, macros with associated buttons, and any functions or formulas that were used.

Practice Questions

Q1 Who is the target audience for your user guide?

Q2 List five things that should definitely be included in a user guide.

Q3 Do two quick sketches to show really bad and really superfantastic layout for a user guide.

Q4 What is electronic documentation? List four things it should contain.

Q5 Explain how technical documentation is different from user documentation.

User Guide to fun — employ your time in a profitless and non-practical way...

This is a chance for you to really shine. Now, while it's true that the moderator isn't going to be impressed with a flashy looking user guide if the content is rubbish, it's also true to say that the moderator will be impressed if the content is awesome and the presentation is attractive and well-planned. Show off a bit, why not? No one else is going to do it for you.

Advice for AQA Unit 1

These pages are for AQA Unit 1 only (just in case you didn't get it from the title...)

It's been a long haul to get this far, but we're almost done now. Just a wee section of friendly advice to help you, then I'll set you free and you can go swimming with donkeys or rollerblading with dolphins or whatever you fancy.

Make Sure You **Understand** How this Unit **Works** — it's a bit weird...

For AQA unit 1 you need to cover all the sections of the **systems life cycle** — **analysis**, **design**, **implementing**, **testing** and **evaluation**.

1) The unit has been designed so that the theory stuff you do **reinforces** the practical work and vice versa. This basically means that you'll be doing real **practical work** (creating ICT solutions) alongside **theory** about the system life cycle.
2) The good news is you **won't** have to produce a **full project** to hand in because everything's assessed in an exam.
3) The bad news is... everything's assessed **in an exam.**
4) You **will** have to take up to 20 pages of **sample work** into the exam from the **analysis** and **testing** you've done.
5) In the exam you'll be asked questions about **what you've done** and you'll have to **back up** some answers by making **references** to your sample work.

It's a bit weird.

What kind of **Problems** can you do?

You can use lots of different types of software, ranging from the more traditional database and spreadsheet applications to more exciting things like podcasts, blogs and web pages etc.

The range of software splits into **three distinct areas**:

E-commerce and transaction processing
Databases
Spreadsheets

Communication
Blogs
Podcasts
DTP
Word processing
Photo galleries

Multimedia
Web pages
Animations
Rolling multimedia presentations
Interactive multimedia presentations

Your **Analysis** and **Testing** Samples can come from **Different Problems**

1) Rather than doing one really big problem, it's probably better to do **several** smaller problems using different software. This will give you a better **range** of software skills and experience.
2) If you want, you can take the **analysis** and **testing** for your sample work from **different problems**.
3) For the project you take the **testing** from, you'll need to have done the **other stages** too really — **analysis**, **design**, **implementation** and **evaluation** — you can't test it unless the thing's been designed and made first.
4) But you don't necessarily have to do all the later stages for an **analysis**. It'd be fine to do a **problem analysis** and use it in your sample work without actually going on to implement the solution.
5) **Analysis** is a lot simpler if you have a **real problem** involving a **real end user**. This way, you can let the end user do a lot of the **hard work** of thinking what needs to be done.
6) **Databases** and **spreadsheets** are generally **easier to test** than websites, say. This is worth bearing in mind for sample work. Testing websites can be **time-consuming**, needing lots of planning, specialist software, etc.

During the unit, you need to gain as much **practical experience** in using a **wide range** of hardware, software and communication technologies as possible. This will help you with the theory stuff.

Advice for AQA Unit 1

Use these Checklists for your **Sample Work**

Analysis	
A statement and basic outline of the problem.	
Initial evidence collected by - studying documentation - interview - questionnaires - observation - researching similar organisations	
A description of the task has been produced in detail.	
An explanation of the software and hardware that is available to the client has been given.	
Client's current ICT skills identified.	
An explanation of how the data will be kept secure in the proposed system has been given.	
An explanation of how Data Protection issues will be addressed.	
A description of any costs that would be incurred by solving the problem e.g. training.	
Clients requirements, recognised, specified and documented.	
Interpretation of the client's requirements as input, processing and outputs are described in detail.	
Suitable objectives (quantitative and qualitative) documented.	
Performance criteria explained in detail.	

Testing	
Test strategy produced	
Detailed test plan produced including - description of what is being tested - suitable test data (normal, extreme, out of range) - expected result - actual result (annotated)	
Testing evidence cross-referenced to the test plan	
Evidence of the client using the solution is given and explained	

You should cover all of these things in your sample work, but the ones highlighted with **pigs** or **cows** are the most important.

Final Things to Remember before Submitting Work

1) Remember, the analysis and testing you take into the exam will be **used to answer questions** on the paper.
2) Make sure you are only submitting 10 to 20 sheets of paper. Producing more **won't** give better marks, and it'll be harder for you to find the stuff you need to answer the question.
3) The front sheet must include a signed **Candidate Record Sheet** to prove it's your work.
4) All the work must have clear **page numbering** to help you and the examiner find things easily.
5) Page numbering should be **sequential** from start to end, **not subdivided** into sections.
6) All work must be concise, clearly laid out and legible.

There's some general exam technique advice on p132-133. Have a spy when you've finished this page...

Practice Questions

Q1 Which elements of the systems life cycle do you need to study for AQA unit 1?

Q2 Give two examples of problems you could solve in each of these areas:
a) e-commerce and transaction processing b) communication c) multimedia

Q3 What elements do you need to include in your sample work? How big should it be?

Q4 What are the most important points to cover in your sample work?

ICT — and when ICT, I drinks it...

Did you like that gag? I'd been saving that one up. Probably a bit disappointing when you know that. You're probably also wondering why I said 'drinks', rather than 'drink' too. Just sounds better that way. Actually maybe you didn't get the gag at all. I'd better break it down just in case: ICT — "I see tea", tea as in a lovely cup of tea. There, you see? It's a good'un.

Advice for OCR Unit 2 — Structured ICT Tasks

These pages are for OCR Unit 2 — or "G062 Structured ICT Tasks" if you prefer its full title.

The structured ICT tasks (G062) make up 40% of your final AS grade. A new set of structured ICT tasks are set each year and they need to be carried out to provide evidence of what you have done. Each year the tasks will use a different scenario.

The Tasks Will Cover **Four Areas** of the Systems Development Process

The table below shows the **four areas** of the system development process you'll be tested on in this module. They're all **covered in detail** in section 9. The specific advice in section 9 is mostly based around AQA, but it's still definitely worth having a **good read** through all the pages referenced below to make sure you really understand what each topic area is all about.

Topic Area	Description	Covered in Detail
Design	Detailed planning about what a system will do	p108-113
Software development	Constructing the system using hardware and software	p114-121
Testing	Making sure that the system works as it was intended	p122-123
Documentation	Instructions on how to use or maintain the system	p126-127

You'll have to do Some **Design** Tasks

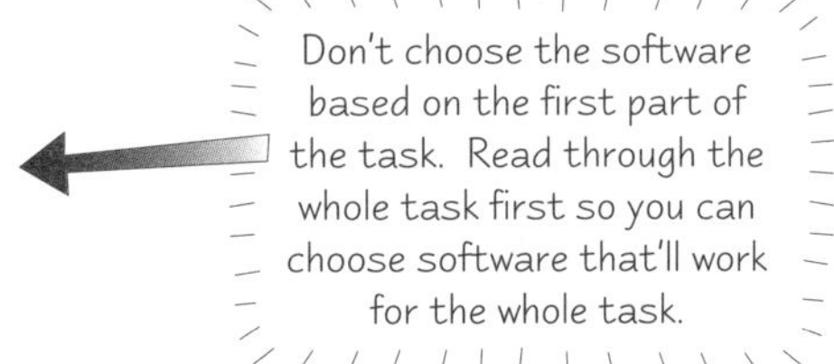

Don't choose the software based on the first part of the task. Read through the whole task first so you can choose software that'll work for the whole task.

1) Before you can produce a design you need to know which **software** you're going to use. Some tasks will tell you what to use, for other you'll need to make the decision.
2) The designs you need to produce will be **sketches** or **plans** of how you want the developed version to look and work.
3) When you've finished your design, ask yourself whether **someone else** would be able to produce the solution you intended without having to come and ask you questions. If not, you need to give more detail.
4) You don't need to worry about your art skills as designs are only sketches, but they do need to be **neat** and **clear**.

Software Development Tasks— also known as the Fun Bits

Software Development is when you make the actual solution based on the designs.
There's two ways you might be asked to do this — either by creating the solution that you've **just designed** or by **following instructions** based on a scenario you're given. Here's a few tips for it...

1) Use any **resources** you like to help you, e.g. books / online help.
2) **Only** do what the task tells you to — there's no point doing extra stuff, you won't get extra marks for it.
3) You **don't** need to show every stage you did to produce the solution (unless the task tells you to).
4) If you're told to produce **screenshots**, make sure they're big enough for someone to see everything clearly.

You'll have to Produce or Follow a **Test Plan**

A task might ask you to produce a **test plan** or you may be **given** a test plan to **follow**.

1) A detailed test plan says **exactly** what you're going to do to test the solution. It will include a short **description** of each test, the **test data** to use and **where** it's entered and the **expected results** for each test.
2) A test plan should include the three types of test data — **normal**, **extreme** and **invalid**.
3) When you're choosing the test data you must give **exact** values, not a range. So if you're testing the validation rule ">70", then choose an invalid data item such as "55", not just "a number between 0 and 70".
4) You might be asked to explain **why** the test data you've chosen is appropriate. Just make sure you understand the **purpose** of the normal, extreme and invalid data so that you can **explain** why you've used them.
5) For some tasks you might be **given** the test plan to follow. You'll probably have to produce screenshots as evidence of the testing. If you get any **error messages**, make sure you include these in the evidence.

Advice for OCR Unit 2 — Structured ICT Tasks

You'll need to Produce **Documentation** on how to Use the System

When a new ICT system is produced, documentation needs to be written to explain how the system works and how to maintain / update it. In the tasks you'll be asked to produce one or more of these types of documentation:

1) **User Documentation** is written for the people who'll be using the system day to day. You have to assume they won't have any specialist IT knowledge, so it needs to be **simple to follow** and avoid **technical jargon**. It should include a contents page and introduction, hardware requirements, software requirements, instructions, glossary and troubleshooting sections.
2) **Help Sheets** are usually 1 – 2 pages long. They contain instructions on how to use all or part of your system. They **don't** need contents pages, hardware / software requirements, glossary or trouble shooting sections.
3) **Electronic Documentation** can be accessed from within an application with no paper instructions needed. It might be accessed through a Help menu or by clicking on a 'Help' hyperlink.
4) **Technical Documentation** is written so that maintenance can be carried out to repair or upgrade the system. It's aimed at an IT specialist so you can include more technical language. It should include a contents and introduction / overview, hardware and software requirements, and configuration settings.

Annotate to Show What you've Done and Why

Some tasks will ask you to **annotate** (add comments to) the work you produce, e.g. screenshots.

You might use annotation to:
- describe **how** you made a printout or screenshot.
- describe the **purpose** of a printout or screenshot.
- give reasons for **choices** you made.
- **label** input and output values or other **features**.

You can annotate your work by:
- **Handwriting** on the work.
- Using text boxes and arrows within a **word processor**.
- **Numbering** each part of a printout or screenshot and then writing the annotations on a separate page.

Finally, some Mostly Useful **Dos** and **Don'ts**

The main ones are highlighted in red.

Do	Don't
Include a cover page with your name, centre name, centre number and candidate number on.	Assume your teacher will provide a cover page for you.
Put your name, candidate number, centre number, task number, page number, in a header or footer, on each page.	**Put "I love Gary Barlow 4 eva and eva" in a header and footer on each page. Yes Rachel, I'm talking to you.**
Hand your work to your teacher in an envelope file or use treasury tags.	Hand your work to your teacher in a ring binder or put every sheet of paper in a plastic wallet.
Print pages in colour if colour is needed.	Waste ink by printing everything in colour for the sake of it.
Separate each main task by using a cover sheet or coloured piece of paper putting all of your work into order.	**Separate each task with A4 prints of Gary, Mark, Jason and Howard.**

Practice Questions

Q1 Which four areas will the Structured ICT tasks cover?
Q2 What should you ask yourself to check your design is detailed enough?
Q3 Name the four types of documentation you might need to produce.
Q4 Put the following Take That members in order of bestness (best first): Jason, Gary, Howard, Mark, Robbie.

Take that advice and party through your OCR structured tasks...

We're almost at the end now. I haven't felt this emotional since the first time Take That split up. Don't be afraid to cry, it's OK. Just let it all out. Yes, I know. There, there. Just remember, ICT will be with you always — when you're downloading Mark's solo efforts, when you're browsing Jason's Blog, when you use satellite technology to stalk Gary. ICT will be with you.

Exam Question Tips

These pages are for AQA Units 1 and 2, and OCR Unit 1.

This double page is filled to the brim with irresistibly sweet, juicy tips to help you in the exam. So get in there and lap it all up like it was a vast lake of molten chocolate orange with floating pieces of popping candy.

Learn the Different Question Types and how to Answer Them

All exam questions include magical **keywords**. They tell you what you need to do to **get the marks**...

1) **State or Identify:** You have to answer with a single word or phrase.

> Q1 Identify **two** factors that affect the quality of information. (2 marks)

Each factor you give is worth 1 mark. 'Two' is even in bold for this one to give you an extra reminder.

2) **Give:** You have to answer with more information than a single word statement.

> Q2 Give **two** methods of validation that could be used with a text-based data entry field. (2 marks)

You must use a **phrase** to answer this question. Each method you give is worth 1 mark.

3) **Describe:** You have to give a bit more detail to be sure of getting the marks with these questions — short phrases won't do. If you're asked to give examples, make sure they match the context of the question.

> Q3 Describe what is meant by a workbook and give an example of how a publishing company could use it in their financial model. (3 marks)

To cover the 'describe' part in the question above, you should state what a workbook is and say what it's used for. That'll get you 2 marks, then the third mark would be for giving a suitable example.

4) **Explain:** These questions want you to give **reasons** to back up the points you make.

> Q4 Explain the problems that could be brought about by a lack of standardisation in hardware. (6 marks)

Simply making a list of problems won't get you full marks here. You need to write a proper answer in continuous prose. For each problem you identify, give some **detail** or an **example** to show **why** it's a problem.

5) **Discuss:** We're getting into the more **meaty** essay-style questions now.
These need to be well-structured using good English and continuous prose again.

> Q5 Discuss the impact on society of using the Internet to shop. (9 marks)

Your answer should include both **advantages** and **disadvantages** (and roughly the same number of each to make it balanced). You should also give a concise **conclusion** (and not one that just repeats what you've already said).

6) **Compare:** When you're asked to compare two things, you need to describe the **good** and **bad** points of each for the situation given, and think about how they're **different** and **similar** to each other.

> Q6 Compare the use of a spreadsheet and a database application for holding data on members of a sports club. (8 marks)

It's no good just randomly listing the good and bad points of each software. Your answers must relate to the sports club **context**, explaining how each application would cope with different tasks. Try to give **equal coverage** to both applications, so four points about spreadsheets and four about databases would do nicely.

Exam Question Tips

A Few Tips for *Longer* Questions

Look at the number of marks

— this will tell you **how much** you need to write. If a question's worth 12 marks this means you need to make 12 **distinct** points. Don't think you'll get the marks by just filling the space, it's **what you say** that counts.

Use good English

— in the essay-style questions you get marks for the **quality of your English**, so you need to produce well-written structured answers. Pay attention to your punctuation and grammar, and make sure you spell technical terms correctly. Don't use bullet points either.

Plan your answer

Jot down the **main points** you're going to make and decide how you're going to **finish** your answer. Otherwise you'll just get bogged down, forget half the stuff you were going to say and start waffling on like a big potato waffle with beans and fish fingers and a dollop of ketchup. Help me... I'm melting.

Read your answer and ask yourself

- does it all make sense?
- have I made enough distinct points to get all the marks?
- have I answered the actual question? Did I miss anything it asked?

Keep your answer balanced

If the question asks you to compare two things, make an **equal number** of points about each. If you're asked to discuss an issue, remember to give **pros** and **cons** and roughly equal numbers of each.

Look at the number of marks.

Three More Tips for the Road...

Doodles — not big and not clever.

Handwriting — make it neat. If the examiner can't read your writing, they won't be able to give you lots of lovely marks will they... Only use black or blue ink.

Doodling — this may seem like a good idea if you finish the paper early, but it's not. If you do have time to spare, go back and check through your answers. Add more detail if necessary.

Crossing out answers — just put a single line through stuff you want to delete. Don't scribble it out because you could get still marks for it if you've not written a new answer. Think before you cross out a large section of text – is it really wrong or are you starting to panic and not think clearly...

Practice Questions

Q1 List six truly magical keywords that might be used in exam questions. For each one, say briefly what answer you'd need to give.

Q2 Give five special tips for dealing with longer questions.

Q3 What should you do if you make a mistake and want to cross it out?

Q4 In exam terms, are doodles a) a really great idea or b) really not that great an idea

Whatever I said, whatever I wrote, I didn't mean it...

Was that a Take That reference too far? Anyway, you can do what you like, but if you really want to shine, you need to learn this stuff for sure. It only takes a minute to plan an answer, so have a little patience with that. Never forget to read over your work. Finally, and this isn't one of my empty promises, if you follow all this advice then you and me, we can rule the world.

Answers

Section 1 — What is ICT?

Page 3 — Data, Information and Knowledge

1 a) *It consists of a set of characters (in this case 8)* **[1 mark]** *and has no context to give it meaning* **[1 mark]**.

b) *It could be a date (e.g. 21st Sept 2002) or it could be some form of ID or reference number.* **[1 mark for any reasonable answer.]**

c) *Information is converted into knowledge by applying a rule. E.g. if the data refers to the date of birth, the age of the person can be found (the knowledge) by applying a simple calculation (the rule) that compares the data to the current date.*
[2 marks available — 1 for explanation, 1 for a suitable example]
The important thing to remember here is that you need to talk about using rules to convert information into knowledge.

2 a) *The questionnaire results are input using an appropriate input device, e.g. a keyboard, scanner, Optical Character Reader etc.*
[1 mark]

b) *Data is then processed (manipulated) using the computer system to group the data together and analyse it — e.g. the different responses may be added up and percentages calculated (to show what proportion of the sample gave each response).* **[1 mark]**

c) *The results are displayed in an appropriate way, e.g. as a table of results or graph, either displayed on screen or printed.* **[1 mark]**

Page 5 — Data, Information and Knowledge

1 a) *Possible answers:*
- *Data may be coded in order to save space.*
- *Data may be coded to make it quicker to enter.*
- *Data may be coded so that it can be easily validated/checked.*
- *Data may be coded so it can be processed more easily.*

[3 marks available — 1 for each point]

b) *Possible answers:*
- *The gender of a person can be stored as M or F rather than the longer "Male" or "Female".*
- *Dates should be coded in numerical format. The computer can be instructed with rules informing it which dates have been entered incorrectly e.g. 09/04/19788 is wrong because "year > 2010".*
- *The questionnaire could give people options to say what country they were born in. e.g. England 01, Ireland 02, Scotland 03, Wales 04, Other 05. Coding this data as numbers will make it quicker to process.*

[3 marks available — 1 for each example]
You can use any decent examples for this sort of question — it's good to keep it as straightforward as possible. I've used gender, dates and birthplace because they're pretty easy to explain. Just because they're basic doesn't make them bad — they cut straight to the chase.

2 *Possible answers:*
- *Precision of data is reduced* **[1 mark]**, *as the codes can generalise the data* **[1 mark]**.
- *The user needs to know the codes that have been used* **[1 mark]**, *because if they do not then they cannot interpret the data* **[1 mark]**.
- *Coding of value judgements* **[1 mark]**, *for example "Is this a good university?" to be coded as a value between 1 and 4. Different people will interpret the values differently, and this will make comparisons difficult* **[1 mark]**.
- *Limited number of codes* **[1 mark]**. *If codes are made up of a range of letters and numbers then there may not be enough combinations to avoid running out of codes* **[1 mark]**.
- *Difficult to track errors* **[1 mark]**. *Validation will ensure the code is entered correctly but the nature of the code will make it difficult to see if the code is actually correct* **[1 mark]**.

[Maximum 4 marks — 2 marks per problem, 1 for identification of the problem, 1 for an example / description]

3 *Possible answers:*
- *A CD-ROM holds a limited amount of information* **[1 mark]**, *whereas a website can hold larger amounts* **[1 mark]**.
- *Hyperlinks can be used on the web pages about each book* **[1 mark]** *and linked to related web pages on the company website* **[1 mark]**.
- *Increase in customer base* **[1 mark]** *as people may find the site through browsing the Internet* **[1 mark]**.
- *Easy to update the website, rather than having to reissue new CDs.*

[Maximum 6 marks]

Page 7 — Value of Information

1 a) *Possible answers:*
- *Tastes / fashion in skiing and ski resorts may have changed in 7 years, and the 2001 data will not reflect this.*
- *The facilities at the resorts may have changed and the data might not now be relevant.*
- *Data from 2001 would not reflect any resort closures / openings.*
- *Using data from a single year makes it hard to predict a trend — it would be better if they could compare figures over different years.*

[2 marks available — 1 for each point]
Hey hey, this looks like a simple 2 marks here, but don't blow it by forgetting to put enough detail in. Basic rule here: just writing "it'll be out of date" won't score you any marks at all...

b) *Possible answers:*
- *Staff would be needed to conduct surveys or survey results would need to be bought from an external source.*
- *Data would need to be validated and verified to ensure its accuracy. This would mean paying out more to staff for the work.*
- *Added storage space would probably be needed to cope with volumes of data.*
- *If the company wants to produce new information from the database, it will need to invest in appropriate software for processing it.*

[2 marks available — 1 for each point]

2 *Possible answers:*
- *It's faster, as it will save time when collecting customer information over the telephone, meaning that more customers can be dealt with.*
- *It's more accurate (unless there were mistakes in the original database) because the road and town names will not have to be physically keyed in.*
- *Customers' details will be more complete because of the data stored in the database.*
- *It will ensure that only customers who live in areas the company delivers to will be able to set up an account, thereby cutting down on cancellation and enquiry paperwork.*

[3 marks available — 1 for each advantage]

Page 9 — What can ICT do?

1 *Possible answers:*
- *They can manipulate / process data to produce information.*
- *They can transfer data from one place to another.*
- *They can search for and retrieve data.*
- *They can store vast amounts of data.*
- *They can deal with different types of data (textual, graphical, audio, video)*
- *They can carry out repetitive tasks.*

[3 marks available — 1 for each appropriate example]
Easy money on this question — there are squillions of possible answers to this one. Anything sensible and properly explained will do.

2 *Possible answers:*
- *Communication Technology is the transferring of data from one point to another via links between computers, such as broadband cables, telephone lines, modems and satellites.*
- *Communication Technology means the transfer of data between computer systems, mobile telephone communications or fax.*
- *Communication Technology in this context refers to the transfer of data between different computer systems, using electronic links and devices (e.g. modems, routers, broadband cables, telephone lines, etc).*

[2 marks available — 1 for a definition and 1 for appropriate examples]
There's 2 marks here — you'll need to say more than "the transfer of data" in order to get both marks, don't forget.

Answers

Section 2 — Hardware

Page 11 — Input Devices

1 *Possible answers:*

- *A mouse could be used to navigate a web page on a home PC. They are designed to fit in your hand and be easy to use. However, the mouse can be slower than using keyboard commands and shortcuts. Optical mice can have trouble working on certain surfaces.*
- *A trackball or trackpad could be used to navigate a web page on a laptop. These can be integrated into the machine, so there is no need to plug in a mouse or provide an extra surface space for one. However, users can find both of these difficult to adapt to if they are used to a mouse.*
- *A numeric keypad can be used to navigate a web page on a mobile telephone. Special keys are assigned to navigate and click on buttons. They are small and convenient to use. However, the keypad itself can be quite slow and offers limited access options for more complicated sites.*
- *Touch screens can be used to navigate web pages on public Internet terminals and mobile phones. These are integrated into the system, so there is no need for detachable devices which could be damaged or stolen. However, it can be difficult to pinpoint particular areas and they are sometimes quite clumsy compared with more precise devices.*

[6 marks available — 1 for each of two suitable examples, then a further 1 mark for a suitable positive and negative point to accompany each one]

Hmm... This is a bit of a stinker. The trick is to look back at the question and work out what it's asking you — it's asking for two examples, and says you need to evaluate them. This is very tricky, as it can feel a little unstructured, but the easy way to think about it is that for each example you'll get 1 mark for an appropriate example, 1 mark for a full and appropriate pro, and 1 mark for a full and appropriate con. Once you've broken it down like that it should be pretty easy to just reel off the facts, one by one...

2 *Possible answers:*

Benefits:

- *Limited keys make it simpler to use than a conventional keyboard.*
- *They can have larger functional areas for people with limited hand movement.*
- *They have a sealed surface that is less likely to be affected by dirt and liquid than a conventional keyboard.*

Limitations:

- *They are limited to the specific system they were designed for.*
- *All applications must be designed especially for the keyboard.*

[2 marks available — 1 for an appropriate benefit, 1 for an appropriate limitation]

Page 13 — Input Devices

1 *Possible answers:*

- *A scanner could be used to input existing photographs.*
- *A digital camera could be used to input new photographs.*
- *A keyboard could be used to input textual slogans.*
- *A pointing device (e.g. mouse / trackball / trackpad) could be used to position photographs and text.*

[6 marks available — 2 for each of three full answers, 1 mark for device and 1 mark for description]

Page 15 — Backing Storage

1 *Possible answers:*

- *They could use magnetic tape for backing up data (global or incremental).*
- *They could use CD-R / DVD-Rs for keeping copies of program software.*
- *They could use CD-RW / DVD-RWs for keeping copies of individual data files.*
- *They could use a second hard disk for backup data.*
- *They could use a second hard disk for mirroring the main hard disk.*

[6 marks available — 1 for each device and 1 for the description]

There's lots of storage media you could give here, the important thing is to match the ones you choose to a suitable use.

Page 17 — Output Devices

1 *Possible answers:*

- *A graph plotter would be appropriate because it can output high quality vector graphics.*
- *A graph plotter would be appropriate because they usually print on paper larger than A4 size.*
- *An A3 laser printer would be appropriate because it is able to output high quality vector graphics.*

[2 marks available — 1 mark for the device and 1 mark for the description]

2 *Possible answers:*

- *Lots of students will want to print at once, and the laser printer is very fast, so it means less waiting around for output.*
- *Laser printers print at a very high quality, which is useful for school projects and presentations.*
- *Laser printers are relatively quiet so it is less likely to disturb other working pupils while it prints.*

[2 marks available — 1 for each suitable reason]

Answers

Section 3 — Systems Software and Processes

Page 19 — Systems and Applications Software

1 Possible Answer:

*Details of customers of the smaller companies (**1 mark**) may be incorrectly passed between different parts of the new company (**1 mark**). This can cause problems for customers as they may be represented incorrectly by the details (**1 mark**).*

*New equipment may have to be purchased (**1 mark**) to ensure that all parts of the new company can communicate and interact (**1 mark**). This will lead to extra costs as a direct result of non-standardisation (**1 mark**).*

[6 marks available, up to 3 marks for each of two effects described].

2 *Possible Answers (many other answers possible):*
- *Compression — A utility program that converts data into a format that takes up far less memory space, enabling faster communication.*
- *File conversion — A utility program that enables applications to open files with different file extensions.*
- *Configuration files — A file which provides information on system parameters that applications should adapt to.*

[4 marks available — 1 mark for the utility and 1 mark for the description]

Page 21 — Systems Software — Operating Systems

1 a) *Possible answers:*
- *It manages all applications installed on the computer.*
- *It monitors the systems input and output devices.*
- *It allocates memory on request.*
- *It schedules programs and resources.*
- *It provides an interface between user, hardware and software.*
- *It logs errors.*

[3 marks available — 1 for each of 3 appropriate tasks]

b) *Possible answers:*
- *An operating system with a Graphical User Interface, as this provides easy-to-use mouse-driven systems.*
- *A single user system, as there is likely to be access from one user at a time.*

Be careful not use trade names (e.g. Microsoft Windows®). You won't get any marks for stating trade names without a full explanation.

[2 marks available — 2 for naming an appropriate system and providing an explanation, 1 for the name or explanation only]

Page 23 — Human-Computer Interaction

1 *Possible answers:*
- *When the user is prompted to do something it must be clear how they do it.*
- *There must be online help that appears at the right time.*
- *All inputs must be validated or must use a method that makes it easy for the user to enter data (e.g. drop-down lists, validation of text input).*
- *It must not require the user to remember sequences of commands.*
- *It should have all required items on screen at once (the user shouldn't have to scroll up and down to find things).*
- *It should conform to general practice for user interfaces on that platform (e.g. work like a Windows application).*
- *It should be consistent in its approach so that new users can begin to understand it intuitively.*

[3 marks available — 1 for each of up to 3 suitable features]

2 *Possible answers:*

Advantages:
- *They are easy to use.*
- *Most controls are fairly intuitive — we know to click on a button, select from a drop-down list, etc.*
- *They don't depend on the user remembering long lists of commands.*

Disadvantages:
- *They require more processing power and can cause software to be slow.*
- *They can be limited in their function and some of the more useful functions can be hidden.*
- *Some users would prefer to enter all data in one way (e.g. type it all) and can become frustrated by some of the graphical controls.*

[4 marks available — 1 for each of 2 suitable pros, 1 for each of 2 suitable cons]

Page 25 — Types of Processing

1 a) *Transaction processing system OR Interactive processing system*

Possible reasons:
- *It is important that a booking is completed before allowing another booking to be made.*
- *The system must prevent two users from booking the same seats on a flight.*
- *Details of seat availability must be available on request.*

[2 marks available — 1 for naming a suitable processing system, 1 for a reasonable explanation]

b) *Batch processing system*

Possible reasons:
- *Changes to the output are not needed immediately.*
- *All processing can take place at once.*
- *Processing can take place out of normal working hours so as not to disrupt the system.*

[2 marks available — 1 for naming a suitable processing system, 1 for a reasonable explanation]

c) *Interactive system*

Possible reasons:
- *It must be able to react to the user when items are moved.*
- *A question and answer interface is needed when items are changed.*

[2 marks available — 1 for naming a suitable processing system, 1 for a reasonable explanation]

2 a) *Batch processing*

b) *Possible answers:*
- *It can be run without intervention from the user*
- *Batches of deposits will need to be collected and keyed in off-line*
- *The processing / output is not time critical*
- *Processing is done periodically when the system is least used*
- *Records of deposits / data will not be up to date at all times (in fact it cannot be with current booking systems)*
- *Large volumes of documents all of the same type*
- *Allows use of serial storage media e.g. magnetic tape*

[3 marks available — 1 mark each for up to 3 suitable features]

Page 27 — Data Backup and Recovery

1 a) *Possible answers:*
- *If there was a disaster, e.g. a fire, then all transactions made during the week would be lost*
- *If they are lost then it would take a long time to key them all back in again because it may be up to a week since the last backup.*
- *Poor organisation of backup discs — the owner doesn't know which is the most recent.*
- *Poor location of backup discs next to the computer makes the backup discs just as vulnerable as the original data.*

[3 marks available — 1 mark each for up to 3 correct problems]

Answers

b) *Possible answers:*
- *Systematically organise the discs, i.e. label and date so the newsagent can quickly find the most up-to-date backup*
- *Move backup media away from the shop*
- *Put backups in a fireproof safe*
- *Put backups above flood level*
- *Backup more regularly, i.e. daily*
- *Take a daily incremental backup and a full weekly backup*

[4 marks available — 1 mark each for up to 4 correct points]

2 a) *Possible answers:*
- *Backup medium*
- *Content / type of backup*
- *Location of backup*
- *Timing of backup*
- *Frequency of backup*
- *Security of backup*
- *Responsibility for backup*
- *Organisation of backup*
- *Testing the backup works*

[3 marks available — 1 mark each for up to 3 correct items]

b) *Possible answers:*
- *Ensure that the hardware is available*
- *Ensure that the software is available*
- *Ensure that the data is available*
- *Ensure that the staff will be available*
- *Ensure that they know their roles*
- *Ensure that the system is still secure*

[3 marks available — 1 mark each for up to 3 correct actions]

Section 4 — Communication Systems

Page 29 — Networks

1 a) *Possible answers:*
- *Centralisation of services, e.g. data and software*
- *Printers and other hardware can be shared*
- *Backups can be done centrally, rather than individually on each PC*
- *More flexible use of equipment, e.g. employees able to use any available computer*
- *Internal e-mail provides a record of communications.*
- *Internal e-mail reduces the need for staff to meet up.*

[4 marks available — 1 mark each for up to 4 suitable benefits]

b) *Possible answers:*
- *LANs restricted to one site or area **[1 mark]**, WANs can be spread over a wide geographical area and cover remote locations **[1 mark]**.*
- *Difference in type of connection — LANs can be connected physically with cables, e.g. co-axial / fibre optic **[1 mark]**, WANs are connected by leased lines or wireless connections, e.g. satellite **[1 mark]**.*
- *Difference in speed of transmission of data — LANs are generally faster than WANs **[1 mark]** —typically a LAN might transmit data at 10Mbps, compared to 1 Mbps for a WAN **[1 mark]**.*

[4 marks available — 1 each for up to 4 sensible points.]

c) *Possible benefits:*
- *head office can provide all local offices with up-to-date information.*
- *easier to ensure consistent systems and policies used throughout all local offices.*
- *search capabilities of local offices become national.*
- *better communication between local offices, e.g. for sharing of data, information and ideas.*

[2 marks available — 1 each for up to 2 sensible points.]

Page 31 — Networks

1 a) *In a peer-to-peer network the computers are linked together but there is no file server. In a client-server network, one central computer (the file server) controls the flow of data in the network and stores the data and usually some of the software on its hard disk.*
[2 marks available — 1 for a reasonable description of a peer-to-peer network, 1 for a reasonable description of a client-server network]

b) *Possible answers:*
- *As there is an increase in the number of computers, a client-server system will be needed to help with the increase in traffic.*
- *A client-server system allows central storage of data which will free up space on individual machines, making them run better.*
- *A client-server system allows automatic back up of data which means an increased level of protection against data being corrupted or destroyed.*

[3 marks available — 1 for each reasonable answer]

2 a) *In a bus topology all the computers are linked in a line to one cable with the file server in the middle. In a star topology there is an individual cable from the hub to each workstation.*
Bus network:

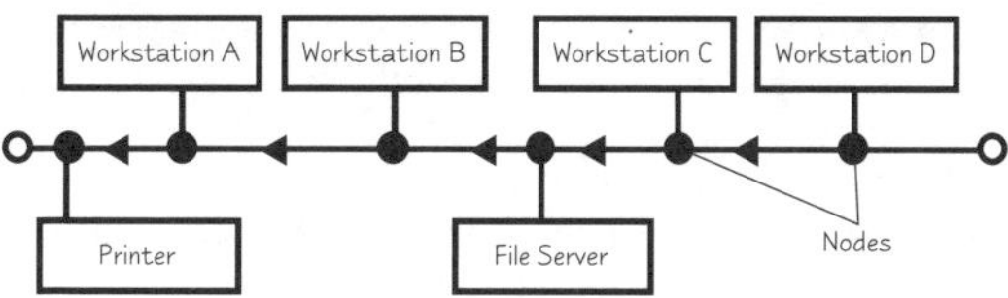

Answers

Star network:

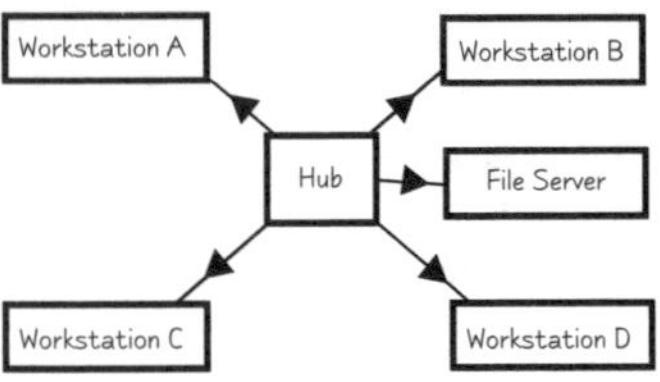

[4 marks available — 1 for a reasonable description of a bus network, 1 for a reasonable description of a star network, a further 1 for each of two supporting diagrams]

Don't get scared if you don't like drawing diagrams. They only need to be very basic. Sketch one out really quickly on some scrap paper before you start, so you've got something to copy from, and make sure you label all the different bits of it really clearly.

b) Possible answers:
- *Fewer physical cables are needed for a bus topology, making it more straightforward to set up.*
- *A bus network is cheaper as fewer cables are needed.*

[1 mark]

c) Possible answers:
- *A star network is often faster because there is an individual connection from the hub to each workstation.*
- *If the cable to one computer fails, it will not affect the operation of any other networked computers.*

[1 mark]

As long as you know your network topologies, you'll be fine here. These "advantage" and "disadvantage" questions are really straightforward and a great way to pick up easy marks, so make sure you revise all the reasons thoroughly.

Page 33 — The Internet

1 Possible answers:
Mobile phone, e-mail telephones / new telephone boxes, digital television, games consoles.
[2 marks available, 1 for each]

2 a) Possible answers:
- *a browser is used to display / view / navigate web pages **[1 mark]** in a readable form **[1 mark]**.*
- *a browser is used to display HTML pages **[1 mark]** in a viewable format **[1 mark]**.*
- *a browser is a piece of software / a program **[1 mark]** that enables the viewing of web pages **[1 mark]**.*

b) Possible answers:
- *A search engine is used to find specific pieces of information / web pages / websites / URLs **[1 mark]** using key words **[1 mark]**.*
- *a search engine is a piece of software / an application / a website / a web page **[1 mark]** used to find websites / words / topics **[1 mark]**.*

Be careful not to refer to the browser or the search engine by trade names (e.g. Google™, Lycos®, Firefox). You won't get any marks for stating trade names without a full explanation. Also, 4 marks are available here, so for each part you need to make 2 decent points.

Page 35 — The Internet

1 Possible answers:
- *It costs less to send an e-mail than a letter (provided the friend has Internet access).*
- *E-mails arrive much more quickly than regular mail.*
- *You can send the same letters / information to many people at once.*
- *You can attach other files and documents to the e-mail and send them at no extra cost.*

[2 marks available — 1 for each sensible reason]

2 Possible answers:
Advantages include:
- *Customers can shop when they want.*
- *Greater choice of goods from all over the world.*
- *Comparison of prices and delivery details are available through shopping comparison websites — saves searching for the best deals yourself.*
- *Goods can be bought using credit or debit cards so there is no need to use cash.*
- *Shopping can still be done if customers are housebound, live in remote areas or if their transport is limited.*

Disadvantages include:
- *The website might not be genuine — fraud may be committed.*
- *Shoppers might experience problems with tax and import regulations if they attempt to buy from countries with different restrictions and rules to their own.*
- *Goods ordered may not arrive at all or the ones that do arrive may not be the ones ordered originally.*
- *Delivery options may not be convenient — alternative arrangements may have to be made.*

[9 marks available — answers should cover advantages and disadvantages to gain full marks. Relevant examples should be given to back up each advantage and disadvantage]

Page 37 — Other Communication Systems

1 Possible answers:
- *It increases road safety **[1 mark]** as it forewarns drivers of problems ahead **[1 mark]**.*
- *It prevents cars from being delayed **[1 mark]** because it alerts drivers to potential traffic problems in advance, allowing them to find an alternative route **[1 mark]**.*
- *It allows better route planning **[1 mark]** because up-to-date information about roads and traffic is available **[1 mark]**.*

[4 marks available — 1 for each of 2 reasons. An additional 1 for each accompanying explanation.]

Remember there are 4 marks available here. You need to back your reasons up properly to get them all.

2 Possible answers:
- *Digital TV produces a better quality picture than analogue sets.*
- *Digital TV provides viewers with more choice.*
- *Digital TV allows the viewer to use the television as a communication device.*

[3 marks available — 1 for each reasonable benefit]

Page 39 — Other Communication Systems

1 Possible answers:
- *She could use her laptop (if connected to the Internet via a wireless connection) **[1 mark]** to send a report by e-mail **[1 mark]**.*
- *She could use a mobile or video phone **[1 mark]** to send messages / images in to the office / relay her report verbally **[1 mark]**.*
- *She could use a fax machine **[1 mark]** in order to send documents **[1 mark]**.*

[4 marks available — 1 for each of 2 acceptable ways. An additional 1 each for a more extended explanation]

Make sure that you read any question on teleconferencing properly. Video conferencing includes moving images but teleconferencing may not include this. Okay. Now take a deep breath and check out the answers...

2 a) Sample answer:
*Videoconferencing is when people at different locations are able to have an interactive discussion **[1 mark]** in which they are able to see each other **[1 mark]**. The discussion will have been enabled by the use of telecommunications **[1 mark]**. Specialised video link equipment and / or sophisticated studios are needed for this **[1 mark]**.*

Watch out — there's 4 marks for this question, so you need to give plenty of detail in your answer. Basically it breaks down like this: 1 mark for saying it's a real time system (i.e. that it's interactive), 1 to say they can see each other, 1 to say that it's enabled by ICT, and the other 1 for saying you need special equipment in order to do it.

Answers

b) *Possible advantages:*
- *It saves the cost of travel.*
- *It saves time travelling to a common meeting place.*
- *It's useful when a quick response is needed.*

Beware of answering this question by saying "you don't have to travel". People don't have to travel to a common meeting place but they may have to travel to the videoconferencing unit — be sure to make this clear.

Possible disadvantages:
- *The quality of the video image can be poor.*
- *There can be annoying minor time delays.*
- *The equipment can be expensive to buy.*
- *Training in use of the equipment is needed.*
- *There is a loss of social interaction.*
- *There may be difficulties agreeing on a suitable time due to the time difference between the UK and US.*
- *It can be harder to control or keep track of the meeting.*

[4 marks available — 1 for each of 2 reasonable advantages, 1 for each of 2 reasonable disadvantages]

Section 5 — ICT in the Real World

Page 41 — ICT in Industry and Manufacturing

1 *Any reasonable examples accepted — for example:*
- *The use of robotic arms to weld and paint car bodies in the automobile industry has eliminated many jobs because the entire manual job is taken over by the robotic arms.*
- *The use of CAD systems has transformed the jobs of draughtsmen and designers. Instead of working with pencil and paper they now work with computers. They can design a product and then make small changes until they are happy with the result. This requires completely different skills.*
- *An example of a new job is the maintenance and upkeep of robotic arms to handle delicate objects. The machines need sensors to be checked and grip and release need to be monitored to be kept in perfect working order so the goods are not damaged.*

[6 marks available — 1 for each of 3 examples. An additional 1 for each explanation]

The trick to these types of question is to remember that you're looking for 6 marks, so break the question into 3 chunks. In this case, it's eliminating jobs, transforming jobs and creating jobs. Then make sure you give a sensible, thorough example and explanation for each one.

2 *Any reasonable answers accepted — for example:*
- *Robots can be used to assemble goods instead of humans. This results in greater output because robots can work day and night.*
- *CAD can be used to design products. The designers are able to see the designs in 3 dimensions and rotate designs so that they can be seen from all angles.*
- *Robots can be used to inspect and clean chemical tanks, which would otherwise need to be emptied, resulting in lengthy downtime. When robots are used to perform the task, the downtime is significantly reduced.*
- *In car plants, CAD can simulate car crashes in safety tests. This is safer and less costly than tests which use real cars.*

[4 marks available — 1 mark for each of 2 examples of a use of ICT, and 1 additional mark each for stating the benefit.]

Page 43 — ICT in Commerce

1 a) *Any one of the following is acceptable:*
- *Reduces strain on staff as certain things can be carried out by ATM e.g. giving a statement, paying out cash etc.*
- *It allows new services which might encourage new customers e.g. quick print of statements, changing pin numbers etc.*
- *It increases the building society's potential market.*
- *It encourages customers to stay with the building society.*
- *It allows the building society to compete with other banks.*

[1 mark available for any of the answers above]

b) *Possible answers:*
- *It allows cash to be obtained 24 hours per day, 7 days a week, whenever the user requires it.*
- *There is no need to queue at branches, therefore it saves time.*
- *It can reduce the amount of paperwork for the customer, as customers can decide whether to obtain receipts from the ATM or not.*

[2 marks available — 1 for each reasonable advantage]

2 a) *Possible answers:*
- *Gordon could have given his details to the company when buying the DVD.*
- *The company could have passed his details on to a different part of the same company in order to market related products.*
- *The company could have given or sold his details on to other companies.*
- *Gordon may not have read the details on the on-line form correctly (or at all), and has thus allowed his details to be passed on.*
- *The company may not be complying with the 1998 Data Protection Act and has passed on his details without permission.*

[2 marks available — one for each reasonable answer]

b) *Most people worry that their credit or debit card details, or their personal information will be stolen or hacked into, and misused* ***[1 mark].***

Answers

Page 45 — ICT in the Home

1 *Possible answers include:*
The friend probably thinks ICT means "computers". ICT is not limited to meaning "computers". Anything with a microchip in it uses ICT. Examples of very common devices with microchips include digital watches, or any digital timing device such as a clock on a cooker, and video machines. Central heating systems are almost always controlled by programmable timing devices which use microchip technology. Other examples include washing machines, burglar alarms, video cameras etc. Most households would include at least one of these, so could not be said to be free of ICT.
[5 marks available — 1 for saying ICT refers to more than just computers, 1 for saying that anything with a microchip uses ICT, 3 each for any 3 suitable examples]

2 a) *Possible answers (for children):*
- *Example: finding information for homework.*
  Benefit: there is more information available on the Internet than in any library.
  Drawback: it's hard to know if a lot of information from the Internet is reliable.
- *Example: using instant messaging systems to chat to friends.*
  Benefit: they can keep in touch with people who may live far away without running up large telephone bills.
  Drawback: most children use texting language so they get into bad habits for writing English.

[6 marks available in total for two suitable examples — give 1 mark for each example, 1 mark for a benefit and 1 mark for a drawback]

b) *Possible answers (for adults):*
- *Example: home banking.*
  Benefit: they can do much of their banking from home at any time of the day or night.
  Drawback: banking is becoming less personal and many people never meet their bank manager.
- *Example: online grocery shopping.*
  Benefit: they do not have to lift heavy goods into the trolley and out again, or to pack the goods into bags.
  Drawback: if the product they order is not available, they do not get a chance to choose an alternative.

[6 marks available in total for two suitable examples — give 1 mark for each example, 1 mark for a benefit and 1 mark for a drawback.]
Other possible examples for adults or children are downloading music, playing online games, using e-mail. As long as you're clear you'll be fine. Remember — 1 mark for a use, 1 for a benefit and 1 for a drawback. ALWAYS READ THE QUESTION to avoid silly slip-ups.

3 *Possible answers:*
- *One use is to monitor and control home security systems. This results in more sophisticated systems which can detect intruders and activate alarms.*
- *Another example of ICT in the home is a games console, which provides entertainment for children and adults by playing films, music and games.*

[4 marks available in total — 1 for each of two uses, and an additional 1 each for stating the benefit]

Page 47 — ICT in Education and the Police Force

1 a) *Possible answers:*
Teachers, head of year, careers staff, pupils themselves.
[2 marks — 1 for each sensible user.]

b) *Possible answers:*
- *Teachers obtain standard reports, such as class lists together with grades. They can also obtain more complex information using the sort and search functions, such as which pupils attained an A grade in maths and in science.*
- *The head of year will be able to produce reports looking at the grades attained for the whole year, looking at a comparison between classes and groups and identifying any problem areas.*
- *Careers staff can find lists of pupils with particular interests and abilities in case of a special event. They can look at pupils' profiles to see what careers advice is needed.*
- *Pupils can track their own progress, identify their own problem areas, and monitor their progress in relation to the average performance of the year.*

[6 marks available — 1 mark for naming the user and 1 mark for a suitable reason]
Because 6 marks are awarded for this question, you know you need to give some pretty meaty examples of how each user will use the package.

2 a) *Possible answers:*
- *Teaching programs provide students with content and questions. Students answer the questions and are given automatic feedback. This means that students do not have to wait for the teacher to grade their answers to find out if they are right or wrong.*
- *ICT provides efficient ways of organising and storing data. Schools can use databases to store information about students which can be used by staff to produce things like class lists, grade sheets, absence lists.*

[4 marks available — 1 for each of two examples, and an additional 1 each for stating the benefit]

b) *Possible answers:*
- *Computerised police databases (e.g. fingerprints and DNA databases) allow detectives to search for matches on samples found. This speeds up the detection of criminals.*
- *Systems such as HOLMES2 allow police to enter the details of crimes onto a database and management system and then search through all the data for similar cases, anomalies in the evidence and other useful information which will help them solve the crime.*

[4 marks available — 1 for each of two examples, and an additional 1 each for stating the benefit]

Page 49 — ICT in Medicine

1 a) *An expert system combines artificial intelligence with a database of specialist knowledge. It is programmed with a set of rules that tell it how to analyse the information in its database and form conclusions.*
[2 marks available — 1 mark for explaining the database aspect, 1 mark for explaining how it uses rules to turn the data into knowledge]

b) *Possible answer:*
The doctor would input relevant details into the system, e.g. the symptoms, patient's past medical history, family history of illnesses. The expert system will search its database and produce the most likely diagnosis based on the data entered by the doctor.
[2 marks available — 1 for a basic description, 2 for a more detailed answer]

2 *Possible advantages:*
- *Patients have easy access to large stores of specialist knowledge without having to visit their GP.*
- *These systems can help people recognise symptoms that point to serious problems which they would otherwise have ignored.*
- *Less patients visit GPs with minor ailments as they can now diagnose these themselves — this give GPs more time to deal with more serious cases.*
- *Expert systems should contain very reliable, up-to-date information as they are compiled and reviewed by medical specialists.*

Possible disadvantages:
- *There is a risk of patient's misdiagnosing conditions as they don't have the specialist knowledge to correctly identify their symptoms.*
- *They are lessening human interaction — patients don't get a one-on-one discussion of their problems.*
- *Many people may take legal action if their misdiagnosis results in a serious illness not being picked up.*

[6 marks available — 1 each for up to 3 suitable advantages and 1 each for up to 3 suitable disadvantages.]
In questions like this, you need to give an equal number of points for and against to be sure of picking up all the marks.

Answers

Page 51 — Working in ICT

1) *Possible answers:*
   - *New workers should be willing to work flexible hours, as user support may require working at times when the users don't need their equipment, e.g. installing new software or fault correction out of office hours or at lunchtimes.*
   - *New workers should be able to communicate well orally to enable efficient and effective communication with users and colleagues, e.g. questioning effectively to obtain user requirements and details of problems.*
   - *New workers will need good written communication skills to record faults clearly and document solutions and actions.*
   - *They will need to be able to work as part of a team, which means being able to exchange views and share information.*
   - *They will need the ability to work under pressure as large problems can occur suddenly.*
   - *They will also need good organisational skills and the ability to multi-task, having several different jobs running concurrently as many users will need attention at the same time.*

   [8 marks available in total — 1 for each of 4 qualities, and an additional 1 for each suitable reason to accompany them.]

   Examiners would also accept other answers like ability / willingness to learn new skills as ICT moves forward so quickly. If you only state the qualities and do not give reasons then the maximum mark you can get is 4. Make sure the reasons are relevant to the job and not ones you just made up.

2 *Possible answers:*
   - *Good communication skills will be needed in order to explain to users exactly what the problems and their solutions are, as well as to advise clearly on future use of ICT to avoid further problems.*
   - *They should be approachable so that users feel comfortable and able to go to them with all their ICT problems, even the ones they consider to be small and insignificant.*
   - *They need to have good written skills so that they can, for example, advise the whole company at once via e-mail about any forthcoming changes to their system.*

   [4 marks available — 1 for each of 2 qualities, and 2 further marks for explanations of why each quality would be needed]

Page 53 — Working in ICT

1 *Possible answers:*

a) *Programmers have to debug code on existing pieces of software that does not meet its specifications for some reason **[1 mark]**. They have to work out why the software is not performing as it should and what has caused the problem **[1 mark]**. Debugging code can range from preventing a system from crashing to working out why a process is performing much slower than expected **[1 mark]**.*

b) *Even software that has been released has to be maintained and in some cases updated **[1 mark]**. Bugs can be discovered in the program after its release and programmers need to fix these so the program carries on working properly **[1 mark]**. Programmers have to document the code they write clearly and accurately so other members of their team can work on it without needing it explained **[1 mark]**.*

2 *Possible answers:*

a) *A web developer would be involved with the implementation and improvement of the website's design. This could extend to new layouts, creating new content or features, and inputting whatever code was needed **[2 marks]**.*

b) *A web technician principally deals with the version of the website that the public can see. They organise the hosting for the website and make any updates to the version of the website that is displayed online **[2 marks]***

c) *In a larger company, the webmaster is more like the manager of the department that looks after the website. The webmaster's job is to develop documentation about the general look and feel of the website, and about how specific parts of it should work **[2 marks]**.*

Page 55 — The Effects of ICT

1 *Possible answers:*

a)
   - *It's easy for people to spend more time at the computer instead of doing other things like reading.*
   - *This could reduce levels of literacy among young people who don't develop reading or writing skills as a result of using computers too often.*
   - *Education standards in general could fall and the abilities of people joining the workforce will be lower, making companies less competitive.*

   [3 marks, one for each reasonable effect]

b)
   - *Society now relies very heavily on technology to do things like manage money, and control machines where people would have previously done the same tasks.*
   - *With technology, tasks can often be done more efficiently and reliably.*
   - *However, there are risks with relying on IT systems too much — there is always the potential for them to malfunction or be manipulated.*
   - *You could argue that we managed fine before IT systems and so we don't actually need much of this new technology. Companies try to persuade us that we must have things like mobile phones, mp3 players and broadband Internet, but is it really giving us a better quality of life, or simply allowing them to make more money?*

   [3 marks, one for each reasonable point]

c)
   - *Communicating over the Internet is so popular that it's possible to shop, book travel, talk to friends, etc, without leaving the house.*
   - *One of the worries of the increasing use of online services is that people will stop being physically active, and become progressively less healthy and fit.*
   - *Communicating solely with people who share your interests through the Internet could be bad for a mixed society, as groups that share the same interests and opinions may gradually interact less with those that don't.*

   [3 marks, one for each reasonable point]

Answers

Section 6 — Legal Stuff

Page 57 — Malpractice and Crime

1 *Possible answers:*
- *By locking doors and keeping the rooms in the office secure.*
- *By using security cameras to monitor rooms and corridors.*
- *Using biometric devices like fingerprint readers or iris scanners.*
- *By installing fire or burglar alarms in the building.*

[3 marks available, 1 mark for each reason]

2 *Administrators can apply the following measures to an IT system to keep the data secure:*
- *Setting files to "Read-Only" so that important data cannot be changed or deleted by mistake.*
- *Encrypting data.*
- *Installing a firewall to help prevent access to the network.*
- *Creating different access levels for different users.*
- *Logging users' activity in an audit trail or monitoring access through a software log.*
- *Keeping security software on the system up-to-date.*

[5 marks available, 1 for each sensible reason]

Page 59 — Malpractice and Crime

1 *Possible answers:*
- *They might not log off correctly, leaving data accessible to others.*
- *They might disclose their password, allowing others to access the data.*
- *They might visit unsafe websites and download viruses.*
- *They might use illegal / downloaded software and download viruses.*
- *They might open e-mail virus attachments.*
- *They might deliberately access data they shouldn't.*

[6 marks available — 1 mark for each security problem, and 1 mark for each description]

2 *Possible answer:*
*A hacker is someone who uses their technical knowledge to gain unauthorised access to a computer system **[1 mark]**. Hackers can gain access to computer systems and use the software illegally, or be able to view or copy sensitive information **[1 mark]**. A cracker is someone who uses their technical knowledge to crack codes like passwords or encryptions **[1 mark]**. After cracking passwords or codes, crackers either pass the information on to a hacker or use it to access a system themselves **[1 mark]**.*
[4 marks available, 1 for each of 2 definitions and 1 for identifying the threats posed]

3 *Possible answer:*
- *A virus is a small program that attaches itself to a known program and can replicate itself. They are often designed to cause damage, e.g. by corrupting files.*
- *A worm is a program similar to a virus that will replicate itself and spread over a network. Unlike a virus, it doesn't need a host program to attach to.*
- *Logic bombs or time bombs are malicious programs that become active at a certain time, or when a particular action is performed, e.g. booting up the system, or opening a certain file on the network.*
- *Trojan horses are programs that appear to be performing a task within the system but are in fact infecting, manipulating or deleting programs whilst the user is doing another task.*

[6 marks available, 1 for identifying each of 3 types of malware, 1 for each correct explanation]

Page 61 — ICT Legislation

1 *Possible answers:*
- *Using a piece of software without the proper licence (e.g. installing and using software on several computers with only a single-user licence).*
- *Software piracy (e.g. professional criminals mass-producing illegal copies of software and selling them through illegal outlets).*
- *Downloading files (MP3, video) from illegal websites to avoid paying for them.*
- *Copying text or images from the Internet and using them (e.g. in a publication) without obtaining the copyright owner's permission.*

[3 marks available, 1 for each of up to 3 appropriate answers]

2 a) *Any of these are acceptable:*
- *It is an agreement between the user and the producer of a piece of software on how that software may be used **[1 mark]**.*
- *It is a legal document which specifies how a purchased piece of software may be used **[1 mark]**.*
- *It is a contract from the producer of software which is purchased at the same time as the software. It sets out the terms of use **[1 mark]**.*

b) *No, it would not be breaking the agreement. The agreement does not actually prohibit them from installing the software on more than 5 machines. It will only be broken if the software is used on more than 5 machines at the same time.*
[2 marks available — 1 for saying "no", 1 for an appropriate explanation]

Page 63 — ICT Legislation

1 *Possible answers:*
- *Transaction can be completed quicker **[1 mark]** as hand written signatures do not have to be obtained **[1 mark]***
- *Increased level of security for transactions **[1 mark]** leads to increase in confidence and more people using it **[1 mark]***

[4 marks available, 1 for identification of the benefit and 1 for further explanation]

2 *Possible answers:*
- *Communication may be secretly monitored and recorded in certain circumstances **[1 mark]** such as interest of national security / crime prevention **[1 mark]**.*
- *Communication may be secretly monitored but not recorded in certain circumstances **[1 mark]** such as a company checking employees aren't misusing their communication system / to monitor help lines **[1 mark]**.*
- *Internet service providers are required to monitor e-mail and Internet activity **[1 mark]** to assist law-enforcement agencies **[1 mark]**.*
- *Cannot intercept telephone calls, e-mails or post **[1 mark]** without authority. **[1 mark]***

[4 marks available, 1 for identification of the provision and 1 for further description]

Page 65 — ICT Legislation

1 *Possible answers:*
- *Consent is not required for the storing of the data, as it must be stored for legal purposes.*
- *Consent is needed for the processing of details for direct marketing, as this is not required by law, and it does identify an individual.*
- *There is a legal requirement for charities to process this sort of data to produce accounts, so data subject consent is not needed for this.*
- *Management analysis will often look at general trends and will not identify individuals so, again, consent is not needed.*

[4 marks available — 1 for each appropriate point]

2 *Possible answers:*
- *The eighth principle states that data cannot be transferred to a country or territory without adequate data protection. As long as data is transferred within the EU there is no problem.*
- *The second principle states that data must be used only for the purposes stated in the register. If data is being transferred to a third party, it can only be transferred if this was stated in the register.*
- *The seventh principle states that appropriate measures must be taken against unlawful processing and against accidental loss of, destruction of, or damage to, personal data.*

[2 marks available — 1 for each of 2 correctly described principles]

Answers

Okay, only 2 marks here, which means you're going to have to fight for them. Just identifying the principle by number isn't going to get you anything — you need to give a proper description in order to get your marks here. Bit of a scummy question really, such a long intro and it's only worth 2 marks. Oh well...

Page 67 — Health and safety

1 *Possible answers:*
- *There should be a smooth changeover from the old system to the new one to minimise stress.*
- *The new system must be an improvement on the old system.*
- *The system should be easy to use, with provision for training if necessary.*
- *The new system must not be unnecessarily slow.*
- *There should be the facility for the user to use shortcuts.*
- *New hardware must be appropriate for the software so as not to cause too much stress.*
- *New hardware must operate within acceptable time limits.*

[3 marks available — 1 for each correctly identified point]

Ooh this is a bit tricky — don't get thrown off by the fact that it's asking about experienced users. Almost all of the same points apply to experienced and less experienced users.

2 *Possible answers:*
- *They can take regular breaks from looking at the screen.*
- *They can use an ergonomic mouse and keyboard or wrist rests.*
- *They should avoid sitting still for too long and should move around during breaks.*
- *They should sit up straight and sit in a chair with back support.*
- *They should make sure that the chair and keyboard are at the correct height.*
- *They should sit with their eyes at least one metre from the screen.*
- *They should make sure that there is adequate lighting and no glare on the screen.*

[3 marks available — 1 for each correctly identified point]

Section 7 — Applications Software for Presentation and Communication

Page 69 — Word Processing and DTP

1 a) *Possible answers:*
Ask, Fill-in, If... Then... Else, Next Record, Skip Record If
[2 marks available — 1 for each suitable word field]

b) *Possible answers:*
- *Data can be taken from sources other than his original database.*
- *Unwanted data can be filtered out.*
- *Standard information, like the date the letter is being printed on, can be inserted.*

[2 marks available — 1 for each suitable benefit]

c) *Possible answers:*
- *Not having to type out every letter by hand simply saves a lot of time.*
- *Using a standard letter format means lots of letters can be created quickly, as he only needs to write one letter which can then be used as the template for the others.*
- *Using a standard letter format reduces the chances of error. As long as he proofreads the original letter, he knows the others will also be correct.*
- *It is important to be able to send letters with personalised information as every customer will have a different balance on their account.*
- *The fact that the data comes from an existing data source also means there is less chance of errors as no data needs to be re-keyed by him.*

[4 marks available — 1 mark for benefit and 1 mark for the expansion]

Obviously the key here is detail. Don't just write down impersonal blah — make sure you back up your answers.

Page 71 — Word Processing and DTP

1 *Possible answers:*
- *Large font*
- *Clear font*
- *Lots of white space on the page to improve readability*

[2 marks available — 1 for each suitable formatting suggestion]

2 *Possible answers:*
- *All work done by each member of the team will follow the same consistent format.*
- *The initial work of setting up different styles can be done by one member of staff and then shared with others, so every member of the team does not have to waste time doing this.*
- *Formatting the document is faster and more straightforward, as team members can apply a pre-set style to a bit of text instead of having to format it the long way.*
- *Using paragraph styles means that global style changes can be implemented easily.*

[3 marks available — 1 for each reasonable example]

Page 73 — Templates, Style Sheets and Wizards

1 *Possible advantages:*
- *Documents can be created more quickly.*
- *The application is more user-friendly for inexperienced users.*
- *Documents can be kept in a house style.*

Possible disadvantages:
- *All documents will look similar, which may mean they become boring and difficult to distinguish from each other.*
- *The wizard's templates may not match the user's needs precisely.*
- *Users are limited to the choices offered by the wizard, so it's harder to make adjustments.*

[4 marks available — 1 for each of 2 appropriate advantages, 1 for each of 2 appropriate disadvantages]

Answers

2 *Possible answers:*
- *Templates could be used to govern layout and ensure that all company documents have a consistent style and "look." The template ensures that everyone is working to the same document format.*
- *Style Sheets can be used in other programs to make sure that different users follow the same stylistic guidelines.*
- *Wizards can be used to create documents — as they have their own pre-set templates, users could agree to use the same one in order to keep their documents looking consistent.*

[4 marks available — 1 for each appropriate example, 1 for explanation]

Page 75 — Clipart and Graphics Tools

1 *Possible advantages:*
- *The diagram will be recognised all over the world **[1 mark]** — the network design company may be in a different part of the world to its clients. **[1 mark]***

Possible disadvantages:
- *The graphics library may not be up-to-date **[1 mark]** — new network components may need to be included in the network **[1 mark]**, the symbols for these new components may not be in the current library **[1 mark]**.*

[2 marks available for an advantage and 2 marks for a disadvantage — in each case, 1st mark for the identification and 2nd mark for an example / description.]

2 *Possible advantages:*
- *The clipart images are available immediately **[1 mark]** so the logo can be produced quickly **[1 mark]**.*
- *The logo does not cost much to produce **[1 mark]** — no designer has to be employed to design the logo **[1 mark]**.*
- *No extra equipment is needed **[1 mark]** — the clipart images are usually included with the software **[1 mark]**.*

Possible disadvantages:
- *The school is limited to the choice of images to be used in their logo **[1 mark]** — the images may not be suitable **[1 mark]**.*
- *Another school may have used the clipart in their logo **[1 mark]** — many people have access to clipart images **[1 mark]**, they are not unique **[1 mark]**.*

[2 marks available for each of two advantages and one disadvantage — in each case, 1st mark for the identification and 2nd mark for an example / description.]

Page 77 — Clipart and Graphics Tools

1 a) *Possible answers:*
- *They could create the outlines of simple graphics by using line tools (either straight lines or drawing "freehand") and shapes tools (like squares and circles).*
- *They could use a "fill" tool to fill graphics in with colour.*
- *They could make the graphics look more sophisticated by using tools to add shadows or 3-D effects.*
- *They could use interactive fill tools to alter the shading within the graphic so that the fills change subtly from dark to light.*
- *The designers could copy and paste a single graphic many times in order to produce a montage where lots of images are layered over each other.*
- *Designers could use a transparency tool in order to layer one image over another without obscuring either.*

[3 marks available — 1 for each suitable use]

b) *Possible answers:*
- *They could alter the brightness, contrast or intensity of the colours in a photograph in order to make it more intense, or to bring out the features better.*
- *They could use shape and line tools to create a frame to put around the photograph, or they could add shapes to the image (e.g. stars or exclamation marks).*
- *They could apply built-in filters or effects to give the photo a sophisticated visual style, e.g. pastel, brush strokes, stained glass, watercolours, etc.*

[3 marks available — 1 for each suitable use]

Page 79 — Multimedia Presentations

1 *Possible advantages:*
- *It's very easy to move between slides.*
- *He's already familiar with creating and presenting with acetates, so won't need new training.*
- *He already has his own equipment so will not need to buy any more expensive projectors or pieces of software.*

Possible disadvantages:
- *The acetates can be easily damaged.*
- *Because new technology exists and is used so commonly, he runs the risk of making his own presentations seem very out of date.*
- *He has to change each slide by hand, which can be awkward.*
- *He can't use any added effects like video or additional sound, which might make the presentations boring.*

[4 marks available — 1 for each of 2 suitable advantages, 1 for each of 2 suitable disadvantages]

Right — this one's quite tricky. Try not to get distracted by multimedia presentations and just focus on the good and bad things about OHPs.

2 *Possible answers:*

a) *Slide Transition*
- *Different types of slide transition can be used to move from one slide to the next in an interesting way. For example, she could set it so that one slide faded into the next, making it look smart and professional.*
- *Slide transition moves the presentation from one slide to the next. The look should be kept consistent through the whole presentation to make it look more professional.*

b) *Buttons*
- *Buttons can be inserted into slides so that something happens when they are clicked on (e.g. activate a hyperlink which takes you to another part of the presentation). The number of these should be limited so that the presentation doesn't get too confusing.*
- *She can use buttons on each slide that will activate a hyperlink when you click on them. The buttons should be bright and clearly labelled in order to be effective.*

c) *Sound*
- *Sound can be used to emphasise an important point or the end of one part of the presentation. She shouldn't overuse the sound or else the presentation will become confusing.*
- *She can use pre-existing sounds or else record her own new ones for the presentation. She needs to think about the audience and make sure the sounds are not unclear or confusing.*

[6 marks available — 2 for each fully explained and supported answer]

Page 81 — Multimedia Presentations

1 *Possible answer:*
- *Slides can be grouped **[1 mark]** so visitors can select the attraction they want to know about **[1 mark]**.*
- *Navigation enables visitors to return to the opening page/other attractions **[1 mark]**, which then enables different routes to be taken through the presentation **[1 mark]**.*
- *Slides about a selected attraction may then have sub-sections **[1 mark]** allowing different information about each attraction to be clearly shown **[1 mark]**.*

[4 marks available, 1 for each of two points and 1 each for explanation of the point. The answer must be given in the context of the question — in this case the tourist information centre]

2 *Possible answers include:*

Advantages:
- *The presentation can be set with timings **[1 mark]**, so no human intervention is required **[1 mark]**.*
- *The presentation can be set to loop **[1 mark]** — it can run continuously during the open evening **[1 mark]**.*

Answers

Disadvantages:
- *The timings might be set too short* ***[1 mark]****, so people may not be able to read the information contained on each slide quickly enough* ***[1 mark]****.*
- *The timings on the slides may be set too long* ***[1 mark]****, so people may lose interest as the information is on screen for too long* ***[1 mark]****.*

[4 marks available for advantages (2 for each), 2 marks available for disadvantage]

Page 83 — Creating Stuff for the Web

1 a) *Possible answers:*

Advantages of web-authoring software:
- *The software is quite sophisticated, so exact effects can be achieved.*
- *The links can be checked and updated automatically.*
- *Web-authoring software can have other packages integrated into it in order to achieve more impressive effects, e.g. animations.*
- *You can choose to edit your page through what appears on the final screen (WYSIWYG) or by editing the HTML code directly.*
- *Specific wizards are included in the software, e.g. one could help the school create a site map for the website.*

Advantages of standard applications software:
- *No additional software costs are involved, assuming that the school already has access to computers with appropriate software.*
- *Less extensive staff training on specific software is required.*
- *If documents which already exist need to be uploaded, then they can just be automatically converted to HTML.*
- *It is easy and quick to create web pages in this way.*

[6 marks available — 1 for each of 3 suitable advantages of web-authoring software and 1 for each of 3 suitable advantages of standard applications software]

Wow — 6 marks up for grabs just for this one question. You'd best make sure you think about making 6 decent points here. 3 advantages for each sounds like a good start to me.

b) *Possible answers:*
- *Using a consistent layout will help users become familiar with how the site works and they'll be able to navigate their way around it more easily.*
- *The consistency can make the site appear more professional.*
- *Following a similar template for each web page reduces the risk of certain elements being left out by accident, provided that the original layout is complete.*

[4 marks available — 2 for each of 2 fully supported explanations]

Page 85 — Creating Stuff for the Web

1 a) *A 'blog' is short for 'weblog', and is an article or piece of writing published online by a user, usually about their experiences, thoughts or opinions on a particular subject.*

[1 mark for appropriate definition]

b) *Possible answers:*
- *Publishing a blog through a website is free.*
- *Using a website means that you can write the blog through your web browser without knowing HTML or any other programming language.*
- *You get a view in your web browser that looks just like a word processor and so is very user-friendly.*
- *You can create new posts or edit old ones.*
- *The website automatically updates your blog page so the newest entry is at the top of the list.*
- *Websites often give the option for other users to leave comments on the blog.*

[3 marks in total, one for each appropriate advantage]

2 *Possible answer:*

Jukebox software is preferable because it can support podcasts directly ***[1 mark]****. If you subscribe to a podcast and you have jukebox software, it will automatically download new episodes without you having to check for updates yourself* ***[1 mark]****. The software then synchronises your mp3 player to include the new podcast* ***[1 mark]****. Jukebox software automatically performs this function every time you connect your mp3 player to the computer* ***[1 mark]****.*

3 *Possible answer:*
- *The equipment needed for making video recordings is generally much cheaper now than it used to be. This means that more people can potentially create their own videos and publish them online.*
- *There aren't any restrictions on how good the quality of the videos are, so people recording clips on their phones or digital cameras can also upload video files really easily.*
- *Vlogs are more widely supported by portable devices that can play videos, so they're becoming more and more popular as more people now have the ability to watch them.*
- *There isn't any censorship or restrictions on the content of vlogs and videos, so you can make one about whatever you want, and post it independently.*
- *Websites exist that remove all the technicalities (and make it totally free) to upload videos, so you don't have to have any specialist knowledge as long as you can get the files onto the computer.*

[8 marks in total, one for each of four reasons, one for each explanation]*.*

Page 87 — Customising Applications

1 *Possible answers:*
- *Buttons could be added to the interface to, for example, take the user to another document, run the selected action or sort data.*
- *Menus could be added to the interface. They give users all the options to choose from in a single list, and limit and direct the user to selected options.*
- *Forms can be added to the interface. Drop down boxes can be used for data selection, and boxes that fill in automatically can be used, depending on what other data is entered.*
- *Macros can be added to the interface. They save time by letting you add information at the click of a single button. For example, you can record a macro to add a header containing the filename, date and page number into all your documents.*

[6 marks available — 1 for each of 3 customising features, an additional 1 each for a description of how they would work]

2 a) *Possible answers:*
- *A spreadsheet with macro capabilities has the ability to record and store a sequence of instructions that can be used to carry out repetitive tasks for a user.*
- *If a spreadsheet has macro capabilities, it means it is able to use macros to carry out certain repetitive tasks so the user doesn't have to. Macros do this by recording a series of commands and then carrying them out when prompted.*

[2 marks available — 2 marks for a full explanation, 1 mark for a partial explanation]

This is a bit of a tricky question. They've allowed 2 marks for it because it's quite a tricky definition to come up with, but there's no obvious way to break it down into what you get the separate marks for. The main thing is to write an explanation in detail — i.e. whatever you do don't just write: "a spreadsheet with macro capabilities is a spreadsheet that can use macros".

b) *Possible answers:*
- *They could be used in a word-processor to change the details in the header.*
- *They could be used in a spreadsheet program to format cells in a particular way.*
- *They could be used in a presentation program to add particular buttons to slides.*

[2 marks available — 1 for each appropriate example]

This is an easy question to pick up marks on — there are LOADS of examples of things you could use macros for.

Answers

Section 8 — Applications Software for Data Modelling and Storage

Pages 89 — Using Spreadsheets

1 a) *Possible answers:*
- *A worksheet is part of a workbook, and can be stored and accessed as a single unit.*
- *Calculations can be performed, based on data from multiple worksheets.*
- *Worksheets can be used to break up related data in a logical way. For example, in a spreadsheet of sales data, there could be separate worksheets for sales volume, sales value, and sales graphs.*

b) *Possible answers:*
- *A workbook is a collection of worksheets.*
- *A workbook keeps related data in one file. For example, a chain of shops might keep a workbook containing information on the whole chain, while individual worksheets would refer to individual shops.*

c) *Possible answers:*
- *A cell range is a group of selected cells.*
- *Cell ranges often appear in formulas, e.g. the formula SUM (A3:B5) uses the function "SUM" and the range "A3:B5" to find the total of all the cells in the range.*

[6 marks available — 1 for each of 3 full explanations, 1 for each of 3 appropriate examples]

There's only 6 marks here guys, and you have to give examples, so remember to make your explanations good or else you won't get the mark for each one.

2 a) *Possible answers:*
- *Absolute referencing is where cells are copied without changing the value in the cell automatically, but are just kept the same.*
- *For example, a constant delivery charge or VAT rate on a spreadsheet that does not change during calculations.*

[3 marks available — 1 for a partial explanation or 2 for a full one, plus 1 for a suitable example]

b) *Possible answers:*
- *Relative referencing will copy the cells in such a way that the cell references change, either by row or column, in relation to where the copy gets placed.*
- *For example, adding up totals in a row or column.*

[3 marks available — 1 for a partial explanation or 2 for a full one, plus 1 for a suitable example]

Page 91 — Using Spreadsheets

1 a) *Bar chart or line graph* **[1 mark]**

b) *Scatter graph* **[1 mark]**

2 *Possible answers:*
- *Label controls and error messages can be added to give the user guidance, e.g. error messages can be included in the cell validation.*
- *Macros can be linked to buttons, assisting the user in performing specific tasks.*
- *List boxes / combo boxes can be used, where users select from a preset list of options. These can be used for validation as the user is restricted to entering certain values.*
- *Option buttons can be used to select options where there is a pre-defined choice like the title of a person.*

[4 marks available — 1 each for identifying 2 methods, an additional 1 each for a full explanation]

Page 93 — Modelling Software

1 *Possible answers:*
- *They can be used to predict future financial events* **[1 mark]***, using 'what-if' questions* **[1 mark]***.*
- *They can be used to show trends* **[1 mark]***, using graphs which change automatically as values are changed* **[1 mark]***.*
- *No specialist software is needed* **[1 mark]***, because spreadsheets are standard packages* **[1 mark]***.*
- *There is less chance of errors occurring* **[1 mark]***, because calculations are performed automatically* **[1 mark]***.*

[6 marks available — 2 marks for each fully explained advantage.]

Okay, six marks here. That means come up with three decent points and make sure you give full explanations of all of them.

2 *Possible answers:*

Functions:
- *Functions are standard routines built into the spreadsheet package.*
- *They have wizards to help the user use them.*
- *Functions can be nested within other functions to create more complicated commands.*

Examples of functions are:
- *SUM, which calculates the total of a range of cells.*
- *IF, which returns one value if the condition specified is true and a different value if it is false.*
- *AVERAGE, which returns the mean or average value from a range of cells.*

Formulas:
- *Formulas are typed directly into the formula bar by the user.*
- *They use mathematical operators in order to prompt the computer to process the data in a particular cell.*
- *They're usually used for simple calculations.*

Examples of formulas are:
- *A3+(B7*RATE_VAT), which would multiply B7 by the RATE_VAT value, then add it to the A3 value.*
- *A3+B3+C3, which would add together each of the values in A3, B3 and C3.*

[6 marks available — up to 3 for functions and 3 for formulas; 1 for an incomplete description or 2 for a full description, plus 1 for a suitable example]

Okay, simple — just break the six marks down into obvious components. It'll be 3 for functions and 3 for formulas — 1 for a lame description, 2 for a full description, then 1 for the example. Easy, eh?

Page 95 — Databases

1 *A primary key is a unique field in a table* **[1 mark]** *that is used to identify a record* **[1 mark]***. A foreign key is a field in a table* **[1 mark]** *that is related to the primary key of a second table* **[1 mark]***.*

2 a) *Product_ID* **[1 mark]**
Cust_ID **[1 mark]**

b) *Any two from:*
Cust_ID in the ORDER table
Product_ID in the ORDER table
Supplier_ID in the PRODUCT table
[1 mark each for up to 2 correct answers.]

c) *i) one-to-many / one customer may make many orders* **[1 mark]***.*
ii) one-to-many / one supplier may supply many products **[1 mark]***.*

Page 97 — Databases

1 *Possible answers:*
- *Relational databases store data only once, which ensures data consistency (there's no danger of data being updated in one place, but not another).*
- *You can store a much larger variety of data than in a flat file database by organising it into separate linked tables.*
- *There is no redundant data / duplicated data because each data item is stored only once.*
- *Relational databases are less time-consuming to update.*
- *The DBMS can ensure that only authorised users are able to access certain parts (e.g. tables) of a relational database.*
- *Searching is quicker as all data is held in one place, and not in different independent files.*
- *It gives different views of the data to different users. This means users only look at the parts that are relevant to them.*

[4 marks available — 1 for each reasonable advantage]

2 *Possible answers:*
- CUSTOMERS
- SUPPLIERS
- EMPLOYEES
- COMPLAINTS
- SERVICES

[3 marks available — 1 for each reasonable table]

Answers

3 Possible fields are: Pupil ID number, first name, surname, date of birth, tutor group, grade, address. Out of these the Pupil ID number would be the primary key.
[6 marks available — 1 each for 5 sensible fields, and another 1 for suggesting the logical primary key]
Wow — how easy is it to pick up marks on these questions! You'd be loving it if you got a question like this in the exam! They do come up, but beware of straightforward questions: it's sometimes all too easy to slip up on them...

Page 99 — Examples of Databases

1 Possible answers:
- PASSENGER (passenger ID, title, surname, phone number, address1, address2)
- COACH (Registration number, driver name)
- ROUTE (Route ID, destination)
- BOOKING (Booking ID, passengerID, routeID, Registration number, seat, date, time)

[5 marks available — 1 for each of three suitable tables. An additional 2 marks for supporting information about relationships and keys]
Now remember guys — this kind of question is especially tricky, as it's not certain where exactly all the marks come from. The best thing is to make sure you don't skimp on the detail. Put in as much as you can about the tables (as long as you're not rambling on or repeating yourself) and you can be sure to pick up all the marks required here.

Page 101 — Entering and Retrieving Data

1 *Possible answers:*
- *Consistent layout to follow existing house / corporate style* ***[1 mark]***.
- *Buttons / icons / menu options should be added to make it easier to use* ***[1 mark]***.
- *The screen should only contain concise and relevant information* ***[1 mark]***.
- *Layout of data entry screen should match layout of paper form with the source data* ***[1 mark]***.
- *Error / help messages should be included to help the user enter the data correctly* ***[1 mark]***.

[4 marks available — 1 for each sensible answer]

2 a) *In parameter queries, the user inputs the value to be searched for* ***[1 mark]***. *It is used for a specific field / value* ***[1 mark]***. *Example: All books about a specified subject* ***[1 mark]***.
[3 marks available — 1 for a brief description or 2 for a more detailed one and 1 for a suitable example]

b) *A complex query uses more than 1 field and may be taken from different tables in the database* ***[1 mark]***. *Complex queries often use logic functions such as AND, OR or NOT* ***[1 mark]***.
Example: All books about ICT written by a specified author ***[1 mark]***.
[3 marks available — 1 for a brief description or 2 for a more detailed one and 1 for a suitable example]

3 *A simple query contains only one parameter* ***[1 mark]***, *a complex query contains more than one / uses AND/OR/NOT* ***[1 mark]***.
The question asks for the difference between the two, so to get two marks you must talk about both of them, not just one.

Page 103 — Data Verification and Validation

1 a) *Possible answers:*
- *House number*
- *Postcode*
- *Customer reference number*
- *Date*

[2 marks available — 1 for each sensible answer]

b) *Possible answers:*
- *Presence check to ensure the meter readings are present.*
- *Range check to check that the meter reading is equal to, or higher than, the previous reading.*

[4 marks, 1 for each of 2 check names. An additional 1 for each explanation]

c) *Possible answers:*
- *The person reading the meter may have read the numbers incorrectly (e.g. they may have seen an 8 instead of a 3).*
- *The person reading the meter may have read the numbers correctly but made an error writing them down (e.g. they may have intended to write down 34153 but instead they wrote down 34513). The data validation software can't spot this sort of error.*

[2 marks available — 1 for each sensible answer]

Page 105 — Normalisation / Data Dictionaries

1 *Possible answers:*
- *Data type* ***[1 mark]***
- *Data validation / Input masks* ***[1 mark]***
- *Relationships between tables* ***[1 mark]***
- *Primary keys identified* ***[1 mark]***
- *Access rights e.g. edit / read only* ***[1 mark]***

[5 marks available — 1 for each sensible answer]

2 *Possible answers:*
- *There is no primary key* ***[1 mark]*** *— no field contains unique data* ***[1 mark]***
- *The fields are not atomic* ***[1 mark]***, *they all contain data that could be broken down, e.g. the customer name field should be broken down into forename and surname* ***[1 mark]***.
- *Repeating data* ***[1 mark]*** *held in the order field* ***[1 mark]***.

[4 marks available — 1 for each sensible answer]

Page 107 — More Uses of Applications Software

1 *Possible answer:*
- *Stock control systems record how much of each product is in stock.*
- *When new products are delivered they can be scanned into the system via a barcode on the packaging. The system then increases the stock level accordingly.*
- *The system decreases stock levels when it receives a signal from the point of sale that a product has been sold.*
- *The system can automatically generate orders if stock falls below a certain level.*
- *Stock control systems can also keep track of patterns in demand — they might start ordering more of certain products just before Christmas, for example.*

[4 marks available — 1 for each sensible point]

2 *Possible answers:*
- *Can get directions in both graphical and text form, e.g. maps and step-by-step instructions.*
- *Routes can be printed.*
- *Distances between different steps of the journey can be shown.*
- *Total mileage of the route can be shown.*
- *Places of interest along the routes can be shown, e.g. hotels, fuel stations.*
- *Routes can be planned to go via a specified destination.*
- *The user can select road types, e.g. motorways / dual carriageways.*
- *The user can select fastest or shortest routes.*
- *Routes can be downloaded to a pda.*
- *Routes can be saved for future use.*

[8 marks available, 1 mark for each sensible point.]

3 *Possible answers:*
- *School administration software can monitor pupils' attendance and produce attendance statistics to help tackle truancy.*
- *It holds every student's details (address, next of kin, emergency contacts) linked to a UPN (Unique Pupil Number) that the pupil keeps throughout their time at school.*
- *It records exam marks and overall performance — the software can be used to produce reports on student progress and performance.*

[6 marks available, 1 for each feature identified and 1 for an explanation]

Index

Index

Index